Riches from God

Decoding God's Plan to Make You Rich

Colonial House Press
1220 Winter Garden Vineland Road, Suite 108
Winter Garden, FL 34787
www.ColonialHousePress.com

For you

Table of Contents

Some people believe that the subjects of God and money should never be mixed. They say it's unethical, immoral, ungodly, etc., but I'm here to disprove that claim...

I know that you picked up this book for one of two reasons: either you want to prove me wrong or you're curious about *Riches from God*. Either way, I'm sure you have some reservations about mixing the ideas of God and money, but I'm going to show you that those two subjects go hand-in-hand. The proof is all in The Bible...

The act of making money scares so many people. The system is set up to make you think that way, and cover up the fact that the wealthy people in our society have their hands in more things than you know. But it's all merely a transparent barrier. You should never settle for a life that oppresses you and enforces the idea that you're confined for eternity to a specific social class. Upper class, middle class, lower class; these aren't categories that define our lives—unless we let them.

The truth is, there's an escape route out of that rat-race that you've been living in, but you've been forced to ignore it your whole life. I took that escape route many years ago, and I haven't looked back since. But it wasn't easy.

There was a single force that was trying to push me back into "working for the man." That force was influence. I was poorly influenced by family, friends, and strangers into thinking that I could never break free from the shackles that the rich establishment had placed on me. Until one day I decided to think outside the box.

If it was influence that was keeping me in the rat-race, then surely it would be influence that could get me out.

So, I started to do some research. I started to read everything that was ever written about money that I could get my hands on. Real estate, the stock market, business, you name it—anything and everything to do with money. But I still didn't feel like I had enough positive influence behind me to push back against the negative.

I pushed on through the rat-race for a little longer until I reached the end of my tether. I was done. I quit my corporate job and decided to really push myself to extreme limits. If I wasn't making enough money to pay the bills, then surely I'd find some inspiration to break free. It was then, at my darkest hour, that I decided to turn to an old friend...

Before I go on, I must please ask you for three very important things:

1. Please suspend your skepticism
2. Please keep an open mind
3. Please listen to what God is saying throughout The Bible...

Successfully doing these is the only way you'll prosper...

Holy Beginnings

I've always been fascinated with The Bible and all its teachings. I've always found new perspectives each time I read psalm after psalm. Each new lesson enhanced my life in significant ways. But things were different this time. I approached my next read with a tone of desperation and frustration.

Until I saw some very special notes on random pages through the book. I had almost forgotten that the copy of The Bible I was reading used to be my grandfather's. These notes soon became the foundation of my 7 secrets system that you'll see throughout the rest of the book.

My grandfather was a very wealthy man, and if there was one thing he couldn't stand it was misinterpretation of the Holy Scripture.

People always misquote The Bible by stating that "money is the root of all evil." I can't help but laugh when I think about the puppeteers who dangled that one down to the middle class. The real quote is actually "LOVE of money is the root of all evil." You can see how that's been misconstrued by a simple little edit.

While it might be a simple little misreading, the meaning of each of those quotes couldn't be any more different.

"Money is the root of all evil" emphasizes that you shouldn't seek wealth at all. "LOVE of money is the root of all evil" states that you shouldn't value money more than everything else in your life. You see how one sets out to oppress you and the other sets out to teach a valuable lesson?

This quote must be one of the most misconstrued in the entire Bible. But the truth is there between the pages. Just go look for yourself; it's located in 1 Timothy 6:10.

This misconception could be the reason why I'd never approached The Bible like I did when I was at the end of my rope. It's thought of as shameful to talk about money and The Bible in the same sentence, but there's a lot to be said about acquiring wealth in both testaments.

As I read on with this newfound mindset, I started to realize something very intriguing. I thought to myself... God wants me to be wealthy.

After I finally came to this realization, I was able to construct a special type of system that I like to call my Biblical Money Code.

This code consists of all the secrets to becoming wealthy, and it explains exactly what I mean when I say God Wants You to be Wealthy.

As I've said, I haven't looked back since then. I now have my own self-sufficient business (it's like a money machine that won't stop printing), I've made millions of dollars from real estate (including my famous commercial real estate investment that paid out enough for me to retire on from that one deal), I'm able to use the stock market as if it were an ATM that has no withdrawal limit, I live in a mansion in Florida with my happy (and set for life) family, and I'm able to choose between a Porsche and a Tesla whenever I walk out my front door.

That's not to say that I didn't put in a lot of hard-work, but luckily for you I've compiled all that hard-work and experience into a single book...

Just take a look at my resume:
- Age 18: Became a pro hockey player in Britain's Premier League
- Age 20: Youngest regional manager in their history at a major auto manufacturer
- Age 22: Became a self-funded airline pilot
- Age 29: Youngest 737 Captain on the fleet of a major airline

- Age 32: Started a multi-million-dollar business from the ground up and retired
- Age 36: Became a 2007 best-selling novelist; the award-winning book was later translated into Chinese, Italian, and Turkish

- Age 37: Bought a small plane and set a world airspeed record, only to land and find out that another world record had been broken mid-air for sales from a promotion I wrote
- Age 39: Produced a TV show

Needless to say, God wanted me to be wealthy, so that's exactly what I did—I followed His word to wealth.

The lavish lifestyle has never been quite enough for me, though. I've always felt the need to consistently give back. Whether it's through charitable donations or by educating people who are in the position that I was once in, it all completes my ideal life. And that's where you come in…

By picking up your copy of Riches from God, you've not only helped me achieve my goal of giving back, but you've taken the first step into your new wealthy lifestyle. As You'll see in the coming chapters, I've outlined each and every little detail that led me to where I am today.

This book is as good as a blueprint for wealth, and if you read every word carefully, I guarantee you'll be exposed to the opportunities that I was presented with way back when.

If I had this sort of information at my fingertips when I was looking to turn my life around, I would've reached where I am today a lot quicker, but I don't think that I'd be able to educate people like yourself as well as I do if I didn't face all the mistakes personally.

The reason I wrote Riches from God is because I want to guide you all the way to that life of financial liberation. I want to help you dodge every landmine that set me back. But before you read any further, I need you to promise me one thing: After you're done reading this book, and you've achieved that financial figure that sets you free from the rat-race, pass on your knowledge; help somebody else in need. You can physically pass on this book, or document your own story, but just make sure you pass along all your experience.

Trust me, there's no better feeling than helping those in need, and by passing along this valuable information you'll understand what it means to influence somebody else toward a better life.

The 7 secrets that I'm going to reveal to you are tools that I've uncovered throughout The Bible. They cover the only 3 true ways to make real wealth in this world, and there's no other way around it.

These 7 secrets guide you through every single step as I decode God's plan to make you rich...

Chapter 1: Clearing Your Path to Freedom

very journey begins with a single step, and you just made
that step into what I aim to make ***the defining journey
of your life***. And it needn't be the first step of many;
I'm here not only to walk you through the steps to the wealth
God wants you to have, but also to show you *why* God wants
you to be wealthy. This is all about working smart using His
guidance, not working hard... by following a proven wealth-
blueprint that's hidden in the most famous book on the planet:
The Bible. This blueprint—what I sometimes refer to as 'God's
Treasure Map'—takes the form of 7 Secrets that I've decoded
from The Bible.

*What better guide to wealth could you have than the
book that has been read more than any other in history, and
changed more lives than anything or anyone in history? God's
power can truly be working for YOU if you understand this. And
there is no greater power.*

I'm not here to covertly make a religious statement;
my mission isn't to convert you to Christianity—The Bible is
simply the source of the power, prophecy, and wisdom that I
wish to pass on to you. This course isn't about me; I'm just the
translator and the messenger. My goal is simply to channel the
Ultimate Financial Power into your life.

In this first chapter, I'm going to tell you what these 7
Secrets are. These 7 secrets can take you all the way to your
financial dreams IF you use them as I instruct you to, in simple
to follow steps.

But that's for later on. Before I personally walk you
down God's path to financial freedom, we need to clear that path
of obstacles or these 7 secrets will have no effect. How so? I'm
obviously going to be referencing The Bible throughout these

scriptures as I decode its secrets, so let me begin with this:

"The legs of the lame are not equal: so is a parable in the mouth of fools." – Proverbs 26:7

The Bible makes consistent reference to "fools," and for good reason. If *you* act like one of the Fools, even if you possess these 7 secrets it won't matter. As that verse states, a parable in the mouth of a fool is worthless. And these 7 Secrets will be worthless in the mouth of a Fool.

So the other purpose of this first chapter is to identify any Fools that are reading this, and to weed out those Fools who are unwilling to change. These 7 Secrets will only work if they're in the right hands, and I trust those hands are yours.

The path to freedom is now right before you, and I'm standing at the start of it with you, holding these 7 Secrets and hoping to guide you all the way with them. But that path is currently full of Foolish obstacles that we first have to clear before we actually start walking.

Don't worry, this book will be revealing secrets you never knew existed, and yes, most of them are proven to put money in your hands instantly. But if you currently find yourself feeling impatient to "just make some money!" right now without any instruction and preparation first, then the first Fool Warning Light should be flashing, because the only path you're standing in front of is the path to financial destruction. Please understand:

This is not some lame get-rich-quick scheme. This is a genuine and total plan for your financial freedom that can take you all the way in simple steps. You WILL learn the fastest ways possible to make money, but you will need to be patient as I explain the secrets.

Get-rich-quick schemes never work because they're aimed at the gullible Fools. If you've ever tried one of these schemes and then complained why it didn't work, then you should now know why, and most importantly, *you should be ready to move on to a solid and proven method instead...*

If you're coming into this with a childish get-rich-quick attitude, then you will fail in ALL your attempts to become wealthy because it indicates you are lazy and impatient.

But that's not to say it will be terribly difficult to get to a comfortable retirement quickly; I'm just saying you can't be a lazy and impatient Fool because haste will cost you dear. The Bible says:

"He becometh poor that dealeth with a slack hand: but the hand of the diligent maketh rich." "The soul of the sluggard desireth, and hath nothing: but the soul of the diligent shall be made fat."

Both those Bible verses say the same thing I've just said. Having a "slack hand" and being a "sluggard" are both references to being LAZY. And in the second verse there, it's a reference to wanting something but being too lazy to get it—being a LAZY DREAMER. If you're a lazy dreamer and unwilling to change, you're in the wrong place.

But look at the full verse from those two I just quoted above. The Bible is saying you can't be lazy if you want wealth, but it's NOT saying that you have to be incredibly smart or work yourself to death to realize your dreams; it's saying you have to be *diligent...*

The key word is "diligent." The diligent shall be made rich. <u>Not</u> the super-smart people, the workaholics, or the privileged, but the *diligent.*

Diligent is defined as: "Quietly and steadily persevering in carrying out tasks."

So can you handle that? Can you quietly and steadily persevere in carrying out the simple tasks I set you? Or are you a slack-handed sluggard looking for the next get-rich-quick fix, *and destined for poverty...?*

If you're not ready to become *diligent* (instead of being a get-rich-quick junkie), then you are destined to make the same mistakes over and over as you become poorer and poorer. Doing the same thing continually, but expecting different results is insanity. To quote The Bible: *"As a dog returneth to his vomit, so a fool returneth to his folly."*

So let's clear your path to freedom before I give you these 7 secrets, and filter out any foolish habits. But wait... how do you know *I'm* not one of the Fools myself...?

Who is This Guy?

"He that walketh with wise men shall be wise: but a companion of fools shall be destroyed."

But who am I to be telling you all this? How am I qualified to be your shepherd to freedom? This is your first lesson: When *anyone* tries to give you advice, ask yourself how they're qualified to do so, and/or if they have any agenda that conflicts with your own agenda.

"Has this person travelled on the path I would like to travel on? Do they know what they're talking about? How do

I know they're not a charlatan or one of the Fools? Do they benefit by giving you poor advice?"

So let me tell you a little about myself so you can answer this question to your satisfaction.

Firstly, I have no other agenda here than to give you all the secrets needed to make it to financial freedom, as decoded from The Bible. I gain nothing by giving you bad advice—quite the contrary, actually. As an example of the opposite case, a financial advisor may get paid more commission on a product that may not be best for you—that person has a conflicting agenda with yours because he benefits from giving you what may not be best for you. Same goes for a doctor who gets paid by pharmaceutical companies to prescribe more drugs. See the difference between them and I? You should always ask yourself this question in *any* situation.

Next up, and more importantly, how am I qualified to walk you down the path to your financial dreams? What I'm about to say isn't to impress you as much as let you know that I truly have been where you want to go and that I'm considered an authority by many.

Here's the mansion I live in today with my beautiful wife and children. It has a $250,000 tropical pool and patio that's modeled on paradise—the costs of this are higher than the average house. I own a top-of-the-line Mercedes and BMW, both paid for. We are millionaires, and we travel through life first-class whenever we vacation, cruise, and whenever I speak publicly at events around the world.

I'm also an international bestselling novelist, my work is published in Chinese, Italian, and Arabic as well as English. I also have a loyal following of thousands of wealth-students around the globe, all readers of the type of material you're reading now. As a former airline captain, I also have owned a private aircraft that I set a world airspeed record with.

I've built and sold businesses; I've made millions. I was making money from real estate ventures way back in 1993—long before everyone else got on the bandwagon (and got burned—whereas I sold everything in 2007 before the 2008 crash, thanks to The Bible), and people all over the world trust me for my predictions for the stock market (again, thanks to The Bible).

Yes, I have a lot to be thankful for. I've made it, and then some. But there's something missing, something I still need to do to complete my life-goal of being all I can be. Want to know what it is?

You reading this now. Letting me give you all the wealth secrets I discovered allows me to *give back*, just as The Bible advises us to.

So I'm not just a random nobody off the street; I'm qualified for the job of leading you down the path I went down—*once we clear your path of obstacles.*

I say this because I *know* you've been stung before by wannabe charlatans who are flat-broke but think they can teach others about wealth! I've been where you are now, and I too have been subjected to a lot of garbage and scams. I'm frightened to add up how much money I've wasted on all that get-rich-quick nonsense over the years.

But everything happens for a reason. If I hadn't been subjected to all the lame schemes and rip-offs, I wouldn't have turned to the ultimate source of truth to find the answers to my financial prayers: The Bible. But it was a long and dark road to finally discover a *genuine* path to freedom.

Just in case you think I don't know what it's like to be in your position, let me say that I probably had it a lot *worse* than you before things got so good for me. I wasn't always living a good life; I was flat broke not so long ago. Whatever money I made from my crummy job I spent on moneymaking systems and seminars that never seemed to work. All the 'gurus' who turned out to be charlatans, all the promises that were actually lies, and all the money I'd invested in schemes that went up in smoke.

I remember the day that was the low-point for me, when I felt I was at the bottom of financial hell. Literally, all I had to my name was a few dollars on the coffee table. I stared at those bills, and I knew it was the end of the road. I'd lost my job, I was up to my ears in debt, and I had no savings, all in the middle of a brutal recession. At least I still had a roof over my head, thanks to my girlfriend at the time, but I could tell even she was losing her patience with me—she was going to work each day to pay for everything. But there's something about being at that low-point in life, something immensely liberating—those few dollars being all I had to my name gave me this strange mental release, like a feeling of letting go, *because things could only get better from here.*

And so my mind suddenly opened up to opportunity...

It was then, at rock-bottom and desperate for help, that

for some reason I picked up a beaten-up old Bible that my late-grandfather had once given me. And something shocking fell out of it.

My grandfather died years ago, and he had left me his scuffed and stained old Bible, but this was the first day I'd picked it up. I don't know what made me do it that day, I'd like to think it was his spirit watching over me, but this was the day that my financial hell started transforming into financial heaven. Grandpa retired early, wealthy, and money always seemed to be abundant for him. He was into everything: businesses, lottery, casinos, property, stocks, you name it. And that's what made this discovery so intriguing. In handwritten notes tucked into this Bible, my grandfather had meticulously extracted and translated all the money-secrets in Holy Scripture, passed down through millennia from the wisest and richest people in history (the *real* wealth gurus!). After all, the Bible is packed with the greatest advice ever known, parts of it written by some of the richest men in history. *But, as I discovered, there's a lot more under the surface; what I believe to be a 'money code' that was skillfully woven into the text, so that the deserving could prosper.*

It was incredible. I had in my hands the most famous wealth-building system ever known to man—more valuable than all those expensive moneymaking seminars put together.

The rest is history, and here I am inviting you to follow in my footsteps. We've just cleared the first obstacle from your path to freedom; an obstacle that perhaps you hadn't even considered until today: that the person who's advising you may not be qualified for the job!

This is why it's so important you take this first step of clearing obstacles in your path. Most people don't even know that the obstacles are there; these obstacles lurk in the subconscious mind and are hard to detect, and their financial dreams just 'mysteriously' never work out. So we need to 'recalibrate' your brain before we begin!

So now that you know this and your confidence in me is hopefully assured, allow me to explain what I have in store for you…

A Money Code Hidden in The Bible…

"There is a God in heaven that revealeth secrets, and maketh known what shall be in the latter days." – Daniel 2:28.

This isn't just about making a bit of extra pocket money; that's only as far as the Fools think. This is a guide that reveals God's wealth-blueprint that's designed to get you to a comfortable *retirement* faster than you imagined. A life that features…

- **No more worries about property and stock market crashes (decoded from *Genesis*)…**
- **Automatic and easy income streams (decoded from *Psalms*)…**
- **Freedom from banks and governments milking you until death (decoded from *Proverbs*)…**
- **No employers or fixed income worries (decoded from *Corinthians*…)**
- **The six-number secret that bought me my mansion (decoded from *Ecclesiastes*)…**
- **Guilt-free happiness, joy, and abundance (decoded from *Deuteronomy*)…**
- **The Biblical money code that gets me regular payouts**

(decoded from multiple Bible chapters)...

- **The simple and proven method that could turn $1,000 into a $MILLION in just ten steps (decoded from *Proverbs*)...**

On that last point, it sounds crazy, I know, but when I show you the consistently PROVEN way to double your money using just one of these **7 *Secrets***, you can see how turning $1,000 into a $MILLION can be done in just ten steps. Let me demonstrate. You could start the levels with any amount you want, but if you started with a thousand dollars, and you kept doubling your money, you'd be just 10 levels from turning $1,000 into $1,024,000:

Level 1: $2,000

Level 2: $4,000

Level 3: $8,000

Level 4: $16,000

Level 5: $32,000

Level 6: $64,000

Level 7: $128,000

Level 8: $256,000

Level 9: $512,000

<u>Level 10: $1,024,000</u>

I know it seems unbelievable, but there's the undeniable truth. That's the power of keeping your money working... IF your money is working the Biblical way. And that's an example of just ONE of The 7 Secrets I'll be giving you. And here's another one...

I just received <u>$1,470</u> within a few days because of an ancient code hidden in The Bible. It worked so well that I did it again, and I got another <u>$1,160</u>. Then I got <u>$920</u>. Then I received $720. <u>The payouts keep coming in</u> within a WEEK of each time I use this faith-based moneymaking secret...

In fact, <u>*every single time* I've used this Biblical money code I've received cash</u>... cash that was once taken from me, and now I am taking it back! It literally takes under ten minutes to use, and it's as simple as it is powerful...

Anyone can use this code, and I really mean *anyone*. As long as they have faith in this hidden message that I discovered in the world's most trusted book: The Bible.

So that's just a small sample of the powerful wealth-secrets decoded from The Bible that I'm going to pass on to you and show you how to use in simple steps. But now let's get back to the task of clearing obstacles from your path to freedom.

There's a *big and common* misunderstanding about The Bible that I need to clear up right away.

<u>Yes</u>, God Actually WANTS You to be Rich

"For ye know the grace of our Lord Jesus Christ, that, though he was rich, yet for your sakes he became poor, that ye through his poverty might be rich." – Corinthians 8:9.

Many people who would like to become rich allow misunderstandings about The Bible to become obstacles in their way and keep them poor. We need to get this confusion cleared up so we ensure you aren't one of those victims! These mixed feelings about money cause guilt and hesitation that become obstacles in the way of your goals, and will end your journey to freedom before it's even begun.

Here's just a *few* examples of The Bible stating that it's not just okay to be wealthy, but that God actually *wants* you to be wealthy. God is on your side if you listen to His advice, and what greater ally could you have?

"Be not thou afraid when one is made rich, when the glory of his house is increased." – Psalms 49:16

"The blessing of the Lord, it maketh rich, and He addeth no sorrow with it." – Proverbs 10:22
"A feast is made for laughter, and wine maketh merry: but money answereth all things." –Ecclesiastes 11:19

If you read carefully, The Bible does NOT say that money is the root of all evil; it says that the LOVE of money is the root of all evil.

Here's the verse that confuses so many people (emphasis mine):

"For the <u>LOVE</u> of money is the root of all evil." – Timothy 6:10.

And I wholeheartedly agree. The Fools, the get-rich-quick junkies, they LOVE money. I say this because they have no clever master plan to get the money they need to be free, they just crave an unknown amount of money ("Just gimme some money!") for a spending spree or to pay off Foolish debt. If a Fool won the lottery they would be broke again just a few years later (you hear of this a lot, don't you?).

I don't *love* money. But I do respect it, understand it, know how to make it, and I appreciate what it does for me and how it can be used as a force for good.

To obsess about money or be miserly isn't why we're here. Money is simply *a means to an end*; it buys freedom, security, and choices. When money becomes an *addiction* simply for the sake of acquiring it, and especially when you screw over others or commit crimes to get it, then it's a problem. As the Bible says:

"The getting of treasures by a lying tongue is a vanity tossed to and fro of them that seek death."
And: *"He that loveth silver shall not be satisfied with silver."*

And here's the other key verse in The Bible that sends a mixed message to the unenlightened, from Matthew 19:24, which quotes Jesus's actual words:

"And again I say unto you, It is easier for a camel to go through the eye of a needle, than for a rich man to enter into the kingdom of God."

I can understand why that puts people off becoming rich! And I'm sure that over the centuries that verse has been conveniently misinterpreted to ease the conscience of many a slack-handed sluggard who'd prefer to vilify wealthy people instead of striving for wealth, while secretly wishing to become wealthy.

Sounds impossible for a rich man to go to heaven, right? About as possible as it is for a camel to go through the eye of a needle, right? And to be sure, far too many people (Fools) take a dishonest shortcut to becoming rich by being unethical or criminal, and needless to say those people are surely not going to heaven!

So where does that leave you and I? How do we reconcile this statement from Jesus' own mouth with what I've explained so far? Well, let's read on and state the very next verse after that famous 'camel verse' that too many people (Fools) omit...

When his disciples heard this they were exceedingly amazed, saying, Who then can be saved? But Jesus beheld them, and said unto them, "With men this is impossible, but with God all things are possible."

In other words, what Jesus was actually saying there was that with God, *yes it is possible* that a camel can go through the eye of a needle (all things are possible), and therefore that *it is possible* that a rich man can go to heaven if they trust in God's word (The Bible).

I believe this was Jesus giving us a big clue about the hidden wealth-blueprint in The Bible. He's openly saying that a person may become guiltlessly rich if they are following God's advice. I believe that this was Jesus saying that discovering and decoding the money-secrets in The Bible is as easy as a camel passing through the eye of a needle. It's a way of hiding the secrets so that only the faithful can use them. Thankfully for you, I believe I have discovered and decoded these secrets.

And that's why you're here; to receive these keys to the kingdom. Now let's clear some more obstacles from your path because I still sense you're skeptical—and if so, that's a big part of your problem if you want to go all the way to freedom.

So, God wants you to be wealthy, and The Bible will help you do so. But there's still a big obstacle in your way that we have to clear before we go any further: your lack of belief in what's possible…

The Power of Faith (and the weakness of doubt)

"Therefore I say unto you, What things soever ye desire, when ye pray, believe that ye receive them, and ye shall have them."
– Mark 11:24

I want to talk about two more obstacles you face: thinking small and not having a coherent logic about money, both of which come down to lacking faith in your financial ambitions and how obtainable they are.

First, let's address thinking small…

Most people think in terms of 'chump change'. They have miniscule goals when it comes to money. For modern proof of this, take a look at what people evidently want to watch on TV: reality shows about pawn shops, bidding on abandoned storage units, rummaging through mud in search of an old coin, searching through the attic in the hope of restoring something, buying stuff you don't want with coupons and cheering about it… it's a frenzied craze of late. **We are clearly in what I call 'The Vulture Culture'.**

People have become obsessed with, and are celebrating, breadcrumbs on the floor of the banqueting hall. We are developing into a scavenger-race like something out of a 'Mad Max' post-nuclear holocaust. And while most people are playing in the dirt, the rich man plays a different game—a faster game, and he never gets his hands dirty.

All because he thinks on a different level, and because he has a coherent philosophy about money.

It's more about a question of how you think, and on what level. If your entire day is spent obsessing about small things and 'chump change', **you're not getting a good return on your thoughts**.

So I must ask you if you're 'big minded'... or 'small-minded'. If your financial goal consists of a running battle from day to day like a Fool, scavenging what you can here and there purely for the love of money, it's time to take stock of your situation, and most of all, your THOUGHTS. Take a 'time out', and evaluate where you are and where you need to be...

Most people are extremely confused about money to an oxymoronic degree. On one hand they crave money, and on the other they feel wealth and wealthy people are somehow corrupt, immoral, and that 'money is the root of all evil'. That is NOT a coherent logic. You have to make a choice, because this confusion in your mind is stopping you growing rich! So which is it? Are you here to make money? Yes? Great! If so, it's time to clear out all that garbage in your head that's holding you back—the cynicism, the laziness, the negativity, the confusion, and guilt you feel regarding wealth.

Look, money is indifferent to you. It's like a beautiful and sophisticated woman who doesn't need men, and she's repulsed by desperation and inconsideration. She doesn't care one way or the other what you think about her. If you want me, come and get me, she says. And if you don't, that's fine too, because plenty of others will if you don't.

The guy with the guts to approach her is the one who'll get her. Do you think she cares if you go and complain about that outcome if you didn't approach her first? She's been around as long as civilization itself, and she's here to stay. And throughout history, any time humans have tried to share her equally, she went into hiding.

The man who has a coherent philosophy about her, the man who knows what she is, accepts her as such, and respects her... he's the one who'll gain her respect and attention.

On one hand you want wealth, and you KNOW that way too many rich people didn't have a privilege over you. But on the other hand, there's a conflict inside you based on what society and media feeds you: that wealth is corruption and rich people are evil. This all adds up to a paralyzing affliction and an incoherent philosophy regarding money that will keep you scavenging for breadcrumbs in The Vulture Culture instead of banqueting with that beautiful woman: wealth. And if you truly don't want to get up on that table, that's fine too, as long as you get out of the way of others who do. At least you have a coherent philosophy now. Just make a decision and end the conflict in your mind.

What are the odds that you'll make a million dollars for yourself? 10-1? 50-1? 100-1? 1,000-1? Which is it for you? All those answers are wrong, and I'd like to explain why, and give you your correct answer. That's right, I'm going to tell you what the odds are of you becoming a millionaire. I think the answer will surprise you.

Older readers may recall the winter Olympics of 1980

in Lake Placid, and the famous gold medal victory of the USA ice hockey team, coached by Herb Brooks. They overcame dramatic odds. At this time, the Soviet hockey team (known as "The Red Machine") was the far and away favorite to win. They had always won, they seemed unbeatable, and 1980 looked to be no different, especially after they'd thrashed an NHL all-star team in a warm-up exhibition match. The specter of growing communist power in the world hung over every victory of theirs.

Team USA coach, Herb Brooks, approached the problem in an unorthodox way. He appreciated that to keep doing things the same way and expecting different results is pure stupidity. He understood that hockey is a team sport, and that all-star line-ups were a bunch of individuals. So he formed a team of young college kids he had figured would work as a cohesive unit. Young guys who could skate hard for three periods and keep up with the Russians. Kids he could mold to play a different style, the European style, to beat the ever-dominating European teams in the event. (The European rinks are generally larger and are more about skating hard and physical fitness than the North American counterparts). He was berated for this approach by American commentators and 'experts', but the results spoke for themselves, and they faced the Soviets in the semi-final. Even then, nobody expected USA to win, the Soviets looked that strong. **The odds were against them.** In the dressing room before the game, Herb Brooks made a speech to his young players...

He knew that his players knew the odds were against them. 10-1 seemed to be the expert consensus. He didn't try to deny these odds with 'rah-rah' positive thinking and invent his own version of reality for them; he acknowledged the 10-1 odds against them. But then he said, "Yes, if we played this team ten times, we would lose nine of those games. **But tonight is NOT one of those nine games. Tonight is that one game that we win.**" They beat the Soviets and then beat Finland in the final (go rent the movie about this: "Miracle").

*In short, Brooks made his players ignore the odds. **And so should you.***

If I'd have listened to the odds all my life, and to people warning me that the odds were against me succeeding, I'd never have got anywhere. In time I developed an answer for people who'd warn me about the "average chance of success." It was this: "Averages are for average efforts. Most people only put in average effort."

So that's what it comes down to, my friend. Averages are literally a measure of what MOST PEOPLE do. So it's really a question of if you're prepared to choose to MAKE yourself a special case. And with *The 7 Secrets* working for you, you *will* become a special case and gain the wealth God wants you to have.

The odds shouldn't bother you, and yet we seem to fixate on them when it comes to getting what we want in our lives. And doesn't everyone want to be a millionaire? I mean, you're crowded out by 'competition'... you'll get killed in the stampede, won't you? No, you won't, and here's why...

Because most people will only put in an average effort to achieve this goal and won't have the Biblical blueprint they need. In fact, they'll be downright flaky about it, most of them putting faith in a lottery ticket. This is the case by definition, not my opinion, as that's what creates averages or odds, right?

And odds can be deceptive. Here's a classic that may have held you back in the past if you hesitated about starting a business: "80% of new businesses fail in their first year." Ah, but what TYPE of businesses is this referring to? HOME businesses are different because they lack the overheads, HOME businesses have a SUCCESS rate in EXCESS of 90% in their first year.

So let me ask you that question again: "What are the odds you'll become a millionaire?" The next time someone tries to tell you that the odds are against you achieving your goal, put yourself in that dressing room in 1980 and hear Coach Herb Brooks tell you: **"Not tonight."** The Bible echoes Brooks' words:

"The Lord is my light and my salvation; whom shall I fear? The Lord is the strength of my life; of whom shall I be afraid? When the wicked, even mine enemies and my foes, came upon me to eat my flesh, they stumbled and fell." – Psalms 27:1-2

Stop the negativity and start believing it can be done! If you keep doing what you've always been doing, then you'll keep getting what you've always been getting! Ready for a change? Then open your mind! Worried about not being like everyone else? Well, if you think like everyone else you'll have what everyone else has, which is years of hard work and a lifetime of debt!

That's what's in store for the Fools if you'd care to join them. So it's time to have a long hard conversation with that person in the mirror and consider if you are a Fool or have Foolish tendencies, and if so, if you're prepared to stop being one so you can come with me down the path to freedom.

No Room for Fools

"All we like sheep have gone astray; we have turned one to his own way; and the Lord hath laid on him the iniquity of us all." – Isiah 53:6

Sadly, the Fools make up the majority of people, and the majority of people are simply too afraid to walk down this path to freedom, let alone remove the obstacles from it. The fear is usually a *fear of failure*.

Imagine, quite literally, that you're at a fork in the road. One road is well paved, brightly lit, and many others are merrily skipping down it. And then there's a less beaten path. There's no lights, it's an overgrown dirt road, and not a soul in sight. Which path will you take? Taking the less beaten path is a lot easier said than done!

Eliminating fear makes you strong. I'm not talking about suicidal 'fool's courage', I'm talking about the fearlessness that stems from superior knowledge (like you will gain here). Most people don't bother to seek knowledge, so they remain weak and vulnerable. And they blame anyone else's success on blind luck…

Forget this idea about luck if you want to break free financially.

This belief obscures the truth because it separates an effect from its cause. When we say someone's fallen on bad luck, we relieve that person of any responsibility for what has happened. Similarly, when we say someone has had good luck, we deny that person credit for the effort that led to the happy outcome.

The key lies in maximizing the areas where we have some control over the outcome, while minimizing the areas where we have absolutely no control over the outcome. Cause and effect.

For example, society has fed you a big lie for as long as you've lived. It goes something like this: "Get good grades at school, work hard, get a job, and save money."

When what you actually should've been told is (IF you want financial freedom): "School is irrelevant because it teaches *nothing* about money or what The Bible offers, you should work smart, stop being a wage slave as quickly as possible, and invest money wisely."

People are brainwashed by the first option—society's Big Lie—and then are understandably frightened of risk and making money. But if you're reading this now, it's my bet that you're in the second camp. The second choice is a choice of controlling your own destiny. And it's my pleasure to help you take that least trodden path. But you don't operate in isolation, do you? You're probably surrounded by the Fools every day, and they can hold your dreams back.

Have you ever heard of or witnessed the phenomenon of crabs in a bucket? If several live crabs are caught and thrown in a bucket headed for a restaurant, and one crabs tries to climb out, do you know what the other crabs do?

I would like to think that they would help out. "Here you go, buddy, let me give you a 'claw up'! Good for you for trying!"

But sadly, this is not in the nature of animals (and humans are animals). What happens is that the rest of the crabs in the bucket pull that escaping crab back down with them. The message is quite different in reality: "Hey, who the heck do you think you are? You're not better than me! You get back down here in the collective bucket with us!"

How often does this happen to you in daily life? People can't help themselves. It doesn't matter if it's your dearest and closest friend, your beloved spouse, your parents, your co-workers (they're the worst), they will all act like crabs in a bucket **because that is human nature**.

And the trouble is that you (understandably) trust those people more than me. You listen to them, you are heavily influenced by their compulsive need to pull you back into the bucket. And if you lost your livelihood, they would also be pushing you to do things the same way all over again even though it led to your demise.

My advice is, and always has been, to keep your blueprints for financial freedom safely tucked away where nobody can see them.

If the crabs can't see you escaping, they won't pull you back down. You're reading this because you're a special kind of person. At the very least, you questioned the existence we've been programmed to follow. But do you take action? That's the key.

And how much of your INACTION or APATHY is because you can feel the other crabs in the bucket pulling you back down? The Bible states: *"He that walketh with wise men shall be wise: but a companion of fools shall be destroyed."* In other words, hang out with people who are more successful than you, not people who are less so, or people who are just plain losers!

Despite The Bible advising otherwise, the Fools live as:

1) **Employees, making their bosses rich.**
2) **Borrowers, making banks rich.**
3) **Taxpayers, making the government rich.**
4) **Consumers, making corporations rich.**

Is it any wonder why the rich get richer and the poor get poorer?! The Fools are disadvantaged by their preconceived ideas about everything. They bleat out a pre-programmed response to every situation in life. Their principles have no coherent logic. "This is the way things have always been," is good enough for them. They then wonder why they never achieve anything. The Fools are skeptical about new opportunities. That is why they are mostly powerless and poor and use disbelief as an excuse for their lack of conviction.

The question you must ask yourself is if you want to be one of them? Or are you fearless enough to be told The 7 Secrets and how to use them to your advantage?

If you're one of The Fools you will have been outraged by the things I have said here and will throw this down in disgust. If you're one of these people, you'll desperately be looking to discredit all I've told you here ("Please let it not be true!") so you can carry on life with your head in the sand.

If you cannot free your mind from the illusions that have been inflicted upon you to keep you living paycheck to paycheck, you will never be free of wage slavery. Once you can see through these illusions, their power over you is lost and you will have taken the first and most important step to true freedom. So, let's talk more about these illusions that have been fed to you… but this involves accepting some shocking truths.

The Truth Will Make You Free

"And you will know the truth, and the truth will make you free." – John 8:32.

To be fair, you can't blame the Fools because the institutions that they trust to look after their interests do nothing of the sort—the only interests these institutions serve are their own, and those interests usually involve making life worse for the Fools, not better. *Remember what I said earlier about listening to people with agendas that conflict with your own…?*

Don't you think it's strange how most people have only just enough money to live from month to month? This is no accident. It's like driving down a tunnel with no sign of light at the other end. The only thing that keeps people going is the fact that one day they hope to retire with a pension to support them through the remaining years of their lives. Depressing.

What's going on? It's all about where people get their information from, and they're clearly *not* getting it from where you are now! The American population has three sources for its information: politicians, corporations, and the media. None of these three will tell you the truth you need to know for reasons that are about to become clear.

A series of illusions and con tricks have been created to ensure that the majority of the population stays poor and in the dark. The American Dream is denied. The very fact that you will not read this information in the press is no coincidence. Are you prepared to sit back and let this happen to you and your family? Then listen closely because we are about to remove a BIG obstacle from your path to freedom...

Corporations, the media, and the politicians have been keeping you in the dark for many years, each with different motives to further their causes. They have systematically spun falsehoods to keep the majority of the population living from month to month. Why should they do this? Let's look at each one's motives in turn...

Beware the Talebearers

"Where no wood is, there the fire goeth out: so where there is no talebearer, the strife ceaseth."

Our beloved media?! Surely these people are the messengers of truth and have the interests of the population at heart, don't they? Ummm... no. The 'scoop' of the century will never be published. Why? Because the <u>only</u> thing the media is concerned with is <u>selling newspapers</u>!

They are businesses and therefore, by definition, their sole purpose is to make a profit. To believe otherwise is extremely naïve. By the way, the media covers a wide range of areas, from the Internet to TV. They're all the same thing. We like to think the **media** exposes any and all secrets out there, but the media is a major part of your problem!

   _   **The media would be flat broke without the truckload of money they receive from large corporate advertisers (especially banks) who have a lot to lose from the public becoming wise about money.**

- Every day, corporations sponsor the nightly news. Is the media going to bite the hand that feeds it by running a story that would conflict with a sponsor's interest?

- And let's not forget now that due to so many mergers and corporate acquisitions, most media outlets are now owned and controlled by large corporations, all in bed together, all needing you to stay in the dark so you keep feeding them your money.

- Most newspapers and media outlets are owned/controlled/influenced by a liberal agenda—in other words, an anti-wealth agenda. What effect do you think their biased stories have on your attempts to become wealthy and break free of the rat-race? You can't want wealth *and* hate wealthy people.

The public doesn't want to know the truth as you do, they can't *handle* the truth. What the public wants is snappy slogans and 'sound-bites'. They don't want to know about the things I am telling you because it would unsettle them and would mean that they might actually have to *wake up and do something to change their depressing lives*. People would prefer to be spoon-fed a constant diet of topics that tear them away them from reality so they can bury their heads and live in denial. The media keeps the population in a constant state of panic and guilt by reporting on the latest 'hot issue,' and many times the facts are completely distorted to sensationalize the story. They have played their part in keeping you in the dark by not addressing the key issues.

And Hollywood is another invisible obstacle in your path, without you even knowing. So often we're told this myth by storywriters: how poor people are so much happier than rich people and how money corrupts people—have you ever seen a film where it's the rich guy who is happy and honest and the poor guy is a miserable liar! Of course not—people would storm out of the theater! Story lines like these have *subconsciously* conditioned you into feeling some sort of guilt or hesitation about becoming wealthy. True, money isn't everything—*happiness is everything* and money plays a part in happiness by taking the pressure off, allowing you to leave a job you dislike and follow your dreams. That's happiness.

The purpose of your life is to find the purpose of your life, and financial freedom will give you that luxury because money buys freedom, security, and choices.

So often, people (who are stuck in the rat-race) say to me, "Oh, I don't care about money." Say what?! So you spend the vast majority of your irreplaceable life working for money and then tell me you don't care about money?! That's more than a contradiction. That's insanity!

Now let's turn to the next villain in this drama: the politicians...

Beware the Pharaohs

"Woe unto him that buildeth his house by unrighteousness, and his chambers by wrong; that useth his neighbour's service without wages, and giveth him not for his work." –
Jeremiah 22:13

The Bible is packed with stories about people in power abusing their position and how their subjects suffer as a result. It was tyrannical Pharaohs and Kings in Biblical times, in modern times our leaders don't send soldiers over to kill your first born son (yet!), but they've since developed more insidious and sophisticated ways to control the population to their liking.

Bill Clinton once said, "It's not acceptable for an American to love his country and not respect its government." What strange (but convenient for politicians) logic! Of course you can love your country and dislike the government that runs it, that's what both The American Revolution and Christianity were founded on!

But governments look after your interests though, don't they? The first thing to stop clinging on to is the naïve belief that governments are interested in the people that elected them. This is the first myth they have let you believe. The one and only thing a government exists for is to stay in power. People only become politicians so they can control other people. Period. The greatest achievement any government ever made was making its people believe that they actually care for them. How can they achieve this? Well, quite simply by giving the voters what they want. In other words, by spending and giving away money. A government is only popular for as long as they have fat treasure chests to play their power games.

And where does this money come from? You, in the form of tax!

Now where do you think the government would be if too many people wanted to escape the 'rat race' and more importantly, <u>they knew how to?</u>

Down the creek without a paddle springs to mind! The government has a vested interest in ensuring that you are an indebted wage slave for your entire life, spending **money with** corporations so those corporations can pay even more tax. No tax = no government. Undeniable fact. They need your taxes to bribe voters with so they can stay in power.

They have to get the balance just right though. If you became too poor, you would revolt and overthrow the government by force, like in The American Revolution (which was the silent agenda for disallowing a population to own firearms). On the other hand, if too many people gave up work and retired, the government would also be out of a job.

So do you think the government wants you reading material like this? Why do you think the government doesn't want The Bible taught in public schools? And why would they want you to be financially educated in school? Knowing The 7 Secrets enables a person to give up work. If too many people paid off their debts, stopped spending, and retired, the global economy would collapse. Period.

So do you now see why the government is a big part of your problem? This is no conspiracy theory garbage. Governments aren't vindictive, they just turn a blind eye. It's <u>convenient</u> if you slave away paying taxes to them your whole life. It's <u>convenient</u> if large corporations rip you off, because corporations pay tax too AND contribute to political campaigns (and many corporations are part-owned by politicians too). Nothing personal. Just a game of musical chairs, with YOU left standing!

An interesting fact for you: the first thing an elephant trainer teaches a baby elephant is not to escape. He does this by chaining the infant's leg to a large log so if the baby elephant tries to escape, he gives up, realizing the log is too big for him to pull. Even when the elephant becomes an adult, all the trainer needs to do is chain it to that same size log, even though the elephant is so large it could easily pull it along and escape.

Why? Because of the conditioning the elephant received as an infant: that it would be hopeless to try and escape. It becomes a prisoner of the past.

Do you see the similarity? You've been chained to a log too, a log that you can now walk away from. You've been conditioned since childhood to get a job and pay taxes until you die. The government has trained you to never escape the rat-race. You just need to appreciate that you're big enough and strong enough to throw off those chains now! The American education system is still based on the Prussian system. The Prussian system was invented with the Industrial Revolution and is designed to brainwash children into becoming compliant drones for a corporate workforce and factories. So it's certainly *not* about developing individuality, creativity, and financial education in children, and if you reflect on your own education with this in mind, I'm sure you'll remember school for being the sausage factory it is.

Here's an interesting thought: the government encourages you to get the largest mortgage you can on your home. They do this by giving you a tax break on the interest you pay on the loan.

All the time you're in debt you have to work to pay tax to them! Plus, a larger mortgage usually means a larger house which means more property tax, so it's not the tax-break everyone thinks it is (but it means more tax for politicians!) Isn't it funny how you get a tax-break for getting into debt?

Please would you take a dollar bill from your wallet and hold it up. Done that? Great, now could you please tell me what it is? The answer is: paper with patterns printed on it. Nothing more. What you're essentially holding in your hand is an "IOU" from the government. You're saying that you trust the government to honor the value of that "IOU" note. Once upon a time, money was gold coins and actually worth something. In those days, your dollar really would be worth a dollar.

In my opinion, the two most important documents in the world are The Bible and The Constitution, and both documents state gold and silver as the only true currency.

As the financial system became more sophisticated though, paper notes were issued based on government's PHYSICAL holding of gold bullion. However, in 1930 this system (known as The Gold Standard) was dropped. Here in the land of the free, gold was even confiscated from anyone known to be holding it. Why was this perfectly honorable system dropped? Because it meant politicians could only spend what they owned. By dropping The Gold Standard, governments created their own credit cards in the form of printing presses. They quite literally gave themselves a license to print money!

The result? Inflation (inflation is defined as the quantity of money in the system). This is why you hear about stories from Germany in the 1930s where a wheelbarrow full of cash was needed to buy a loaf of bread. Since 1930, governments, in their quest to win votes by printing their way out of their incompetence, have systematically destroyed the wealth of generations. Your dollar bill buys far less than it did in 1900, right? However, an ounce of gold pretty much buys today what it did 100 years ago! Can you see how powerful belief is? Belief enables the whole world to think that paper money is actually worth something! Governments want you to believe that the idea of gold is a silly relic of ancient times. Why do you think that is? And if that's the case, why do governments themselves hoard hundreds of tons of gold?? Paper money is a huge house of cards and every now and then, those cards tip over and the price of gold rises. The house of cards has not yet fallen though; it's just started wobbling.

How about the money the government promised you in later life in the form of Medicare and Social Security? Well, Social Security is expected to be bankrupt by 2032 and Medicare is already bankrupt. Why? Politicians all claim to want to save Social Security and yet still carry on raiding it! That's right, all that money you pay in tax isn't going to Social Security; it's just the government's credit card! As an insider, Senator Ernest Hollings pointed out, "Obviously the first way to save Social Security is to stop looting it."

I don't want to start a revolution against the government (they would kill me in cold blood if I tried, as sure as the Romans killed Jesus); I just want you to see the truth and have clarity of thought in the real world, because this clears your path to financial freedom.

Now let's turn to the big-banks and corporations they control…

Beware the 'Money-Changers'

"The rich ruleth over the poor, and the borrower is the servant to the lender."

The financial system is simply a function of human psychology—supply and demand, fear and greed. And what is The Bible if not the ultimate guidebook and record of human psychology. Furthermore, the financial system was very much in place at the time The Bible was written, albeit in a less developed way. There were bankers, currency traders, merchants, trade agreements, and the laws of supply and demand (and pricing) were as much in play then as they are today. Most of all, the deadly sins of pride, greed, and fear haven't gone away, and you'll learn to become a beneficiary of these deadly sins being committed in the financial system, not a victim of them.

The Bible refers to the big-banks as 'money-changers', and there's a well-known tale in The Bible about Jesus flipping over the trading tables of these 'money-changers' for their greed. Banks take *your* hard-earned money and return you a pittance on it while they manipulate events for their own fortune, and then use *your* money to gamble on those events. And with the fat profits they make from their manipulations, they lend it back to you at high interest rates, after borrowing even *more money* from the government at low interest rates—and where did the government get the money from to do that? You, in the form of taxes!

I can see where Jesus was coming from when he smashed up their trading tables! The whole system is a shameless racket, and you're the target. Think back over your lifetime. Add up how much money the banks and their government buddies have taken from you over the years. Wouldn't you like to get some of it back? Then let's do it...

Clear the Path of Obstacles
"Surely the Lord God will do nothing, but he revealeth his secret unto his servants the prophets." – Amos 3:7

Knowledge is worthless unless you act upon it. If I told you what the lottery numbers were for next Saturday, what would you do? Why, you'd run to the nearest gas station to buy a ticket! This is exactly the same principle here. I will gladly tell you what *The 7 Secrets* are, but they are worthless and meaningless unless you learn how to use them, and that is what the rest of this book is about.

Please resist the temptation to draw your own conclusions from what you are about to read. We have already discovered that to bleat out a pre-programmed response through complete dogma would be an act of one of the Fools! To help you to avoid this temptation allow me to show you what the classic Fool responses are to reading *The 7 Secrets*:

Fool Excuse 1) "Well if it's that easy why isn't *everyone* doing it?!"

I wish I had a buck for each time I've heard this ridiculous question. It's ridiculous because it's completely hypothetical. The wealthy will always be a *minority* and they will always be so because the majority are too busy making silly excuses for inaction, like this one! Do you see? The masses are so busy being skeptical about opportunities they miss all the opportunities that come their way. And so they become even more skeptical about the next opportunity and the whole thing becomes a downward spiral. The question is do *you* want to be one of the financially free? Remember what I said about being *diligent*?

Fool Excuse 2) "Oh, I already know that!"

Please! You may think so, but if that is the case why are you not already wealthy? If you're hoping to skim through, looking to pick morsels out here and there you will not gain anything. These are the actions of the slack-handed and sluggards, and The Bible rightly forecasts their imminent poverty:

"The way of a fool is right in his own eyes: but he that hearkeneth to counsel is wise."

Fool Excuse 3) "That won't work—you can't beat the system!"

The only way you are qualified to say this would be if you had already tried to use the knowledge I will be giving you in the true sense and knew what the outcome was. As you do not yet know what the true sense is (because I have not yet told you) it logically follows that you are not qualified to say this. The argument of a skeptic is often destroyed immediately by the use of logic. Beat the system? If you call the system something that forces us all to go to work in some form or another every day then you're wrong. Myself and many others are a living testimony to the contrary, and The Bible contains several famous stories about minorities of clever people beating the system, the most famous one of all being Jesus himself, of course. He was seen by the Romans as an enemy of the state, and yet a few hundred years later all of the Roman Empire was forced to convert to Christianity…

"Trust in the Lord with all thine heart; and lean not into thine own understanding."

Fool Excuse 4) "My friends say this is a waste of time."

Are your friends all wealthy? Have they used the information I'll be giving you here before? No? Then how on earth are they qualified to state this?

There are two types of people in this world: eagles and chickens. Eagles are fearless and chickens live up to their name and live by fear. An eagle's first step to living the life of an eagle is to face all fears. And an eagle's number one fear is: What will my chicken friends think if I start to live differently?

The skepticism of others close to you is something I cannot help you with, so it is best that you don't tell anyone what you are studying; their skepticism is contagious and threatens to condemn you to mediocrity. The sooner the eagle flies the coop, the sooner the eagle lives the life of power and freedom he was born for!

Remember, the system is designed to keep the vast majority at the grindstone through lack of education. So it stands to reason that the majority of people you mix with will think all this is a waste of time (read: "I can't be bothered to change my life and you're unsettling me by making an effort to change yours"). The Bible told me to always mix with people who are more successful than I was, not less successful:

"He that walketh with wise men shall be wise: but a companion of fools shall be destroyed."

Fool Excuse 5) "It's alright for some—I haven't got a head for money/business."

Now we are coming to the simply feeble excuse of the sluggard. You can insert any one you like here, such as not being educated, not being the right sex, color, or age. The list is endless. The current state of our society is increasingly bringing out the weak and needy side of human nature that makes us think nothing is our fault anymore; something that is highlighted by the outrageous lawsuits getting through the system. A person becomes obese from eating too much... hey, it's not his fault; it was all because of that evil fast-food restaurant that forced him to eat 50 of their hamburgers a day! No, you're NOT too old either. Colonel Sanders didn't make it until he'd lost everything in his 60's!

Money isn't prejudiced against sex, color, or age. It just wants a master who will understand and nurture it. The only way you'll face prejudice is when you let another body control your destiny. Financial freedom takes the upper hand away from the prejudiced:

"For ye know the grace of our Lord Jesus Christ, that, though he was rich, yet for your sakes he became poor, that ye through his poverty might be rich." Corinthians 8:9.

Fool Excuse 6) "I haven't got the time for all this!"

I'm sure you haven't! The system is set up that way. Hey, the rat-race is a busy place to be. Just one thing to add: MAKE TIME!

It doesn't matter how fast you get to a place if that place isn't where you want to be! You need to take a step back and look at the bigger picture here. You're thinking on a different level now. Sure, you need to pay the bills, so no-one's asking to quit your job. *But you must make time.*

It's funny, but I often hear people make this excuse about having no time and money, but those same people are happy to wait in line for half an hour to pay $7 for a coffee at Starbucks!

And there always seems to be enough time and money to go shopping, eat donuts for the heck of it, smoke cigarettes, get drunk, etc. Time is now the most precious commodity you have. A key difference between those that succeed and those that fail in life is what they do in their spare time. Prioritize. What's more important to you?

The Fools can always find something 'better' to do, like change the oil in their car. Jiffy Lube charge around $30 to do this and the supplies to do it yourself can run at $28, but 43 million Americans still change their own oil instead of educating themselves about money. The same 43 million Americans who live paycheck to paycheck most likely! I talk about financial freedom; they talk about changing their oil. I find it hard to sympathize when they then complain about being poor!

You are quite right when you say your time is precious. What you do with your time is your future!

Is that part-time job necessary enough to deprive you of learning about escaping the grind altogether? What's the hourly rate of that part-time job? Now deduct tax (at the higher rate most likely). Now deduct what it costs for childcare (both emotionally and financially). Now deduct costs of transport (fuel, tolls, etc.), dry-cleaning, and subsistence. Is it worth it? Or are you too brainwashed about the work ethic to learn about money and freedom?

Besides, one of the skills you'll learn here is how to 'compress time'—to do in one year what it takes most people ten years!

God wants you to be wealthy, but you'll need to adopt the tools and characteristics that allow you to gain that wealth.

"Hope deferred maketh the heart sick: but when the desire cometh, it is a tree of life."

The 7 Secrets
"Wisdom hath builded her house, she hath hewn out her seven pillars." – Proverbs 9:1.

If you've honestly digested everything I've said so far we should have cleared your path of obstacles. I can now put the secrets in your hand and then teach you how to use them, but that crucial step we just took was of extreme importance unless you want these secrets to be worthless, as they truly are in the hands of a Fool.

IMPORTANT: If you ask others what these verses mean they won't tell you what I've told you. All you will hear are the words of people (some of them Fools) who only know the common and confused interpretation of these verses. Their (common) interpretations have not been decoded into the financial secrets

I will teach you. You will not find the financial truth behind these secrets anywhere else because they are closely guarded by those who use them.

So read *The 7 Secrets* that follow with an open mind, not as one of the Fools. And remember, they have little meaning without the in-depth study of them that will follow in the coming chapters…!

The 1ˢᵗ Secret:

"Wilt thou set thine eyes upon that which is not? For riches certainly make themselves wings; they fly away as an eagle towards Heaven."
- Proverbs 23:5

Do you ever feel like your bank account is mysteriously a bucket full of holes and your paychecks are but a small tap desperately trying to fill it up in vain?

This is no accidental occurrence; it's how The System is designed, to keep you scraping by from paycheck to paycheck, paying your taxes to the government, paying your interest to the banks, and buying products from corporations. And when you're too old to do that, those same institutions will throw you on the scrap-heap (just ask a health insurance company, and good luck if you're counting on welfare or Medicare not being totally raided by then).

It's now a statistical fact that most people will not even have enough assets or income to retire at 70. You need to get a grip on this <u>now</u> or you won't be taking your grandkids to McDonald's in retirement, *you'll be serving the burgers there instead.*

The Fools are totally unaware how or why their "riches certainly make themselves wings" and fly away from them. It just always seems to be the case that there is always too little money left at the end of the month. Sound familiar? It doesn't have to be that way and it doesn't have to be hard work to hotwire The System to your advantage instead of disadvantage—you just need to be taught this secret and things will take care of themselves.

Understand: money has a homing instinct. It will always fly back to its master—the people who understand it, have learned about it, and respect it.

This is the reason why so many lottery winners end up flat broke a year later, right? And listen, it's not a case of just spending less and paying off debt or whatever—anybody can do that. No, it's much more subtle and it's more about applying some simple secrets and uncovering the illusions The System feeds you… it's about slipping through the cracks and opting out of what is a rigged game.

What's the secret then? The secret is in the first part of that Bible verse: "Wilt thou set thine eyes on that which is not?" The verse has multiple secrets, all of which I will teach you, and here's just a couple of them:

- *"That which is not"* refers to illusions, and lies and scams perpetrated by government, corporations, banks, and the media. You need to see through these illusions and make some simple changes to get you on the path to freedom.
- *"That which is not"* also refers to the fact that money isn't real. It sounds odd to hear that, I know, but as long as you see money as real, the harder you will work for it! When you understand that money isn't real you can

attract more of it and will work LESS for it. It's a bit like sand—the more you tighten your grip on it the more it will slip through your fingers. As I said, I know it sounds strange, which is why I will dedicate much more time to this later in the book, where I'll also reveal this to you...

- **How in one simple step you could enjoy a luxury, tax-free retirement TODAY with a mere fraction of what you thought it would take to retire.**
- **How your retirement account can pay you at least DOUBLE the income you expected.**
- **How your Social Security card could be like an unclaimed lottery ticket and pay a minimum of $5,000 instantly and thereafter.**
- **The forgotten document that could be somewhere in your home and worth over $100,000.**
- **The government loophole that pays you $620 a month for doing nothing.**
- **Specially developed software that brings your retirement closer.**
- **How to make the big-banks pay you crazily high rent on something you don't even own, and make them start owing you instead of you owing them all the time.**
- **The big secret of money-flow that makes or breaks peoples' bank accounts—how to position yourself to have more money enter your account each month and work LESS for it.**

Would you like to know how to clip the wings of your money so it doesn't fly away, attract more money, and take money from the banks and government instead of them taking from you so that you may build wealth at a rate you never thought possible? *Then I will show you...*

The 2ⁿᵈ Secret:

"That which is far off and exceeding deep, who can find it out?"
- Ecclesiastes 7:24

If I was only allowed to use one of these seven secrets I would pick this one! Though all seven are crucial, this one binds them all together. This is the secret that got me that mansion I showed you earlier! This is a really BIG secret, but very few people know it, and those that do don't understand it fully or know how to use it. You must not make this same mistake...

The main reason much of The Bible is open to interpretation and debate about meaning is that many verses, I believe, are a riddle to be solved by those in search of its treasures, and this is a classic example. What is "far off and exceedingly deep" is a matter of *perception*, and that's why a Fool will never find it out, and never make it to freedom.

It's precisely because the dream of accumulating wealth (or anything) is perceived as being impossible or extremely difficult to achieve that people get overwhelmed before they've even taken a single step down the path to freedom. Every journey begins with a single step, and without this secret you won't take it.

In case you're wondering, I'm not talking about self-belief and all that other happy-clappy stuff you hear in motivational seminars or books. In fact, those things are a big part of the problem because they're usually written by charlatans who haven't travelled the path themselves. No, what I'm talking about is a *concrete, 1-2-3 step method* that's proven to get you to freedom as quickly as possible.

"Who can find it out?" Exactly the point. Hardly anyone can find it out! The Fools have about as much chance as finding this out as a camel passing through the eye of a needle. The application of this secret doesn't come naturally to human beings; it's like swimming or riding a bike; it has to be *learned*. I will teach you this, and here's just a few examples of what you'll learn:

- **How a simple task that took me under a minute a day led to me getting my mansion.**
- **The 6 numbers that most people don't know and are causing them to fail and fall behind.**
- **The one word that supercharges your ride down the path to freedom.**

Would you like to learn this powerful secret—the secret of secrets? *Then I will show you...*

The 3rd Secret:

"A prudent man forseeth the evil, and hideth himself: but the simple pass on, and are punished." - Proverbs 22:3

"The evil" is the shenanigans of big banks. You know the effects of this all too well, but you probably don't know how and why it happens, and how you can engineer their actions into your favor...

On the surface it seems obvious, but in a financial context there's a lot more to this verse than meets the untrained eye. *Ignorance of this secret is what will deny you the retirement you deserve and keep you a slave to the banking establishment your whole life!* If you'd have known this secret in May of 2008 you'd have not only escaped the brutal financial crisis that followed, you'd also have made an absolute fortune from it, perfectly legally and ethically.

Here's how the big-banks use this "evil" secret against you in 1-2-3 steps:

1. Entice you into sending them checks each month for some sort of investment/retirement account. You've seen the glossy brochures with happy retired couples walking down the beach at sunset; you know what I'm referring to.

2. Just in case you don't write them those checks, they lobby (read: bribe) the government to make it mandatory under law and to give you tax-breaks for doing so.

3. The banks then tell you that the investment is a *long-term* proposition, and you have to just stick to it, keep paying those checks in, if you want to look like that happy retired couple on the brochure, that is. In other words, *do not take the money out.*

4. The banks then take those monthly checks of yours and trade with it in the stock market. So the stock market rises with all that cash coming into it—and they call that a "bull market." When the stock market eventually gets too high, the banks then need an exit strategy— they need someone to buy all this now-overpriced stock from them. So they promote it to the public and they

support prices up by continuing to buy stocks at tactical times. Only when they've offloaded all their stocks on the unsuspecting public do the banks stop buying, and the market crashes (after the banks have made special kinds of trades that profit from a crash). Note: it's only the banks' money that was saved, not yours. Your money goes up in smoke, and all those little checks you sent them are now worth half what they were. Sorry, you'll have to work a bit harder and a bit longer to be like that couple on the brochure—read the small print.

5. But the government is happy because the banks have paid huge amounts of tax to them for all that money they just made. The politicians are obliged to make some noise and even make a few arrests for the cameras, but the party must go on or they'd lose all that tax (to buy votes with) as well as those political contributions (read: bribes).

6. The government charges you tax at the rate of around a third of all you earn, as you well know. They then give some of that money to the banks…

7. So, because the politicians are in the banks' pockets, the government lends the banks money at virtually zero interest—and the banks can borrow all this cheap money (your money) at seven times the cash reserves they have. If a bank has a million dollars, it can now borrow another seven million dollars from the government (read: YOU) at let's say 1%. So it now has 8 million dollars to lend YOU and is only paying 1% for it. It lends YOU and everybody else that eight million dollars at anywhere from 5-20%. Nice work.

8. But then the banks get greedy with all that cheap and easy money and start lending million-dollar mortgages to car valets who earn $20k a year. This causes demand for a lot more properties to be built. When the inevitable happens and the car valet can't pay his mortgage and defaults on the loan, foreclosures hit the market and the property market crashes. But not before the banks have secretly realized this would happen and have packaged up all this 'toxic debt' into an investment product that they sell to someone else through the stock market. Eventually both the stock market and the property market crashes, and then the whole cycle starts over.

This goes on all the time, it will never stop going on, and the banks will get richer and richer while you get poorer and poorer. All you can do is *switch sides.*

The trick is to be able to see these cycles taking place, to see what the banks are doing and when. If you can accomplish this, then you will be the one getting rich by riding on the back of the banks, 100% legally and ethically.

"A prudent man forseeth the evil, and hideth himself: but the simple pass on, and are punished." You need to be that "prudent man."

Learn this secret and I promise you, you will NEVER again be blindsided by an event like the 2008 financial crisis— you will expect it, and you will profit by it.

The big banks constantly slaughter Fools like cattle, but I'm going to teach you to turn the tables to ride on the back of their game so you can aim to take those ten steps to a million I showed you earlier. Remember:

Starting with just $1,000, if you could double your money just ten times, you'd have over a MILLION DOLLARS. Undeniable FACT.

So, literally, the million-dollar question is, *"How can you consistently double your money? And without crazy risks to do so!"*

Well, there are *hundreds* of examples of the people who know this secret doubling their money over just the last couple of years alone! Most of them were bankers. I will show you these examples and how to follow them later on in this book.

Would you like to use this secret to be that "prudent man" who can see these cycles taking place, who knows how to profit from them, and not one of the "simple" who gets punished? Would you like to turn the tables on the banks and ride on their backs and turn $1,000 into a $MILLION? *Then I will show you...*

The 4th Secret:

4-50-70-100

Inside that old Bible my grandfather gave me were bookmarks on certain pages, and on those pages he'd underlined certain passages...

... And each of those passages referred to certain numbers that seemed to be repeated throughout The Bible...

There were four numbers. These numbers seemed to pop up all over The Bible, and my grandfather had underlined them all.

I wouldn't have thought anything of this had my grandfather not been such a financially astute man. Had I just stumbled on his big secret? Was he trying to pass it on to me by leaving me this Bible? But what use could those four numbers possibly be? They looked like a combination to a bank vault or something!

Little did I know at the time, but 'bank vault code' was closer to the truth than I could ever have imagined...

I use these four Biblical numbers to LEGALLY *take back* my money from the banking establishment whenever they become most greedy. I am constantly raiding the 'money-changers', and reclaiming riches.

Ready to fight back? Want to reclaim some of what 'the money-changers' took from you? These four Biblical numbers are your ticket out of this rigged game. Based on my experience, this Biblical money code can turn your life around *fast*. I'm talking about *within a week...!*

I'm looking at my bank statement now, and this code just made me another fast $720 within a week of using it. I didn't break a sweat to get it, I just punched a few buttons at the time that this Biblical money-code told me to. Easy. So how can you follow my footsteps and use this Biblical money code...?

Here's how. I opened a special kind of account that gives me a kind of direct line into the heart of the banking establishment—all 100% legal. Then I set it all up so it works on autopilot. When an opportunity to use this Biblical money code arises I get an automatic alert. Then I push a few buttons and wait for the banker greed to begin... so I can take back.

It's that simple. I've never waited more than a week

or two to get the money into my account, and I've never been worried I wouldn't get it because these Biblical numbers work so well. Just like me when I first discovered this, you won't believe it... but you'll believe the money when it hits your account after using this code...!

Would you like to learn this Biblical Money Code? *Then I will show you...*

The 5th Secret:

"Behold, there come seven years of great plenty throughout all the land of Egypt. And there shall arise after them seven years of famine."
- Genesis 41:27

This secret is indeed a prophecy, but a prophecy about what? In the modern day financial context, it's too general to say this is talking about the overall economy. When you apply this prophecy to the continually proven and ancient wealth-building secrets I'll show you, it's so ridiculously accurate in its timing it puts shivers down your spine...

This uncannily accurate prophecy will make or break you, it's that simple.

Time your plans according to this consistently correct prophecy and *this secret alone will make you free* with what I'll be teaching you here (this was how I first became financially independent). But be on the *wrong* side of this prophecy and the path to freedom will become so long that you won't have enough years left to make it to the end—your dreams will die with you.

And you want the *really good news?*

As I write this, this prophecy is saying NOW is the time

to use this secret!

In the coming chapters, I'll be explaining this secret a lot deeper, but more than that I'll be passing on the 1-2-3 step systems that are supercharged by using it. When you combine this super-accurate secret with the clever tricks I've used in the past, this one secret could be all you need to retire. I really can't emphasize the power of this highly enough. You'll have solid income from doing virtually nothing... then I'll show you how to instantly DOUBLE that income without lifting a finger. You're going to *love it.*

And I'd like to share a follow-up verse to this secret that talks about a specific way to retire in the fastest way possible—if you're crazily desperate to escape the rat-race NOW, this one is just for you:

"The spider taketh hold with her hands, and is in kings' palaces. There be three things which go well, yea, four are comely in going."

The smallest creature—a spider, an underdog—can live the life of a king. And the key is in the second part: *three plus one.* Later on I'll show you how powerful this is.

Would you like to learn this accurate, powerful, make-or-break secret? *Then I will show you...*

The 6ᵗʰ Secret:

"Let the extortioner catch all that he hath; and let the strangers spoil his labor." - Psalms 109:11

I will walk you down the path to freedom, but thieves appear along the way as you progress. These thieves will try to mug you and take what you've made for themselves—the closer you get to freedom the greedier they will become. You have to protect against these "extortioners," and "the strangers" will help you do that.

If you don't have this secret, then all the other secrets are in danger—if you're looted along the way then it will all have been for nothing. But there is a simple way to ensure it doesn't happen.

Who are the extortioners? Anyone who would take money from you by force, and that includes the government in the form of taxation!

Don't you think your path to freedom would be drastically shortened if you didn't have to pay ONE THIRD of everything you make along the way?! You might even find you could retire NOW when you recalculate things with this in mind.

Please understand: there is nothing illegal about paying the least amount of tax possible—it's your God-given right and what this country was founded on. The trick is knowing the law and the legal loopholes, but:

It's very easy and 100% legal to pay ZERO TAX if you know how. In some cases, the government actually *incentivizes* paying zero tax! You don't have to be rich to enjoy rich peoples' tax-breaks.

But the government isn't the only mugger you have to worry about, there are many more, and those thieves can have a much more devastating impact on your newfound wealth if you don't set things up properly *right from the start.*

Would you like to learn how to do this and discover how "the strangers" will LEGALLY spoil the efforts of these extortioners? *Then I will show you...*

The 7ᵗʰ Secret:

"But thou shalt remember the Lord thy God: for it is he that giveth thee power to get wealth, that he may establish his covenant which he sware unto thy fathers, as it is this day." - *Deuteronomy 8:18*

This is the secret that will change your life the most. It can also *multiply* your wealth as if by magic without you doing anything. I can explain how the other secrets work, but I can't explain exactly how this one works; I just know that it *does* work incredibly well and I know *what to do* to make it work. Why it works is still a mystery to me—maybe there are some secrets in The Bible that are powered by something bigger than ourselves and are intended to remain a mystery...

I compare this secret to the gates of heaven because it's what's waiting for you as you approach the end of the path to freedom. More importantly, you *must* know how to pass these gates if you're to complete your journey, and that's something I will be honored to teach you.

As well as that, if you pass these 'gates' I will invite you to work alongside me and receive a potentially infinite stream of income and joy. More about that later in the book.

Would you like to unlock the power of this most mystical secret and have the opportunity to prosper alongside me? *Then I will show you...*

The Path to Freedom is Clear. Will You Walk Down it with Me?

Even though you now know The 7 Secrets, let me emphasize that you do not understand the <u>true meaning</u> of them or how to use them yet. Do not attempt to use them at this unprepared stage in your training!

God wants you to be wealthy, but it will take some diligence on your part to enjoy the treasures he's left you.

The Bible states: *"An inheritance may be gotten hastily at the beginning; but the end thereof shall not be blessed."*

IMPORTANT: If you ask others what these verses mean they won't tell you what I've told you. All you will hear are the words of people (some of them Fools) who only know the common and confused interpretation of these verses. Their (common) interpretations have not been decoded into the financial secrets I will teach you. You will not find the financial truth behind these secrets anywhere else because they are closely guarded by those who use them.

If everyone knew and used these secrets now, this country and the global financial system would collapse. Stopping all that tax revenue from banks alone would topple what is a fragile house of cards. Do you think 'they' want you reading this? No. But are you going to let them get away with that and let them pillage you and your family?

No? Then let's do something about it, let's quickly change course. And that's what the next chapters will teach you: how to actually use these 7 secrets.

Don't worry, all will become clear as this book progresses. I didn't expect the secrets to have much meaning to you yet, but I appreciate the strong curiosity that exists in most people. I could have tempted you along to make you wait for the last chapter to tell you them, but as I said, I prefer to be honest and to the point.

Now that you know *The 7 Secrets*, you must learn how to use them to your advantage. Your only other choice now is to go on living a lie month to month in the full knowledge that others are taking you for a ride. It's time to stand up and fight. You are 'through the looking glass' now. You've started to discover the truth; to give up at this point would only be suitable if you wish to join the Fools in their life of ignorance and poverty.

Don't allow yourself to be taken advantage of any longer—you don't *deserve* it.

We will declare your own Independence Day. Being who you want to be and doing what you want to do is self-respect.

Do you have what it takes to become a Disciple of *The 7 Secrets, and to truly understand why God has a plan to make you rich*?

Yes? Then I sincerely hold my hand out to you. Come with me and let's walk down this path to freedom together.

"Hear instruction, and be wise, and refuse it not." – Proverbs 8:33.

Chapter 2:
The Foundation
of Wealth

"The thoughts of the diligent tend only to plenteousness; but of every one that is hasty only to want." – Proverbs 21:5

Well done for taking the next step in the ultimate journey. To be here now you've passed the first stage that should've filtered out any get-rich-quick Fools, and, through the dispelling of many common false perceptions, you've cleared the path to financial freedom. You are poised at the beginning of our journey. But you're carrying a lot of weight that will severely limit your progress, so our next task will be to get rid of that weight.

Imagine setting off on a walk, but before you take the first step you fill up a backpack full of heavy rocks, and sling it over your shoulder and take it with you. Why would you do that? You're so busy focusing on the road ahead of you that you forget to take a look at yourself and your preparedness.

Or, to use a different comparison, would you diligently build a house with the finest quality materials on a bed of wet sand and without any foundations? Ridiculous, right? This house would be a house of cards, and all your labor would be wasted.

And yet, financially speaking, that's precisely what most people do every single day of their lives *without even realizing it.* And that is why they remain poor—because of this "invisible saboteur" that we will eliminate in this lesson.

Let me explain. You gain financial freedom when your expenses are covered by your passive income (passive income is income which requires virtually zero effort). Once you have enough passive income coming in to cover your living expenses, you're free forever!

So there's two parts to our quest:

1. Bring your expenses down
2. Bring your passive income up

And when the two meet, our objective is met, as you can see here on this simple chart...

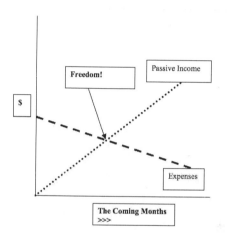

Take a second to digest this simple chart, for this is our mission. The rest of this course is devoted to increasing your passive income, and this lesson is dedicated to getting your expenses in line. Listen, we could make thousands of dollars a month come your way right now but if it's all headed for a financial black hole, what's the point? We'd be building a grand house without any foundations.

This is why most people who win the lottery are flat broke just a few years later: because they're tipping water into a bucket full of holes. To quote The Bible:

"Ye have sown much, and bring in little; ye eat, but ye have not enough; ye drink, but ye are not filled with drink; ye clothe you, but there is none warm; and he that earneth wages earneth wages to put it into a bag with holes." – Haggai 1:6

But a slack-handed sluggard—a Fool—wouldn't take the step you're taking now. They are too impatient and lazy, and that is why they continually fail. But not you; you have the power of the 7 Secrets behind you, and here's the first one as a recap from last time.

The 1st Secret

"Wilt thou set thine eyes upon that which is not? For riches certainly make themselves wings; they fly away as an eagle towards Heaven." - Proverbs 23:5

Do you ever feel like your bank account is mysteriously a bucket full of holes and your paychecks are but a small tap desperately trying to fill it up in vain?

This is no accidental occurrence; it's how The System is designed, to keep you scraping by from paycheck to paycheck, paying your taxes to the government, paying your interest to the banks, and buying products from corporations. And when you're too old to do that, those same institutions will throw you on the scrap-heap (just ask a health insurance company), and good luck if you're counting on welfare or Medicare not being totally raided by then.

It's now a statistical fact that most people will not even have enough assets or income to retire at 70. You need to get a grip on this <u>now</u> or you won't be taking your grandkids to

McDonald's in retirement, *you'll be serving the burgers there instead.*

The Fools are totally unaware how or why their "riches certainly make themselves wings" and fly away from them. It just always seems to be the case that there is always too little money left at the end of the month. Sound familiar? It doesn't have to be that way and it doesn't have to be hard work to hotwire The System to your advantage instead of disadvantage—you just need to be taught this secret and things will just take care of themselves.

Understand: money has a homing instinct. It will always fly back to its master—the people who understand it, have learned about it, and respect it. And unless you learn to become its master, it will always fly away from you, no matter how much of it you accumulate.

But there's a good reason why most people will never become the master of money: because they must first pass a test, and passing this test requires acceptance of inconvenient truths. It requires *faith* in what The Bible teaches.

So let me first prepare you for that crucial test...

The Gorilla in the Room
"And because I tell you the truth, ye believe me not." – John 8:45

Those are Jesus's own words I quoted above, and they are highly significant. For over fifteen years now tens of thousands of people have come to me for guidance on wealth, goal-setting, motivation, and other self-help matters. I have many testimonials as evidence of this. I've reached out to these students through courses, books, manuals, DVDs, and face-to-face in seminars in a genuine effort to help people. And I've observed a constant behavior in my students that's always intrigued me.

When I explain certain truths about the world, the system, "the Man," the mind of the masses, and the rigged game, I'm not met with astonishment as much as anger and upset because people can't handle the truth, and resultantly won't accept it. You must not be one of these people.

As a demonstration of what I'm talking about, I'd like you to try to imagine what follows very clearly: You walk into your bedroom right now. You open the bedroom door and there's a big, fat gorilla sitting on your bed looking at you. What would you do?

If you're like most people, the blood would drain from your face, you'd turn back, and you'd slam the door shut in a cold sweat. Why? Okay, there was fear from the possibility of getting killed, but this wasn't the primary cause of your reaction.

The answer is because your **mental model** of what it means to walk into your bedroom does not involve gorillas sitting on your bed. The terror you felt as you slammed the door was from *the conflict in your brain between what you thought you knew to be true, and what appears to be a new truth.* That mental model just got smashed. Your brain has developed these mental models since when you were born as a survival mechanism, so that you know your environment.

Therefore, your mental model is based entirely on *perception*, how you *perceive* things to be, not necessarily how they ARE. *But to your mind, the impact is as if it was real, not just perception.*

Good writers of horror stories know that the best way

to scare their audience isn't with blood and guts, but rather showing you images that conflict with your mental model of the world, thus terrifying you at a deep psychological level. I think that the horrific events of 9/11 were mostly terrifying for people because none of us had a mental model of airliners being deliberately flown into skyscrapers. The innocents dying isn't what frightened people; it made them sad. The images being outside our mental model are what caused deep, psychological terror. How would it have been if you'd only heard about it on the radio?

Now let's go back to you standing outside the door of the bedroom with the gorilla on the bed. You're feeling braver now you've got over the shock of this conflict with your mental model. You open a crack in the door and peak inside.

On closer inspection, it seems that the gorilla was a stuffed animal, just sitting there, lifeless. You breathe a sigh of relief and start wondering how the heck it got there. "Honey, did you just buy a stuffed gorilla?!" New problem, different feelings. BUT, and this is important, your earlier terror was very **real**, even though the gorilla was not. Your perception was faulty; it was in conflict with the truth. But your reaction was the same because it was based on that perception.

But now you're calm; now you know your perception of the gorilla is false. And this is how I've often found it goes with students when I deliver disturbing and inconvenient truths. At first they want to kill me. Next, they're my best friend, once they see that the gorilla in their bedroom was there, but that they didn't have to be frightened of it because it wasn't real. By examining the matter closely, unemotionally, they were able to see that the inconvenient truth doesn't have to be a problem, as long as we use it to our advantage, and not be in denial about it.

So let's proceed, and let's *observe* our mind's often-faulty perceptions and mental models about things as we go, because this lesson contains some inconvenient truths…

Point "A"

"The way of peace they know not; and there is no judgment in their goings: they have made them crooked paths: whosoever goeth therein shall not know peace." – Isaiah 59:8

We have to get you from Point A to Point B. Point A is where you are right now, and Point B is financial freedom. The shortest distance between two points is a straight line, and that's why this course makes everything happen for you as simply and quickly as is legally possible. But before that, consider something even more basic: that the successful completion of *any* journey requires two pieces of information: **the location of Point A and the location of Point B.**

Sound obvious? Yes, I agree. Just imagine this phone conversation:

Mr. Sluggard: "Hello, I'd like a taxi please."

Taxi Company: "Okay, where do you want to be picked up from?"

Mr. Sluggard: "I don't know."

Taxi Company: Click.

Did that conversation sound highly unlikely and ridiculous? Of course it did—if you don't know your starting point the journey can't take place.

But this is how most people run their financial lives! Is it any wonder why they never get anywhere? They don't even know their Point A.

Do YOU know your Point A?

You can *never* become money's master unless you know your current relationship with money. Money's master is the person who understands money, who has the financial education that school doesn't provide. You're here to get that missing education, so don't feel bad if you don't know your Point A, but our very first order of business must be to figure that out, wouldn't you now agree? So let's do that.

Accounting has to be one of the driest subjects out there, but it doesn't take much to get a grasp on the basics that you need to know. There are really just two words that matter: *assets* and *liabilities*. Now please stay with me, because this is going to be far from boring—in fact, what I'm going to say will surprise you.

I have an unorthodox definition of assets and liabilities. It's unorthodox, yet logical when you appreciate that I focus on INCOME, not NET WORTH. Why? Well, when a corporation goes broke it's hardly ever because of low net worth; it's because of LOW CASH FLOW. Cash flow, or income, is what it's all about. Income is what you need to live, not net worth. Look at that chart earlier—notice how it's a plot of INCOME, not net worth?

So with that in mind, let's consider assets and liabilities in terms of INCOME...

Look at it in this simple way: an asset is something that generates income for you. A liability is something that generates expenses for you. Compendia? If you keep this in mind, you will have a clear idea of when you're acquiring assets and when you're acquiring liabilities.

And the name of the ultimate game is to acquire (income-generating) assets. When you have enough income-generating assets to meet your expenses, you've won the game.

So, for example, when you buy a TV or a sofa on credit, you are adding to your liabilities because these are things that take money from your pocket. If you'd bought shares in Wal-Mart with the money, you would be adding to your assets because the dividends would be putting money IN your pocket. Make sense? Or if you came up with an invention for a product that Wal-Mart sold and generated you a royalty, you have just *created* an (intellectual) asset.

Think of each dollar you make as an employee that must work for you. If that dollar takes money from you, then YOU are the employee of that dollar!

So, let's run a few examples to look for the exceptions to this rule...

If you own a business, is that business an asset or a liability? This is a good question, because I don't consider a business that you have to work in every day to be an asset. Yes, it may put money in your pocket, but if the whole idea is to gain financial freedom, then PASSIVE income is what we need; automatic income that requires little or no involvement from you.

Okay, so time for another test question: is your *home* an asset or a liability?

I can hear you cry: "duh! It's an asset, dummy!" Really? Shall we apply my rule about assets and liabilities and find out?

Does your personal residence that you own put money IN your pocket, or take it OUT?

Your home that you own takes money out of your pocket in the form of property tax, HOA, mortgage interest, maintenance, etc. So that constitutes a LIABILITY. This truth is something that the middle classes will never understand, and why they will be forever living hand to mouth!

I live in a nice house because I want a nice life for my family, and I only did so *at the end of my financial journey*. I'm not saying to live under the expressway. But when I look at a personal residence I just see a big fat bill, from an unemotional perspective. But your personal residence IS an emotional thing, I respect that, I'm just clarifying my point about assets and liabilities, because understanding this principle is KEY to your financial freedom.

USING MY DEFINITION, maximize assets, minimize liabilities. This is the inside track to freedom.

A rental property on the other hand, DOES put money in your pocket, and so this would truly be an asset. Now, if recent "investors" had been thinking ONLY in terms of income from rental property, they would NOT have been burned in the property crash because they'd have only bought a property if the price was low enough to make an income. Most of the property in the boom was priced too high to make a profit from renting, but people just bought anyway and prayed for prices going up forever. Wrong!

This is why you should ALWAYS think in terms of cash flow, income, **return on investment**. I stopped buying rental property and sold some of my properties way back in 2005/6 not because I'm a fortune-telling genius, but because the numbers stopped making sense, and most of all, because a long-proven prophecy in The Bible said to do this. More about this later on in the book.

I expect some of this comes as an inconvenient revelation. As Jesus said, *"And because I tell you the truth, ye believe me not." – John 8:45.* Jesus also said, *"The foxes have holes, and the birds have nests; but the Son of man hath not where he lay his head." – Matthew 8:20.* Now, we obviously all need somewhere to lay our heads; the point Jesus is making there is that a residence is not a requirement to take the righteous path, and certainly is not a priority when you consider everything from an assets and liabilities standpoint.

Here's an example of the sort of objection I receive at this point:

"Jim, what nonsense about your home being a liability, not an asset. I asked my accountant and he said you don't know what you're talking about."

And I wouldn't expect any other answer from your accountant. Accountants are trained to provide data, among other things, and they are following the academic model they learned at school. When any accountant hears the words "assets" and "liabilities," they think of a balance sheet, which is a statement of your NET WORTH. It's not rocket science—here's where your accountant would list your home on your balance sheet:

ASSETS	LIABILITIES
Home	Mortgage (if applicable).

But that's not what *I* was talking about, was it? I was specifically using the INCOME definition of assets and liabilities, and I stated that on this basis, at any given time, an asset puts money IN your pocket, and a liability takes money OUT of your pocket.

You see, the accountant's definition of a balance sheet is a purely academic statement as far as I'm concerned because it doesn't represent daily life. Your balance sheet says what your net worth would be **if you liquidated everything**. If you're liquidating everything you own—your home—something has gone terribly wrong. It's a worst-case scenario, useful for that scenario, and definitely something to have in mind, but it's hypothetical and not useful for our purposes. But if you focus more on the INCOME definition of assets and liabilities, your balance sheet will take care of itself.

The other document your accountant prepares is a "profit and loss." This is a measure of your income against expenses, which is what that chart plotted earlier. *So, if you still don't accept my definition of an asset, now let's see where your accountant puts your home in your profit and loss statement:*

INCOME	EXPENSES
	Interest
	Property Tax
	HOA
	Energy bills
	Insurance
	Etc. etc. etc.

Hmmm, your home's not looking so hot anymore, is it?

Your profit and loss statement, your statement of INCOME regarding assets and liabilities, is REAL, DAILY LIFE. This is the measure of whether you eat tonight. If you don't get a grip on this statement you'll be heading for that liquidation of assets we just spoke about, and you can then use that balance sheet that your accountant is pointing out for the worst-case scenario!

If you bought an investment property and took a monthly loss (because you paid too much for it), and you were just praying that prices would rise forever and investing only for capital gain and not INCOME, you abused your profit and loss statement and were only thinking of your balance sheet. And that didn't turn out too well for folks, did it? That's why so many fledgling property "investors" got burned in 2008.

So you must accept this new definition of assets and liabilities, you must have faith in this truth. Next, I must ask you to face another inconvenient truth as we determine what your Point A is. You must be brutally honest with me now.

"For if any be a hearer of the word, and not a doer, he is like unto a man beholding his natural face in a glass: For he beholdeth himself, and goeth his way, and straightway forgotteth what manner of man he was. But whoso looketh into the perfect law of liberty, and continueth therein, he being not a forgetful hearer, but a doer of the work, this man shall be blessed indeed." – James 1:23-25.

What that verse above is basically saying is this: *look at your reflection, be honest with yourself, and then act accordingly to take the right path—the path of liberty. Truth and freedom are as one.* Let's define your Point A.

Take a blank piece of paper and draw a line down the middle. Write on one side of it *"Assets"* and on the other *"Liabilities."* Now think about all of your income generating assets and put the value of them under "Assets," and all of your expenses and put them under "Liabilities." Include everything, and remember that your house does not count as an asset unless you're planning on selling it, perhaps to downsize (which is something you may well consider!). Subtract the liabilities from the assets to get your *Net Worth*.

When you have that figure of your net worth, write it out:
$_____

Now, you have just created something called a "Balance Sheet." Balance Sheet is one of those CPA terms you've probably heard at some time. It is a "snapshot" of what a company is worth at a given time. Companies produce this document to know their Point A. Running your personal finances the same way a successful business does can only be a good thing, no?

I do urge you to properly complete this little task as I know you will find it a clarifying experience—don't bury your head in the sand—it's just you and me in the room, so be honest. If you have a load of debts, write them down. Don't worry, by the end of this course you should be well on the way to clearing them forever.

I'm going to introduce you to another accounting term now, as further guidance to your freedom figure. It is something called an income/expense sheet. The income/expense sheet goes hand in hand with the balance sheet—they are the first things a CPA looks at when assessing the strength of a company. The balance sheet is a snapshot in time of the finances, but the profit and loss tells you what went on over a period of time, in order to get to that situation in the first place. There's nothing complicated about it despite the fact that CPAs use it and it has a fancy sounding name. It is simply: Income minus Expenses.

In other words, how much money you earned in a specific period and how much you spent. If a company produces revenue that is more than its expenditure and resultantly makes a profit, it is said to be solvent. In other words, it is steadily growing richer.

Sounds basic, doesn't it? I mean, would you like to work for a company that was **in**solvent? Would you invest in shares of a company that was continuously **in**solvent? No, you wouldn't because this is, of course, an extremely precarious way to arrange your affairs.

So can you explain why so many people allow themselves to become technically insolvent?

That's right, insolvent; their outgoings exceed their income. They spend more than they earn. As already explained: if you are solvent, you are steadily growing richer. It therefore stands to reason that if you are insolvent, that you are steadily growing *poorer.* Which path will get you to freedom?

So what I would like you to do is to complete your very own profit and loss statement to see if you are solvent or not. It is vitally important that you are completely honest here—you are only fooling yourself unless you include absolutely <u>every</u>

expense. The best way is to go by your most recent 2-3 bank statements—this is the harsh reality, not the fantasy you're maybe trying to concoct!

This exercise may sound simplistic, but many people are astounded by the result. Therefore, an essential part of your training is to complete this exercise before going any further! The rest of this course will not have the value to you it should unless you do this honestly. You may *think* you know this already. Many insolvent individuals think so too.

Take a blank piece of paper and draw a line down the middle. On one side, write down your regular monthly outgoings and on the other side write down your regular monthly income using your <u>bank statement</u> for reference. The amounts you enter should be the average monthly figures. If you have credit card debts, enter the amount you would usually pay per month.

You should then end up with a total expenditure figure and a total income figure. Compare the two. When you have completed this, you will be in one of three groups:

1) You spend more than you earn.

If the profit/loss figure is a negative, you are technically insolvent—you spend more than you earn and are steadily growing poorer. You are living from month to month on *borrowed* money, which is only compounding things.

Needless to say, this situation must be corrected before you are able to be free.

You can do this by doing one or preferably both of two things: increase your income and reduce your outgoings. I'll be showing you how to increase your passive income with great ease in the remainder of the course. In this lesson though, I want to concentrate on reducing your expenses.

If you have discovered that you are insolvent, please don't worry, as you are one of millions of people in the country—I was once one too! The important thing is that you are making an effort to correct the situation by being here now.

2) You spend as much as you earn.

Once again, this situation must be corrected if you want to grow steadily richer. Furthermore, I expect that your income would *exceed* your outgoings if you didn't have those debts. This lesson will ensure that you reduce your outgoings and turn this "break-even" situation into a "profit-making" one.

3) You earn more than you spend.

If you have just discovered that you are solvent then I urge you to do that exercise again, *honestly*. If you claim to be in this group, you are saying that you are in the minority of people that actually have money left to spare at the end of the month. If you have debts, why do you have spare money? Why aren't you paying off those debts with it?

Don't beat yourself up about the result because the system has been designed to put you in that position, all thanks to the three institutions I explained last time: the politicians, big banks and corporations, and the media. The pay-off these three groups get from making you insolvent is as follows:

1) **The politicians.** By ensuring the population doesn't retire until as late as possible so that "contributions" to the tax coffers are maximized; i.e. you pay income tax until you are physically incapable of doing so. This can be achieved by keeping the population in a permanent state of financial ignorance and living from paycheck to paycheck for as long as possible. If you stop paying them tax, or pay them much less tax (by retiring, spending less, etc.) you are no use to them. "Keep going to Disneyworld," as one president famously said. "Keep working so you pay us tax, and keep spending so that the corporations will pay us tax on the profits."

2) **The big banks and corporations.** The banks make money from your debts and by you remaining in financial servitude. The corporations make more money when you spend beyond your means.

3) **The media.** A vast portion of their profit comes from advertisers, which are corporations and big banks (see above).

Let's look at each villain in turn, and free you from the yoke they placed around your neck...

Deny The "money-Changers"
"If thou hast nothing to pay, why should he take thy bed from under thee?" – Proverbs 22:27

The Bible doesn't have a good word to say about debt. In fact, The Bible states that the people who lent you money should forgive the debt after seven years, which is, oddly enough, almost the exact time when bankruptcy, foreclosure, and bad credit can be erased.

"At the end of every seven years thou shalt make a release. And this is the manner of the release: Every creditor that lendeth ought unto his neighbor shall release it; he shall not exact it of his neighbor, or of his brother; because it is called the Lord's release." – Deuteronomy 15:1-2.

So you should have no problem with taking an aggressive approach to eliminating your debts, especially when it comes to making your creditors forgive part or all of them.

The purpose of this lesson is to slash expenses in order to expedite your financial freedom—recall that chart earlier where expenses and income need to meet in the middle to become free. Debt is one of your largest expenses, so let's deal with it.

By asking you to analyze your current financial situation, I have made you admit to the fact that you have debts. No one likes doing that openly and thoroughly, so well done. I've done a bit of debt counseling, so I know how you feel right now. These debts are hindering your path to wealth because you have to pay the interest on them. A proportion of your income (which could be invested instead) is taken just to pay for the privilege of having these debts. This is like having the proverbial backpack of rocks over your shoulder when you're trying to make this journey. I should know, I've been there.

I was once in a dead-end job that I hated. Most of the money I earned from this miserable existence went on paying interest on debts; bank loans, car loan, credit cards, etc. I thought this was just part of life. My parents never told me not to get into debt, neither did any of my school teachers and I certainly don't recall seeing a government information film warning me off. Besides, how else was I supposed to afford the "necessities" of life? Almost everyone around me had a nice car, nice clothes, and the latest TV. If everyone was doing it, it couldn't be that bad. But it sure felt like it when it came close to the end of the month!

I felt depressed and trapped. I didn't know where to turn next. As soon as I had paid one bill, another one showed up. I would hide bills in the depths of a filing case hoping that the fairies from Wonderland would take them away overnight.

There simply was no light at the end of the tunnel—I was slipping further into debt every month. I didn't even know how much I owed in total—I didn't want to know! Denial is a very convenient method of mental survival, isn't it? It's like taking drugs or getting drunk every day—you protect yourself from the reality of the cruel world out there. Credit card companies would write to me to ask if I wanted a higher limit every now and again. Instead of saying, "Thanks, but no thanks," yours truly would tear their arm off.

If you think that was dumb, I'm just warming up. One day, I decided to sit down and work out my finances. I was tired of sticking my head in the sand. I calculated that over the next six months I would be approximately $9,000 too short for my expenditure. I was due a promotion in six months so all I needed was nine grand to see me through until then, for my monthly expenses. I know, I thought, I'll get another loan! No. Make it two loans; one to pay off one of my cards because the bank had a cheaper rate than the credit card did. After all, I wasn't completely stupid.

The thing is though, I never got the promotion and I had spent $9,000 of borrowed money on junk. Worse, the credit card debt I had cleared was spent up again! I was a whole lot poorer than when I started. I was fed up with having no money, hiding from the mailman, and being threatened with court action. Enough! Something had to give... was it going to be me?

I had reached... that point. The point when a person finally decides to change.

In short, from that day forward, I hacked my way out of debt by doing whatever it took and I vowed never to return to that dark chapter of my life. It was either that or a one-way ticket down a black hole to oblivion. I later discovered what I now call The 7 Secrets and have never looked back.

So I've been there. I'm not preaching to you from a moral high ground, I'm simply telling you what you need to know to accumulate the wealth you require. This fact cannot be denied. I have proven to you by using simple logic that the first step to wealth is to maximize your solvency; to make your income exceed your outgoings as much as possible.

You know this already? So why are you in debt then?

As soon as you stop paying interest and saving money instead, you can make income for yourself (as you will be trained to in the remaining chapters). Paying off ALL debts is essential to your goal.

If you have, say, a $10,000 loan and you pay 12% interest on it a year (APR), that equates to $1,200 interest a year. Let's imagine you earn $8 an hour after tax. That means you have to work for 150 hours each year just to pay the interest! If you work the average week, that means you have worked for almost a whole month just to pay the interest. *In other words, you were working as a slave for a "money-changer" for a whole month.*

One month's hard work all for nothing! How do you feel about that?

Slavery is not dead, after all. In fact, it's never been more common…

"Ye have sown much, and bring in little; ye eat, but ye have not enough; ye drink, but ye are not filled with drink; ye clothe you, but there is none warm; and he that earneth wages earneth wages to put it into a bag with holes." – Haggai 1:6

It's relatively easy to accept the truth about other people and the world around us but when it comes to accepting the truth about ourselves it's a different matter. It's about having emotional maturity, really. I know how you feel because I've been there. Perhaps you would much rather I talk about rainbows or bunnies. Anything but face the harsh truth. Anything but *grow up,* really. If you're still having trouble with the fact that you must eliminate all debts, allow me to tell you about one of the biggest "get-rich-quick" scams ever.

The Bible clearly tells us that charging high interest and exploiting innocent people in the process is not the righteous path:

"He that putteth not out his money to usury, nor taketh reward against the innocent. He that doeth these things shall never be moved." – Psalms 15:5

And yet it goes on all the time. Banks—the "money-changers"—make hundreds of millions of dollars every year by taking the money paid in by regular savers and paying them a low rate of interest, and then lending this money to other people at extortionately high rates of interest! More than that even, because they charge the merchants 3% on every transaction as well.

The banks (credit card companies, all the same thing) hate it if you regularly pay off your credit card because they want to make money by charging you interest. Of course this rarely happens; people don't pay it all off because they are greedy and impatient. They want everything and want it now. Sound anything like a spoiled child?

When you've spent up to your limit, if your bank truly had your interests at heart, they wouldn't lend you anything anymore. But do they do this? No, they throw more credit at you! If that isn't "loan-sharking," I don't know what is. Why do you think that many cards now offer rates as low as 4% or even 0% if you transfer your existing card balances? Because they know that once you have cleared your old balance, you will spend up to the limit on it again and that you will be forced to become their customer when the low rate expires.

Now, of course, credit cards are useful. I have several. They are back up for a debit card, useful for emergencies and travel, and they let us buy larger items for convenience or short term cash flow issues. So I'm not going to ask you to cut them up; I'm going to ask you to ONLY use them for those situations I just gave you. Here are the problems with credit cards and how NOT to use them.

1) **Credit cards let you spend what you haven't got.** That's right. This money is not yours—it is someone else's. Why are you spending money that doesn't belong to you and *paying* for the privilege? As you know, God wants you to grow wealthy, how do you possibly think this can happen if you are spending money you don't have?

2) **Buying with cards doesn't feel like you are actually spending money.** Think about it. If you paid for all those goods with hard cash, actually handed over a fistful of bills, you would be far less likely to buy it. If you think about the times you have paid for something in cash, you will know what I'm talking about. We live in the age of the $500 impulse purchase. People want the approval of other people; the credit card becomes a symbol of their status and power. Don't be a sucker.

3) **It's expensive!** 2% a month doesn't sound like a whole lot, but that's 24% per annum! Double what a bank loan is! Let's say you have the average card balance of $8,000. That means you are paying $160 a month just for the interest on that debt—or if you prefer (which you probably don't), nearly a whole week's work! (Assuming you are on the national average salary with the average working week.)

4) **Money burns holes in people's pockets.** Basic human nature. If anyone ever wins any money on a TV or radio

show, the first thing they are asked is how they're going to spend the money—it's just the way we are. Fine, but borrowed money is not free!

Listen, I'd like to share with you a big money secret: **Do not buy anything for over $100 unless you intended to do so when you woke up that morning.**

Adhering to this rule will keep you out of trouble because a lot of the credit card spending is for random pleasures. What's wrong with a bit of "pleasure?" Nothing if it's free! But "pleasure" really refers to fleeting fixes, impulse, and excess. JOY is not fleeting though; JOY is what really matters and is lasting—love, beauty, creativity, grace, these *natural highs* are far more rewarding, and FREE.

"He that loveth pleasure shall be a poor man: he that loveth wine and oil shall not be rich." – Proverbs 21:17.

The trouble with so-called "retail therapy" is that you're not treating the cause of your dissatisfaction, only the symptom (just like pharmaceutical drugs). So your "disease" is never cured.

"He that loveth silver shall not be satisfied with silver; nor he that loveth abundance with increase: this is also vanity." – Ecclesiastes 5:10

And this is a good time to remind ourselves of the first secret we began this lesson with:

"Wilt thou set thine eyes upon that which is not? For riches

**certainly make themselves wings; they fly away as an eagle
towards Heaven." - Proverbs 23:5**

"That which is not" is empty pleasures bought with
money that is not yours.

At the end of the day no amount of nagging by me is
going to make you stop borrowing money—you have to want to
stop! A bit like someone trying to give up smoking really; there
is no "quick-fix," you just have to stop—and you can only do
this if you want to. If you have reached... that point. You have
to get a little angry. Unless you are, you will never break free
of the debt-servicing cycle that keeps you from true financial
freedom. Debt, at best, stops you building wealth. At worst, it
will eventually make you destitute.

You are not a child anymore. No one is going to turn this
thing around but you.

So what is next for you? Well, you must see the logic
in my argument as well as the ancient wisdom of The Bible,
and make a declaration to get yourself out of the hole you have
dug yourself into. Get angry. Understand that you are being
manipulated by "money-changers" who want to keep you
trapped purely to further their own interests, and they're fully
supported by "pharaohs" (politicians) and "talebearers" (media).

The government turns a blind eye to the crippling effect
of debt because it is good news for the economy—domestic and
international loan-sharking is a massive earner for this country.
It also happens to have the convenient effect of ensuring that the
population doesn't become too wealthy and retire before their
time (= no income tax).

The corporations—the loan sharks who dignify their existence with the title: "banks"—*want* you to be in debt—that is how they make their living. The banks in this country do not concern themselves with the long term effect of this practice—their greed always gets the better of them.

The media doesn't want to be party-poopers. If they announced the truth and that everyone should stop spending money they didn't have, they would not sell many newspapers—not exciting enough, you see. People prefer to read about celebrities who can't string a sentence together, along with the contents of their trash can. Their huge advertising revenues would be seriously damaged, too.

How do you feel about being conned and manipulated this way? Can you see that you can never increase your wealth if you are throwing your money away on interest every month? Do you want your freedom or not?

Let's blast you out of debt and never return. How? Let's start by answering the following question: Why are you in Debt?

Probably several reasons, but they all boil down to one thing: You are in debt because you *chose* to spend more than you earned. Instead of saving up for something, you bought it on credit.

The first step to getting out of debt is to admit that it was your fault that you are there in the first place—no-one else's. Everybody is responsible for their own actions and they have no right whatsoever to blame other people or make others pay for their stupidity. Circumstances are irrelevant. If times are hard, you spend less—simple. I've been there. You adapt to the situation by whatever means you can. Sure, it's easy to say in my position but I wasn't always here—I've been a gardener, a house painter, a bartender and a general laborer—to name just a few. I took these jobs when times were hard and I would do them again if I had to because I know from bitter experience as well as The Bible that borrowing money to finance a lifestyle I cannot afford will only make me poorer.

You are in the brave minority who has decided to stop living life in Disneyland, while the Fools choose to carry on the charade and complain about how they never catch a break.

Anyway, do you agree that it's *your own fault* you are in debt? Or did one of the older kids in the playground or your dog tell you do it…? Were you made to sign the forms and spend the money at gunpoint? *The first step, and half the battle, in fighting any unhealthy addiction is an admission of the problem.*

After this admission, you now have two choices or a combination of the two:

1. Consolidate the debts
2. Get the debts written off.

First, here's how to consolidate your debts. By this I mean combine them all into one low interest rate loan. The best way to do this is by re-mortgaging your home or if you don't have a home, to get a low interest bank loan.

You've probably seen commercials for this sort of thing. Companies calling themselves "debt consultants" miraculously free the population from various debts by paying off their loans with one big loan, at a low rate of interest, secured on their home. Before we move on, allow me to tell you what these commercials don't. This loan is, in effect, a second "lien" on the property. Meaning that if you defaulted on the payments, the "debt consultant" could confiscate your home. Also, this is not a long term solution because you are repaying this "incredibly low monthly payment" over maybe 25 years!

So use this as a short term solution to drastically reduce your monthly interest charges. Remember, the aim here is to pay this loan off as soon as possible, so be sure that there are no penalties for early repayment. Easy enough? Now comes the "hard" part: Do not ask for any more money than the value of your debts.

These ads for "debt consultants" kill me, they really do. You know the scene. Some brainless TV star, earning several million dollars a year, rambles on about the financial pressures of making ends meet and how all your problems can be solved with "debt Busters!" Then enter the rejuvenated wife who tells her neighbor how she paid off all her loans and, "Even had enough left over for a vacation!!" That's one expensive vacation, ma'am. Needless to say, she then proceeded to spend until her cards were up to the limit again.

A recent survey of 4.2 million American homeowners who had taken out second mortgages for this purpose: to pay off debts. Only three-quarters of these people actually *did* use the money for this purpose and even then, eleven months later, 70% of them had run up their debts to nearly the same level as before! Right back where they started, with the painful addition of a larger mortgage now too. Learn from this, please.

Next, getting the debts written off. As a reminder, these "money-changers" shouldn't have exploited you in the first place:

"At the end of every seven years thou shalt make a release. And this is the manner of the release: Every creditor that landed ought unto his neighbor shall release it; he shall not exact it of his neighbor, or of his brother; because it is called the Lord's release." – Deuteronomy 15:1-2.

So you should have no problem with taking an aggressive approach to eliminating your debts, especially when it comes to making your creditors forgive part or all of them.

Firstly, I must caution you against breaking any laws or committing any fraud. Sadly, the laws in society are not always based on The Bible, so you can't take God's word as law. So, provided you're within the law of your land, you could consider bankruptcy, especially if your spouse is able to maintain their credit, because credit is useful for later on in our journey. If you're married, usually only one of you needs good credit.

If there's any way to put all debts on just one person in the marriage and have that person legally default on those debts to wipe them out in a single move, this is something you could consider. Job done.

If that isn't an option for whatever reason, persuade the lenders to write off some of the debt. If you are having trouble paying loans, approach the lender and offer them a reduced full and final settlement (by about 25-50%) They can only say no. And very often they will accept, just to get some cash in. They will need to be convinced that this is all they're going to get from you because of your situation.

If the lender was irresponsible in any way by giving you this money (by not doing enough due diligence on your application), they can be sued for the full amount, and this too shall write off the debt in one move. Job done.

So, to summarize, first get very aggressive and look at ways to get the loans completely or partially written off whilst at the same time ensuring the credit of either you or your partner remains intact. Once you've done the most amount of damage to the total debt using those methods, get a low interest loan (ideally against your home) to pay off the remaining debts. Then we must pay that off.

Okay, now that you've arrested the downward spiral, you can concentrate on paying it off. This section will also apply if you do not own any property and cannot get a consolidation loan. You got into debt by spending more than you earn. So what do we do to get out of debt? Reverse the situation of course! Earn more than you spend! As soon as you do this, you can pay off your debts and this, in turn, will further increase your monthly disposable income.

In the next chapters I will be showing you several ways to massively increase your monthly passive income without taking massive risks. Have faith—I won't let you down. This will go a substantial way to getting you out of debt. Until then, there are many other ways of increasing income and reducing outgoings:

- ✔ If you can't borrow the total amount required to pay off all the debts, pay off the debts with the highest rates of interest first. Credit cards charge the highest, followed by hire purchase, bank loans and then overdrafts.

- ✔ Postpone buying all essential items for as long as necessary. Buy economy food and make do with your clothes. Stop eating take-out for a while. You may think that you are only just surviving now. Take a trip to a third-world country to discover what "only just surviving" *really* means.

- ✔ Don't see the debt as one large sum, break it down into manageable lumps and set yourself monthly targets to pay each one off.
- ✔ No amount of money saved is too small. Even ten bucks. Take it straight down to your savings account. Little amounts add up to big ones you can pay off debts with.
- ✔ When you get extra income, don't spend it! Be disciplined.

On that last point: it's a strange phenomenon but when people feel flush with cash, perhaps due to the value of their house rising as it has been doing in recent years, they spend more and on credit, too. This is a total illusion. *On paper* they may feel worth more and for some bizarre reason, this makes them more comfortable about getting into debt. If you think hard you will recall times when you *felt* hard up and spent less, or when you *felt* flush and spent more—all the time though, the reality was that your fundamental situation was no different. It is this strange psychological behavior that has led to so many in this country to getting so far into debt.

I want you to go and open a savings account with at least one month's notice required for withdrawals, so you can't get your hands on the loot when the next impulse purchase grabs your eye! Next I want you to plan a budget from the income/expense sheet you created earlier. Enter what your new monthly payments will be when you've consolidated the debt, as described already. Also enter into it any anticipated extra income you think you can get by using some or all of the methods shown on the previous page. Then, plan a strict food and spending budget and *stick to it.* Start a direct debit from your current account into the savings account—this part is very important. I want you to aim to save 10-20% of your salary every month here. Don't complain, just do it. Even if you aren't in debt this is a great thing to do.

The trouble is, I expect, that the majority of people you mix with *regularly* are not financially free and more importantly, they are very skeptical of becoming so. This is damaging. Either mix with like-minded people or not at all. You may lose some friends in the process but what sort of friend are they to deter a person from improving themselves, anyway? One thing's for sure: if you admit failure in your endeavors at any time they'll welcome you back with open arms and an, "I told you so," for good measure.

When you pay off that final dollar of debt and vow never to do it again, you will feel an almighty rush of freedom. Life will suddenly become fun again—you don't realize the burden you have until you get rid of it. You have been trained to think that debt is something normal! However, I would hope that you are starting to realize that whatever the crowd thinks is invariably wrong, you should therefore feel proud to be different. Different because you have a mind of your own. And governments don't like it when you think at all, let alone when you think differently.

A financial reality is that the economies of Western countries are based on credit. If suddenly all debt were eliminated, there would probably be a prolonged and severe recession. Banks would collapse and governments would be voted out of office. Is it any wonder why you're conned into debt?

The government taxes you for saving money but gives you a *tax break* for borrowing! I wonder why…

So with that, let's turn to the next villain who enslaves you…

Use The "Pharaohs"

"We have borrowed money for the king's tribute, and that upon our lands and vineyards... and lo, we bring into bondage our sons and our daughters to be servants... neither is it in our power to redeem them, for other men have our lands and vineyards." – Nehemiah 5:4-5.

The government prints as much money as it wants, and the result is the inflation that is steadily destroying the middle class. Even though both The Bible and The Constitution warn that gold and silver is the only true currency, this goes on, and at a rate never seen before in history. For this reason, *money is not real.* And this is another good time to remind ourselves of the first of the 7 secrets we began this lesson with:

"Wilt thou set thine eyes upon that which is not? For riches certainly make themselves wings; they fly away as an eagle towards Heaven." - Proverbs 23:5

"That which is not" is government-printed paper that they laughably refer to as *"money."* If you focus on the pursuit of attaining something that is being made more and more worthless over time, you will become poorer and poorer over time.

So if we're not pursuing money, what are we pursuing? We're pursuing what is real: *true wealth.* I will explain...

This is the pharaoh's greatest trick, and barring a revolution, there's nothing we can do about this legalized scam, but simply exposing it and working around it is all you need to do. Understand that money isn't real, and that by working for money you are working for something that isn't real. But how do you not work for money? Simple: you make money work for you instead. It's about getting your head around a concept I'm about to explain...

Apart from literally having a license to print money (and destroy its value), governments" other great power is the ability to make laws. They will always make laws to benefit themselves, and these will be laws that ensure they remain in power and that the most amount of taxation occurs with the least amount of complaining from their subjects. This is the way it has always been, and the way it will always be. Governments who have not done so have been overthrown, one way or the other.

Our task therefore is to legally pay the least amount of tax, prosper from the money printing, and align ourselves with how the government makes laws.

From a financial perspective, from our perspective, another way of looking at how the government makes laws is seeing them as *incentives.* You see, the tax system is the secretive way that a government *incentivizes* people to behave financially.

The big secret that the middle and working classes will never know is that the government actually incentivizes the system for corporations and owners of assets (which are unaffected by money-printing).

When you acquire or create assets, money is pursuing you, you are not pursuing money. And the money pursuing you becomes greater the more that the government devalue it, so you're compensated.

They would never advertise these incentives to the middle and working classes because that's not what will get them votes, but the incentives are written into law because corporations and asset owners (the wealthy classes) make massive campaign "donations" and pay large amounts of tax.

"Wilt thou set thine eyes upon that which is not? For riches certainly make themselves wings; they fly away as an eagle towards Heaven." - Proverbs 23:5

"That which is not" is the incentives given to the people for remaining in financial servitude to the ruling classes. There are none.

Now, you can either get angry about this fact (as many people do), or you can accept it and take advantage of the fact. The Bible certainly doesn't have a problem with you doing so because all you would be doing is making yourself wealthier, and as we discussed last time, **God wants you to be wealthy**. So, let me explain how the system is incentivized and how to not work for money.

Imagine two islands connected by a bridge. On one island the people live in slavery, day in, day out. On the other island, the people just sit by their swimming pools without needing to lift a finger if they don't want to.

There are two types of people on the slavery side, and two types of people on the swimming pool side, so let's see which group you're in and how to cross that bridge, shall we? On the "slavery" side of the bridge we have these two types:

1) Employee
2) Self-Employed

Let's talk about each in turn…

Employee.

The first group is the one most people are in, and they are obviously the most trapped of all four types. An employee has to work for a superior, has limited time off and even needs approval for that, and they are, by definition, a liability on the corporation's profit and loss account. Usually paid an hourly rate as low as the market will stand. Fixed income unless promotions can be engineered through the minefield of office politics.

One of the biggest ways employees are incentivized NOT to be employees is to do with how they're taxed on the (printed) money they earn. An employee must buy many things with money AFTER they've been taxed already. An employee *works for money* that the government is continually devaluing, then the government taxes that devalued money, and only then, the employee can spend whatever is left (usually on servicing debt that benefits the banks).

"Wilt thou set thine eyes upon that which is not? For riches certainly make themselves wings; they fly away as an eagle towards Heaven." - Proverbs 23:5

The benefit of course is PERCEIVED security—you go to work, receive a steady paycheck that you "know" will always be there each week. As a legacy of grade school, an employee usually wants to show up and suffer from 9-5, and then be able to switch off for evenings and weekends.

This isn't to say you can't be perfectly happy if you enjoy your work and have no great financial ambition, but I suspect the reason you're here is because you're NOT happy to be an employee.

Eventually, some employees (the smarter, more ambitious ones) wake up. They see themselves being fleeced like sheep by the boss who keeps all the money that their hard efforts are creating, and they decide they'd be better off being their OWN BOSS with their own business. And so it's only natural that this group of people then falls into The Big Trap. Enter the second type of person on the slavery side of the bridge.

Self-Employed

This is where most budding entrepreneurs and professionals get stuck. They now work for themselves, but note the operative word I just said: "work." They still work, only for themselves.

Having a corporation or LLC does NOT mean you're not in this group! Unless you pass a test I'm going to give you now, you may as well be employee or a 1099 contractor, I don't care what kind of corporate structure you have. "I have my own corporation/LLC" is a phrase I hear a lot of people boast, but it's a meaningless statement in most cases. They may as well be employees.

So how do you know if you're in this group? Simple. Just answer this question:

If you didn't touch your business for a month and stayed in bed instead, would it still be there when you got back?

Very few people who have corporations/LLCs can say "yes" to this. If you answered "no" to this question, YOU DON'T OWN A BUSINESS, YOU OWN A JOB! All you've achieved is changing employers.

Sure, you *may* earn a bit more money now. You might even be able to goof off a bit here and there. You're in charge of your own destiny now. So it's certainly better than being an employee in most cases, but you're still a slave. You may be the slave master as well now, but you're still a slave. In fact, many self-employed people work much harder than employees, and in some cases earn LESS. If many self-employed people did the math, they'd be better off going back to having a job, especially when you take benefits into account. Just ask my landscaper.

This is NOT financial freedom. You have to work on your business or you won't have a business. This is why doctors, lawyers, and other professionals will NEVER be financially free. They will NEVER cross the bridge to the swimming pool island. Sure, they may all have swimming pools, but they're unable to sit gazing into it all day (or doing whatever they want).

Here's another good question to ask yourself about your "business," in case you're in doubt:

Is your business saleable? Could someone realistically buy it or would it fall apart without you?

Again, most people would say "no." In which case, you don't have an asset, you have a JOB. You're still a mouse on a treadmill.

You pretty much spend what you earn, often because you work so hard and need things like cleaners and childcare. This is The Big Trap for most people who graduate from being an employee for this simple reason: BECAUSE THEY HAVEN'T STOPPED THINKING LIKE EMPLOYEES. And that's where they'll stay in most cases—on the slavery island. Because they have no **exit-strategy**.

These people are somewhat better off than an employee financially, although they are still slaving away *for money* that the government is continually devaluing, and then that person is heavily taxed because they often use an S Corporation for this business (ask your CPA about the different types of corporate structures). But this person can now make their business pay for expenses such as gasoline and computers and entertaining. The key point is this: *they are buying those items with PRE-TAX money.* Before the government takes a bite out of the money made, certain expenses are allowed to be deducted from that profit. This is a big advantage over the employee, but the type of expenses allowed are quite restricted compared to the people on the other side of the bridge.

Now, on the swimming pool side of the bridge, we have two groups of people that I'm sure you'd prefer to be with because they don't have all the disadvantages the people do on the slavery side of the bridge. They're able to sit by the pool all day because they have used the Pharaohs to their advantage.

In later chapters I'll explain this group of people and how you can quickly join them. For now I simply need you to understand how the system works *against* you if you're on the wrong side, and how money is "that which is not." By being positioned incorrectly in the government's system, and by not understanding it, money will mysteriously fly away from you. So yes, we are USING the government, and aligning ourselves with their system if the system benefits us.

"And Jesus answering said unto them, Render to Caesar the things that are Caesar's, and to God the things that are God's. And they marveled at him." – Mark 12:17.

But, moving on, now consider this: *your government isn't the only government.* There are other governments that have their own set of incentives for you to benefit from, and here's one example of this that could mean you retire TODAY.

This amazing retirement loophole can allow you to retire today for two reasons:

- You will live tax-free
- Your expenses will dramatically decrease

When you don't have to pay tax, it's like getting 50% more income! And decreased expenses means your dollars will go further. The secret is retiring overseas. And I'm not talking about some ridiculously poor, dangerous country. I'm talking about a tropical paradise like Panama.

Contrary to popular belief, you DO NOT have to give up your U.S. citizenship in order to retire in Panama. All you have to do is not stay in the United States for more than 30 days a year, and you can live tax-free in a tropical paradise. And you are allowed to earn up to $78,000 a year abroad without having to pay income tax. And that goes a long way in a place like Panama! Panama has everything you need, from proper healthcare to certified banks, and even beautiful beaches. But even better than that, Panama has a great incentive program for retirees. The benefits of this program include:

- Import tax exemption for household goods
- Tax exemption to import a new car every two years
- 25% discounts on utility bills
- 25% discount on airline tickets
- 30% discount on bus, boat and train fares
- 1% reduction on home mortgages for homes used for

personal residence

- 20% discount on doctor's bills
- 15% on hospital services if no insurance applies
- 15% off on dental and eye exams
- 10% discount on medicines
- 20% discount on bills for technical and professional services
- 25% off restaurant meals
- 15% off at fast food restaurants
- 50% discount on entrance to movie theatres, concerts, cultural and sporting events
- 50% discount at hotels from Monday to Thursday, 30% on weekends

So you will get all the benefits of being a U.S. citizen, all the benefits of living in a tax haven like Panama, the benefits of living on a tropical paradise where you will have more buying power, and you can return to the U.S. for up to 30 days each year to visit family and friends.

That's just one example of how a *shift in your beliefs* could change the rules of this game in a single stroke. The objective is to get you to retirement as quickly as possible by lowering your expenses and raising your passive income, and retiring to Panama achieves both goals. This could mean you retire NOW. But this is just one option of many I'll cover. As I move forward, you'll find many more shifts in your beliefs like this, and what you thought impossible before will suddenly look possible.

"With men this is impossible, but with God all things are possible." – *Matthew 19:24 (regarding the impossibility of a camel going through the eye of a needle).*

Now it's time to consider the third and final villain that holds you back in this journey by insidiously making your money fly away from you and constantly showing you "that which is not."

Disempowering The "Talebearers"

"Naked came I out of my mother's womb, and naked shall I return thither: the Lord gave, and the Lord hath taken away; blessed be the name of the Lord." – *Job 1:21*

Have you stopped to ask why people feel so bad about themselves that they become "retail addicts?" Could it be the fact that we watch so much television that we can no longer tell the difference between reality and fiction? I am, of course, talking about advertising. The advertising agencies first think of an *image* that their customers want and then use the advert to coerce people into thinking that this product will give it to you. For example:

Driving this boring family sedan will make strange exotic women attracted to you.

Eating this food will make you lose weight and enable you to be as attractive as the model that is shown eating it.

Sex sells. It is a common theme and at the heart of most commercials. But the way it is used is by displaying seemingly perfect men and women (after hours of make-up, lighting, fake tan and plenty of air-brushing) to make us feel inadequate and so crave the product in question, to make ourselves "better" people. Of course most people know deep down that just because you buy a certain product you won't magically become a better person, but they prefer to buy the illusion and the advertisers know it.

"He is a merchant, the balances of deceit are in his hand: he loveth to oppress." – Hosea 12:7.

When people find that these products didn't actually turn them into a movie star, what do they do? They feel inadequate once more and are ready for another product to make them feel better! Great news for the companies in question though. Are *you* addicted to image? The corporations can only use this weapon against you if you are weak and unintelligent enough to be taken in by the con.

"Hell and destruction are never full; so the eyes of man are never satisfied." – Proverbs 27:20

Fantasy, by definition, is "that which is not," and this is what the media sells you every day, consciously and unconsciously. The real world seems undesirable only to the Fools, who are helpless prey to those that would manipulate them to extract value. The real world is a fantastic place! Knowledge of it not only gives you clarity of mind, it gives you the confidence and happiness to believe in yourself—who and what you are—which, ironically, makes you more attractive to the opposite sex, which is, after all, what drives a lot of our spending at an unconscious level. For example, throwing money away on an expensive sports car purely for the purpose of impressing others—this won't accomplish anything other than make you poorer and appease your vanity.

"There is that maketh himself rich, yet hath nothing: there is that maketh himself poor, yet hath great riches." – Proverbs 13:7

And the thing about vanity is that it's a deep hole in your soul that will never be filled in this way.

"When goods increase, they are increased that eat them: and what good is there to the owners thereof, saving the beholding of them with their eyes." – Ecclesiastes 5:11

The media is responsible for shielding you from the truth and encouraging you to waste precious moments of your life, worrying and pontificating about the latest "hot issue" they have chosen for you on any given day. You already know that the media exists solely to make a profit and that they do this from the price of the newspaper, or whatever, and also by selling advertising space. But let's look at exactly how they get you to buy: Fear and guilt are the weapons they use to make you buy. Fear of anything new is present in most people and they therefore flock to see what this change is. Guilt is used by writing shocking headlines about one of the thousand horrible things that happened yesterday to make you feel bad—if you buy the paper it eases your conscience.

Of course, the media encompasses a wide variety of guises. Entertainment is one I want to give an airing next. You are regularly exposed to storylines with distinctly Socialist undertones (= wealth is a bad thing). This does not affect your conscious mind but rather your subconscious mind, and therefore affects your behavior without you knowing.

"The words of a talebearer are as wounds, and they go down into the innermost parts of the belly." – Proverbs 18:8

Notice how self-made rich people are continuously portrayed as evil, bossy, selfish, money grabbing, unhappy, dysfunctional, lonely, pompous pigs who always get their comeuppance? In fact, the TV show "Shark Tank" is the only production I can find that is even remotely positive towards wealth building (although everyone gets excited by big prize money—what hypocrisy!)

TV and film producers aren't bothered by truth, all they want is something that people will enjoy watching or reading, and this sort of stereotype is popular because it is comforting for folks to think that their dreary and powerless existences are great because wealthy people are truly despicable. I love movies—I have an extensive DVD collection and regularly visit the movie theater, and I certainly don't want to ruin your enjoyment of films. I just want you to see a philosophically flawed storyline when you see one and not let it affect you and your efforts. Without you even knowing, your subconscious mind is being poisoned and is influencing you to believe that money is worthless and being rich is awful. Hardly desirable for someone targeting financial freedom!

So one of the biggest reasons that money flies away from you is your own mind, and that means we need to re-evaluate ourselves, our habits, and our beliefs.

Life Rethink

"A sound heart is the life of the flesh: but envy the rottenness of the bones." – Proverbs 14:30.

Whether people are aware of it or not, a lot of the money they waste is spent on acquiring stuff that they believe will impress other people. In fact, it's often the case that the true self, the person underneath this façade, doesn't even want the stuff they're buying, but they want respect and acceptance from others, and they think the purchase will accomplish this.

But as someone who's owned outright an Aston Martin, a 30-foot Sea Ray boat, a private aircraft, etc., I can tell you now, my friend, NOBODY IS IMPRESSED. That's right, NOBODY. Before I saw the light, I focused too much on "that which is not."

You won't impress people with toys, you will make them jealous, and that will make them hate you, not respect you. This is the harsh reality of people, especially men. So if a shiny new Mercedes is on your goal list, whose goal are you aiming for? Yours or The Joneses? Forget the Joneses. The Joneses are a bunch of superficial Fools who are treading water on credit—if they lost their month-to-month existence tomorrow all that stuff would evaporate in a puff of smoke! And that life is fine for them because they're not taking the journey that you are; they are the proverbial hare and you are the proverbial tortoise.

The Bible says:

"Though while he lived he blessed his soul: and men will praise thee, when thou doest well to thyself. He shall go to the generation of his fathers; they shall never see the light. Man that is in honor, and understandeth not, is like the beasts that perish." – Psalms 49:18-20.

Behind the shiny façade of the Joneses, in the part of their life you don't see, is a lot of stress: worry about servicing all the debt and worry about losing their job they need to do that servicing. There's even a film called *The Joneses* that makes this point eloquently and risibly. Both that film and *American Beauty* should be on your watch-list this week.

The Joneses are an illusion, they are "that which is not."

"Better is a dry morsel, and quietness therewith, than an house full of sacrifices with strife." – Proverbs 17:1

The Joneses *appear* wealthy, but they are actually *destitute* from both a balance sheet point of view and a spiritual one. Listen, you don't even need a million dollars to live like a millionaire. When you're doing something you love every day (that's YOU, not anyone else), you are living a richer life than most millionaires. A big house and a fancy car will only give you so much. If you discover your lifelong dream always was to live in a cabin in Montana and do oil paintings all day, then you may even have enough to retire already.

You see, if you can get your head around this, that all the trappings probably don't need to be in your goals, something amazing happens: your goalposts scoot a LOT nearer, a lot more achievable. Remember our chart of expenses and passive income from earlier? That cross in the middle where the two lines meet is going to happen a lot sooner if you can understand this.

In the rest of this book I'm going to reveal some astounding money secrets from The Bible that will raise your passive income level on that chart we saw earlier, but if you can bring your expenses down too, then your remaining days of slavery will be crushed down to a minimum! But when the money comes in is when you'll face a new challenge that I must make you aware of.

As you start to acquire a little money, every instinct in your body will be driving you to spend the loot somehow. Your pockets will be on fire—all those things out there: a new car, etc. Stop right there. You've just fallen into the trap.

There is an invisible threshold for every person's wallet that makes them "sell out"—they give in to the "well, I might be dead tomorrow," excuse and spend the money they've built up through saving and investing it. The amount is different for everyone, but for the majority it seems to be around $10,000. When people see this amount in their accounts, it just gets to be too much. They start to dream up ways to make it fly away. Have you noticed how the first question people ask when they discover that you've received even the slightest amount of money is, "What will you spend it on?!" It's just our nature.

In your current position, you could well be looking at a figure like $10,000 and say, "I'd be grateful for that alone." I remember when $10,000 represented a handsome life's savings to me. But believe me, once you finish this course and get under way with your plans, $10,000 will soon seem to be petty change—especially when you see how easily it can be acquired—and the danger will be to say "easy come, easy go."

Put yourself in that position now. What is your "sell out" point? Let me re-phrase my question:

Are you here to gain a bit of trivial spending money or are you going to go all the way to freedom?

As I see it, it is now my job to equip you to go the distance. Once you've paid off those debts and started to make your income exceed your outgoings, even by a mere $50, I want you to see the value in saving that money rather than spending it. Moreover, I want you to see the con-tricks that exist to make that money fly away from you while you're busy focusing on "that which is not."

Have you heard about the power of compounding? Let me ask you a question to demonstrate this power:

You have a choice. You can work for $1,000 a day for the next 20 days OR you can work for just $1 a day for the next 20 days but compounding by double each day. Which do you want? Make a decision before reading on.

Let's see how the two options work out:

1) **20 days @ $1,000 a day = $20,000.**

2) **20 days @ $1 a day compounding by double =**

Day 1 = $1, Day 2 = $2, Day 3 = $4, Day 4 = $8, Day 5 = $16, Day 6 = $32, Day 7 = $64, Day 8 = $128, Day 9 = $256, Day 10 = $512

Had enough yet? After all, if you'd gone with the first option you'd have $10,000 by now, not $512! You can switch back to the first option now if you wish... But let's see what would happen if you stuck with it:

Day 11 = $1024, Day 12 = $2048, Day 13 = $4096, Day 14 = $8192, Day 15 = $16,384, Day 16 = $32,768, Day 17 = $65,536, Day 18 = $131,072, Day 19 = $262,144

DAY 20 = $\underline{$524,288}$.

It's like magic, isn't it? Those who chose the first option will fail in their endeavor and you must listen closely to this lesson to rectify this approach. Those who chose the second need to appreciate why and how important it is that they make this approach central to their daily life. If you take the cash out too soon before reaching freedom, you will never make it—you'll be back to square one—I bet you would have been quite tempted to pull out at day 15, ($16,384) wouldn't you? But you were only five steps away from $524,288!

Don't reward success by undoing accomplishments.

It's the equivalent of sticking to a diet so well that you reward yourself with a huge piece of chocolate cake! You know the power of compounding so let's make it work in your daily life. During the 1960s an interesting experiment was conducted with the most conclusive and revealing results. On the Stamford University Campus, Psychologist Dr. Walter Mischel tested a class of four-year olds and then tracked them periodically through their lives.

The experiment itself was simple. The class of youngsters were presented with a single marshmallow each by their teacher and then given a choice. They could have **another** marshmallow upon his return if they waited patiently for him to do an errand. Alternatively, they could have only that one marshmallow but they could have it **now** if they didn't want to wait. They were left alone in the room then with their single marshmallow while the teacher left the room for fifteen minutes. Some children covered their eyes or sung to distract themselves, while others gave in and simply ate the marshmallow.

Those children that still had not eaten their marshmallow upon the teacher's return were rewarded with a second. Many years later, the children that had waited were compared to those that hadn't and the results were dramatic. Those that had waited were generally far more successful in every aspect of their lives.

I call this concept "pleasure postponement." The Bible refers to this discipline in many ways on many different occasions.

"And when the people were come into the wood, behold, honey dropped; but no man put his hand to his mouth: for the people feared the oath." – Samuel 14:26

An example of pleasure postponement is that of full-time study for a qualification to further your career—it may mean that in the short-term you are not as well-off as your counterparts, who are in employment, but in the long-term you will be better off than them because of your studies.

The wealthy are disciplined. To get to where they are, they temporarily postpone certain pleasures to create freedom in the future. That future comes around quicker than you may think and those disciplined people who are able to keep their hands off the single marshmallow are soon able to enjoy their two-marshmallow reward. Meanwhile, those that chose to simply grab the marshmallow as soon as it was offered look in envy at the "lucky" people with two marshmallows and become bitter about this (they then probably vote for politicians that offer to steal marshmallows by force from people with "too many" and redistribute them).

You need to have the clarity and focus to see this through without giving in to pressure. When you see friends and family buying new cars, clothes, etc. will you be able to resist not joining in? Or do you have the depth of character to think single-mindedly about the long-term goal?

One of the most little known secrets about wealthy people is that they actually don't spend very much, and I don't mean miserly. You see, once you liberate yourself from the need to work and start to live a fulfilled and happy life doing the things you actually want to, you won't need the comfort that buying loads of consumer junk gives you. Don't confuse lifestyle with wealth. Big incomes and big lifestyles don't necessarily mean that you are actually worth very much. What's the point in earning $100,000 a year if you owe $105,000? Many of the world's millionaires live below their means.

"And (Jesus) commanded them that they should take nothing for their journey, save a staff only; no scrip, no bread, no money in their purse." – Mark 6:8

I write this as I stare at a long line of cars at the coffee shop drive-thru at 8:45 a.m. These are no doubt people on their way to a job. People who complain about having too little money, too much fat, not enough time, and that gas costs too much. Yet here they are, engines running instead of walking in, wasting time to buy expensive coffee that they could make at home for less money. This land is so rich with irony you could cut it with a knife, and everyone misses the daily comedy.

"Wilt thou set thine eyes upon that which is not? For riches certainly make themselves wings; they fly away as an eagle towards Heaven." - Proverbs 23:5

So are you ready to go for it? Or are you just aimlessly searching for the next ten bucks to blow in the shopping mall? I invite you to become a player in the big game now—that was my aim here—to make you lose the Fool mentality by breaking free of all the "hang-ups" that mass-society infects you with.

Chapter 3: Mountains into Molehills

"If ye have faith as a grain of mustard seed, ye shall say unto this mountain, Remove hence to yonder place; and it shall remove; and nothing shall be impossible to you." – Matthew 17:20

A t a seminar I was speaking at recently one of the students pulled me aside, thanked me, and said, "I'm just so confused as to why I'm in such a financial mess. I mean, I did everything right—worked hard at school, got a good job, paid into a pension... I did everything they told me to do..." I replied, "The answer to your problem was in that statement you just made: *you did everything THEY told you to do."*

Perhaps you relate to that guy? I've now lifted the veil so you can see clearly. As you now know, if you do everything THEY tell you to do you play right into THEIR hands, merrily following their script. The government (the "pharaohs"), the banks (the "money-changers"), and the media (the "talebearers") each have their own selfish agenda, and it does NOT match yours. THEY tell you to get good grades at school so you can get a good job (so you can pay tax forever, buy products, be a good drone for the labor pool, and work for devalued and after-tax money). THEY tell you to then buy the biggest house you can afford with the biggest mortgage you can get (to trash your profit and loss statement to ensure you keep working, paying tax, etc. etc.). THEY need you to stay on the side of the game where you work for money, but I'm working on transferring you across to the other side; where money works for you.

If you've been following all the steps so far you've already come a long way—actually, you're already in the minority of the population! You should now have strong foundations on which to build a solid plan for financial freedom using the many financial secrets I'll be showing you as you follow this ancient money-map. You've cleared your path to freedom by learning the truth about the world, and you've thrown off the dead weight from your back by clarifying your current financial situation and knowing your starting point—your Point A. And now there's one last crucial thing to do before we set off on this journey and start making money.

Here's just a few examples of what you'll learn in this chapter:

- **How a simple task that took me under a minute a day led to me getting my mansion.**

- **The 6 numbers that most people don't know and are causing them to fail and fall behind.**

- **The one word that supercharges your ride down the path to freedom.**

To ensure we actually succeed in getting you to retirement as fast as possible, we are using the 5 "P"s: *Perfect Preparation Prevents Poor Performance.* Most people fail *purely* because they set off on this journey without being prepared. Their path is cluttered; their load is heavy... *and they get lost because they don't carry a map.* This month we are going to create your money-map so you can cross the apparent mountains that lie between you and a comfortable retirement.

I know you want to start making money, and we shall indeed start doing that soon, but the preparation part is essential for success. Those who are impatient for the rain to grow their crops, but unprepared for it when it comes (and when it doesn't) are the real Fools.

"Make this valley full of ditches. For thus saith the Lord, Ye shall not see wind, neither shall ye see rain; yet that valley shall be filled with water, that ye may drink." – Kings 3:16-17

The wise farmer who digs irrigation ditches in preparation for the rain does so in faith, without any payoff for his labor—he does so anyway so he may reap the maximum benefit for when the day of rain inevitably comes.

So we have a mountain to climb. Let me begin by asking you to consider why so many important events in The Bible involve mountains. A few famous examples:

"And the ark rested in the seventh month, on the seventeenth day of the month, upon the mountains of Ararat." – Genesis 8:4 "And he said, Take now thy son, thine only son Isaac, whom thou lovest, and get thee into the land of Moriah, and offer him there for a burnt offering upon one of the mountains which I will tell thee of." – Genesis 22:2 "And the Lord came down upon mount Sinai, on the top of the mount: and the Lord called Moses up to the top of the mount; and Moses went up." – Exodus 19:20 "And after six days Jesus taketh with him Peter, and James, and John, and leadeth them up into an high

mountain apart by themselves: and he was transfigured before them." – Mark 9:2

Like much of the stories and statements in The Bible, it's a metaphor. A mountain is a metaphor for a seemingly tough obstacle that must be crossed to get to one's goal. But, as some of those previous verses showed, great and spiritual things happen on mountains too—on a mountaintop, close to the heavens in silence, one can experience important reflection on their life. In fact, one of the big secrets to crossing this mountain lies in this spiritual act, as we will see shortly. As a recap, here is the "mountain" we have to conquer:

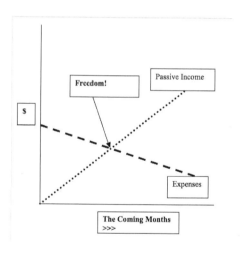

When your expenses are the same as your effortless income you're free to retire. So it stands to reason that if we bring your expenses down, and bring your effortless income up, we are on the fastest path. Last chapter we focused on getting your expenses as low as possible without sacrificing lifestyle (assuming you don't want to change lifestyle). Most importantly, we established the first piece of information you need to complete a journey: we created your "Point A," your starting point. If we were looking at a map, we would know where we are because we'd have a "fix" on your position.

So that was Point A. This chapter we are going to create your "Point B" so we know *precisely* where we are going, so we can start working on the other line in that freedom chart: raising your effortless income. In other words, considering your personal financial situation, *how much money do you need to retire?*

For most people, just the thought of answering that question is intimidating. They imagine it must be such a large amount that it scares them off from even trying! *And that's a big part of the problem.* If you know how to turn this apparent mountain into a molehill, or a series of molehills, you will conquer this mountain.

The 2nd Secret:

"That which is far off and exceeding deep, who can find it out?" – Ecclesiastes 7:24

If I was only allowed to use one of these seven secrets, I would pick this one! Though all seven are crucial, this one binds them all together. This is a really BIG secret, but very few people know it, and those that do don't understand it fully or know how to use it. You must not make this same mistake.

The main reason much of The Bible is open to interpretation and debate about meaning is that many verses, I believe, are a riddle to be solved by those in search of its treasures, and this is a classic example. What is "far off and exceeding deep" is a matter of *perception*, and that's why a Fool will never find it out, and never make it to freedom.

It's precisely because the dream of accumulating wealth (or anything) is perceived as being impossible or extremely difficult to achieve that people get overwhelmed before they've even taken a single step down the path to freedom. Every journey begins with a single step, and without this secret you won't take it.

In case you're wondering, I'm not talking about self-belief and all that other happy-flappy stuff you hear in motivational seminars or books. In fact, those things are a big part of the problem because they're usually written by charlatans who haven't travelled the path themselves. No, what I'm talking about is a *concrete, 1-2-3 step method* that's proven to get you to freedom as quickly as possible.

"Who can find it out?" Exactly the point. Hardly anyone can find it out! The Fools have about as much chance as finding this out as a camel passing through the eye of a needle. The application of this secret doesn't come naturally to human beings; it's like swimming or riding a bike; it has to be *learned*.

Point B

"The wise man's eyes are in his head; but the fool walked in darkness." – Ecclesiastes 2:14

Climbing a mountain is a much bigger challenge if you don't know where the mountain is or what it looks like, and yet that's how The Fools attempt to climb a mountain!

The Fools think something so "trivial" as setting goals

is either easy or a waste of time. So why do so many fail so miserably in achieving their goals then? Do you think setting a goal is irrelevant? Do you even know how to set a goal properly? When people fail dismally, they look around them and see a minority that *have* made it and assume (for the sake of comfort) it must all be down to dishonesty or luck, after all, they're no more intelligent than you, are they?

No, but that "lucky" minority believe in effective planning and more importantly, *they know how to!* Most people have not even tried to plan, and then they wonder why they fail. Please don't make this classic mistake. Last month we imagined this phone conversation:

Mr. Sluggard: "Hello, I'd like a taxi please."

Taxi Company: "Okay, where do you want to be picked up from?"

Mr. Sluggard: "I don't know."

Taxi Company: Click.

But now you know your Point A, so we can move on with this phone call:

Mr. Sluggard: "Hello, I'd like a taxi please."

Taxi Company: "Okay, where do you want to be picked up from?"

Mr. Sluggard: "1234 Main Street."

Taxi Company: OK. And where are you going?

Mr. Sluggard: "Well... somewhere far from here, I guess...?"

Taxi Company: Click.

Now you know where you want to be picked up from, all you need is a destination! And so enters the part where so many fail. Ask the average person what they want or where they want to be and the answer will invariably be, "I want to be rich" or "I want to be successful." Yes but, "*How* will you achieve your financial freedom? *What* will you do with it when you get it? *How* wealthy do you need to be to have financial freedom?" Those are my questions to them.

They will then give me a blank look and say, "I don't know." Vague, vague, vague. They don't know exactly where they want to get to, is it any wonder why they never arrive?

"That which is far off and exceeding deep, who can find it out?" – Ecclesiastes 7:24

Please don't think I'm being fussy. This is exactly the same principle as ordering a taxi to take you somewhere without a specific address! These people will never arrive, and later on in life they will blame external factors for their failure.

So, Point B. How wealthy do you actually need to be? You know, this is a question that many people who have already become wealthy have foolishly overlooked a long time ago. Imagine owning a machine that produced a crisp fifty-dollar bill each time you pulled a lever. Would it not be totally pointless to keep pulling that lever constantly for the rest of your life and die next to a massive pile of fifty dollar bills!?

And yet this is exactly what so many wealthy people do—they don't know when to stop, and they never reach their goal of retirement—and *they fail even though they've succeeded because they didn't make the first critical step that you are about to make.*

So let's calculate exactly how much you personally need to retire. Here's the formula based on using the powerful secrets I'll be teaching you in this book:

1. **Annual total expenses when you're retired (calculated from last time, and this amount may drop if being free means you can, for example, move to a less expensive house or location. Also, account for eliminating your debts as discussed last month): $_____**

2. **Multiply that amount by 5.88 = $_____ = YOUR "POINT B"**

You have just created your "freedom figure," your Point B, *your own personal mountain.*

This is the amount you would need to achieve a suitable <u>passive income</u> that meets your expenses so you can retire. A passive income—an income that requires little or no effort to attain.

Are you surprised it's that low? I expect you are! But

why is it that low? Why did you multiply your retired living expenses by 5.88? All will be revealed as we progress, but the important thing is that you now have a precise destination. You now know your Point A *and* Your Point B—doesn't that feel immensely clarifying? Half the battle is having a precise goal! Most people don't even begin because they are overwhelmed by not knowing *where* to begin and *where* to end.

Don't worry, I'll be showing you how to build this amount in the rest of the book. The objective for now is to come up with a financial objective that virtually guarantees a passive income suited to your needs. As the lessons roll on you'll see how such a seemingly small sum can easily liberate you from the grind. You don't need a million dollars to be free! We now have an exact destination for the ride ahead.

The aim here isn't to change the world or to be the richest person in that world. It's about withdrawal from THEIR game, and living life on your own terms. We're not wasting our energy getting upset about "them," we're just washing our hands of the whole thing by becoming financially free and living independently in abundant joy. Tell me that *that's* not worth fighting for!

Please don't be put off by the amount of your "freedom figure." I guarantee that by the end of all this you will have everything you need to make this figure a reality, without leaving your job if you don't want to. Not being afraid or intimidated by a seemingly big ambition is where this verse is coming from:

"Enlarge the place of thy tent, and let them stretch forth the curtains of thine habitations: spare not, lengthen thy cords and strengthen thy stakes. For thou shalt break forth on the right

hand and on the left; and thy seed shall inherit the Gentiles, and make the desolate cities to be inhabited." – Isaiah 54:2-3

Congratulations. You now know where you are and where you're going. Now, and only now, we can concentrate on conquering the mountain—because you know what the mountain looks like. And a large part of conquering that mountain comes down to a *single word*.

Success from a Single Word

"Ask counsel, we pray thee, of God, that we may know whether our way which we go shall be prosperous. And the priest said unto them, Go in peace, before the Lord is your way wherein ye go." – Judges 18:5-6

I need you to believe me when I tell you what I'm about to tell you, because I speak from long and hard experience:

You are GUARANTEED to fail if you are making this journey for the wrong reasons. You need it to be for the right reasons, and you need to have those reasons locked in your head.

You now have your "freedom figure" but that's just an arbitrary number. That number and the thought of being free isn't powerful enough to be the driving force that will make you go the distance.

You WILL give up on this journey without what I'm about to explain here, so please bear with me as we go deeper.

This course is about freedom. More specifically, how to regain the freedom you were born with, and that has systemically been taken from you as your life has unfolded. Perhaps that wasn't what you were expecting to hear, but that is exactly what God wants for you. Yes, He is devoted to making you a wealthy individual. But here comes an interesting question: *Why* do you want to be wealthy?

Sound like a silly question? Okay, let's say you've just won the lottery. You've just won ten million dollars. What are you going to do with it? May I suggest the following?

1) **Buy the house of your dreams.**

2) **Buy the car of your dreams.**

3) **Buy all your friends and family whatever they want.**

4) **Resign from your job and never work again.**

Your actual list may vary from this somewhat, but I would say that the majority of people have a very similar list. Let's say that your list is the same as this one. What will you do now? When you wake up every day, how will you spend it? After you have grown bored with polishing your Ferrari and having glamorous house parties, what then? (And believe me, you will get bored.)

The point I am making is that God has provided you with everything you need to become as wealthy as you require. Because I know how wealthy God wants you to be, it is my responsibility to prepare you for the time when you have this money and ask the question, "What will you do when you get there?"

The single word that's the key to your success is "WHY?"

You must know WHY you're doing this, and saying the reason is "freedom" is too vague—the mysterious power in the universe that turns our focus into reality doesn't know what to do with that word, "freedom." This is the very essence of setting goals and succeeding in making them a reality, so stay with me. "Why" is more important than "how," trust me!

I know a married couple. Very admirably, they have worked extremely hard for at least twenty years of the prime of their lives to put themselves in a situation where they never have to work again. The reason it took so long is that they achieved this through brute force—i.e. working every hour in the day as opposed to using these Biblical wealth secrets. Anyway, they are now in this comfortable position. How do you think they choose to spend their time? Yep, you've guessed it, they carry on working their butts off day in and day out because they don't know what else to do. They have, in effect, become wage slaves once again.

This is a classic and tragic scenario. To come all that way only to find that the cupboard is bare and, in their case, to discover that they didn't need to work as hard and for as long to get that freedom! Do you want this to be you? But what is the answer then? To stay as you are, living month to month in forced servitude? Of course not. Money is nothing but paper printed with pretty patterns and numbers in a fantasy world. In other words, it is worthless on its own.

We have been conditioned to believe from birth that our sole purpose on this planet is to get a good job, pay into a pension and a mortgage so that when we have reached an age where we are so close to death that we cannot care for ourselves, we are in a financial position as not to be a burden to anyone. The little boy or girl you once were never disappeared, they've just been forgotten about. You can still hear their cries sometimes though, can't you? When you're stuck in traffic on the way to work, do those broken dreams come back to you? Didn't you want to be a world explorer, a famous writer, to sing in a band, to paint, to dance, to live in a lighthouse, to be a beach-bum, fly planes, play football all day, be an actress, open a children's home, just simply to "be free" or maybe just have the time to be a great parent/partner/friend?

I want you to daydream for a bit. Nothing wrong with this at all. It's only when you want something badly that you get motivated to achieve it. That becomes your WHY.

These "fanciful" and "unrealistic" dreams have been expelled from you by the way society is and what we have made it. If you think back in time, school really is about beating the individuality out of kids. They come in one end as open books: unique beings full of exciting dreams just dying to come true. But they come out the other end as docile corporate work-units, just as the system needs them to be. Why? Because to achieve this ultimate happiness you would need total freedom. To gain total freedom, you would need enough money to escape wage slavery and this is deemed to be a "pipe-dream." I want you to rediscover those dreams and make them your WHY.

The accumulation of wealth is our main concern here, but it is only a means to an end. We need to take it further than just "money" or "freedom."

MONEY = FREEDOM = **ABILITY TO FULFILL YOUR TRUE PURPOSE IN LIFE= <u>PASSION TO ACHIEVE YOUR GOAL</u>**

Why can't we just focus on getting your freedom figure and leave it at that?

Because the problem with that monetary goal we just set is that it's not going to get your juices flowing once you get started, it's not going to pick you up from the floor when you fall down, it's not going to motivate you enough because the end result is not exciting. What you need is a vivid picture of something to strive for, something that will excite you, and simply paying off debts won't suffice. And neither will being financially free or retired. These are vague goals.

So you have to explore your soul a bit, and this can be tricky. What do you *love* doing? What would you do on your ideal day? *What did you love as a child?* Any career dreams you gave up on? Who is the real you—before "THEY" sunk their fangs into your soul?

Answer these questions honestly and you will suddenly be energized enough to make it happen. Your inner soul will awaken and will fuel you towards your *passion*.

WHAT IS THE ONE THING THAT DEFINES YOU AND EVERYTHING YOU ARE?

By definition, you're here because you want wealth and success, and you're doing the right thing by listening to someone who's achieved the things you seek. The big secret to achieving your goal is the one deep inside you—that little boy or girl who's desperately trying to be heard, for you to be true to yourself. Do you think that forgotten kid inside you cares about having a grand house? No, that kid just wants to be happy by doing what they LOVE doing each day.

Stop what you're doing. Go within, go deep, and challenge the artificial processes going on within you. What are your opinions and why? Who's saying those things in your head?

We all have a true purpose in life but it's so very rare that anyone actually discovers what it is. Your purpose is determined by your gifts—and we ALL have a gift. You'll know what it is because you feel most like yourself when you're using it. Like you've come home. If you won the lottery tomorrow, you wouldn't stop doing it. And it doesn't have to change the world, fit in with other peoples" wishes or beliefs, or be anything grandiose—as long as it fills you up with lasting *passion and joy*.

There has never been and will never be another one of you ever again, and your gift is just as unique; often, no-one else can understand why it means so much to you. Once you identify your reason for being, you'll quickly realize two things:

1. **Working toward your goal and/or using your gift reinforces the best and deepest elements of yourself.**

2. **You love doing this so much that you simply can't get enough of it.**

Many people are excellent at setting goals in an attempt to "Make it happen," but are those goals the kind that make them *automatically* look past discomfort and risk? The goal needs a "pilot-flame" to keep the fire burning—if that goal is not self-perpetuating through passion, the result will be (surprise, surprise) NO ACTION. If you follow this logic, an interesting point arises:

Most people believe that their dream goal is to acquire more wealth. But if that's the case, why aren't they more motivated to get it? *Because it isn't their dream goal—they just assume it is because they haven't found their gift in life.*

So how can you discover your purpose? For starters, the more new things you experience in life, the more likely you are to find yourself! If you insist on doing the same mundane job, living in the same town, going on holiday to the same place etc., how will you know what you love and what you hate if you've never tried anything different? Change seems scary because there is a perceived risk involved. However, the greatest risk you face in life is not finding your true purpose.

You MUST clearly know WHY you want freedom, for that will be the fire in your belly and the light at the end of the journey.

Know your personal WHY and I promise you, all your mind then needs is a specific task you give it and suddenly it goes to work all by itself. To take an example you can immediately relate to, let's say you're suddenly in the market for a red Honda. That day, as you drive around you'll notice red Hondas everywhere! Now, have the amount of red Hondas on the road dramatically increased overnight? Of course not, but because you had a specific task in mind (researching red Hondas), your awareness of them was dramatically increased. In other words, it was your perception that changed, not the reality.

Forgive the length of this verse below, but it really captures the relentless feeling of emptiness and disappointment from not achieving something for the right reasons.

"And whatsoever mine eyes desired I kept not from them, I withheld not my heart from any joy; for my heart rejoiced in all my labor: and this was my portion of all my labour. Then I looked on all the works that my hands had wrought, and on the labour that I had labored to do: and, behold, all was vanity and vexation of spirit, and there was no profit under the sun. And I turned myself to behold wisdom, and madness, and folly: for what can the man do that cometh after the king? Even that which hath been already done. Then I saw that wisdom excelleth folly, as far as light excelleth darkness. The wise man's eyes are in his head; but the fool walked in darkness: and I myself perceived also that one event happeneth to them all. Then I said in my heart, as it happeneth to the fool, so it happeneth even to me; and why was I then more wise? Therefore I hated life; because the work that is wrought under the sun is grievous unto me: for all is vanity and vexation of spirit. Yea, I hated all my labour which I had taken under the sun: because I should leave it unto the man that shall be after me." – Ecclesiastes 2:10-18

Without the WHY fanning the flames in your belly, you will find it hard to conquer your mountain. Once you have the WHY, we can move onto the next step: the HOW.

The BIG Secret

"Jesus answered and said unto them... if ye shall say unto this mountain, Be thou removed, and be thou cast into the sea; it shall be done. And all things, whatsoever ye shall ask in prayer, believing, ye shall receive." – Matthew 21:21-22.

Of course, it's easy for a Fool to set himself a goal. He just picks a random number out of thin air—say, a million dollars—and he tells himself that's the mountain he has to conquer. He doesn't know why he wants it or why that's the amount—that's his "Point B." He's still set to complete the journey, albeit a flawed journey, isn't he?

No, he isn't, because he doesn't know the BIG secret I'm about to tell you. Many people have set themselves goals and failed. Perhaps even you. Setting a goal and then simply going about accomplishing it isn't simple, after all.

"That which is far off and exceeding deep, who can find it out?" – Ecclesiastes 7:24

So, we've created your freedom figure, your own personal mountain to conquer, and you know *why* you want to conquer it. But it's still a mountain... or more specifically, we *perceive* it as a mountain. And that's the problem.

I realize that at this early stage it will be hard to see the way in which you will achieve your freedom figure. Don't worry, we'll get to that. Break your figure down into months, however many months you give yourself to achieve it. Then divide into weeks, then days. Chip, chip, chip. You <u>will</u> get there.

An essential skill of highly successful people (whether they are aware of it or not) is their trick of breaking large tasks into smaller ones. They see a goal to be achieved sometime in the future, but they don't look at the size of it and go and cry in a corner! No, they divide it into "bite-size chunks."

Let's say your mountain is $300,000 and you make that your goal. Great, your mind gets to work on making it happen...

and then it fails because of "indigestion;" that amount is simply too big to swallow in one goal, so your mind gets overwhelmed, and things "mysteriously" don't work out.

If you're faced with an objective that appears to be "far off and exceeding deep" then "who can find it out?"

What we must do then is change our *perception* of it. We do this by turning mountains into molehills—we break up this objective into smaller, more "digestible" chunks.

Transform your mountain into several molehills. We are going to break this down into *daily* tasks so that you arrive at retirement as quickly as possible. And here's how we're going to do that.

We're going to aim to double our money 3 times a year. How you're going to do that is explained later on—for now, it's just our vital planning tool. Here is a table of what it looks like to double your money, starting with just $100 and going all the way to $1.63 million in just 14 steps:

1. $200
2. $400
3. $800
4. $1,600
5. $3,200
6. $6,400
7. $12,800
8. $25,600
9. $51,200
10. $102,400
11. $204,800
12. $409,600
13. $819,200
14. $1,638,400

In this example the *mountain* of $1,638,400 was broken into 14 *molehills* that began with just $100! That's the power of doubling your money, a power that is proven on public record many times over, as you will see later. Now we're going to calculate, based on this table, how many steps you are from retirement:

Amount of starting capital (check your net worth number that we calculated earlier or consider any savings you can spare): $_____

Now keep doubling that amount until it reaches your freedom figure. Number of steps required to reach your freedom figure: _____ steps to freedom.

How many steps away from retirement are you? Whatever freedom figure your mountain is, you've just broken that mountain up into that many molehills.

So your mountain is no longer a mountain.

"And I will make all my mountains a way, and my highways shall be exalted." – Isaiah 49:11

Your goal is no longer "exceeding deep," is it? Now we can move onto the next step, and you will see that neither is it "far off."

The Secret of 6 Numbers

"But the liberal devised liberal things; and by liberal things shall he stand." – Isaiah 32:8

The other main reason why even the people who set goals fail is because they're missing 6 important numbers: the numbers that make up a date.

A goal isn't a goal without a deadline. If you don't set a deadline, then you give yourself an excuse to keep saying "Tomorrow" and never get anywhere. How many people do you know who say, "Oh, I'll start that diet tomorrow" and never do? And when I say set a deadline, I really mean it. Saying, "By the year 2018..." is not good enough. The deadline must be as exact as, for example, "1st September 2018," or to make it six numbers: 09/01/18.

The reason why so many people don't do this part is because it's a hard thing (for them) to figure out. I mean, they don't even know how much money they need and why they need it, so what chance do they have of knowing WHEN they aim to get it by?!

Fortunately, you already figured this out just now when you calculated how many steps you are from retirement.

Number of steps required to reach your freedom figure: _____ steps to freedom.

Now divide that by 3 = _____ years from freedom. Add that number of years to today's date and you have your deadline.

**Enter that sacred deadline date as six numbers here: ___ /
___ / ___**

Don't be disheartened if your deadline seems far away!
You might want to reconsider your living expenses in retirement
and rework the freedom figure, as that would bring the deadline
closer. Remember that retirement could mean moving to a
smaller home in a less expensive area, or it could even mean
moving abroad to a sunny tax haven, so think carefully about
those retirement expenses you listed. Will you be spending so
much money on junk when you're living your life as you please
in abundant joy each day? Will you care about impressing your
friends with toys at that time, and will you even be living near
them? The other thing to remember is that we're taking this one
day at a time, molehill by molehill, and when you're diligent at
this process the time will pass faster than you think:

*"For a thousand years in thy sight are but as yesterday when it
is past, and as a watch in the night." – Psalms 90:4*

Powerful stuff. You now know exactly *how much* you need to
retire, *why* you want it, and *when* you will get it by. Only now
that you have this specific Point B can we begin the journey
from Point A. And it begins with a special prayer.

The Secret Prayer

"Therefore I say unto you, What things sever ye desire, when ye pray, believe that ye receive them, and ye shall receive them."

We're going to pray for our arrival at Point B. But there are prayers that are heard, and prayers that are unheard. What's the difference between the two?

In my humble opinion, the difference between the two is that God needs to know exactly *what* it is you want, *why* you want it, and *when* you want it by. How could He grant you your desires if you're not clear about what they are? I'm sure He *knows* what they are, but I think He wants *you* to know.

People who don't pray or who say that prayer doesn't work when you ask for things are making the classic mistake of not being clear. I know some people who just pray for "finances" and then wonder why God doesn't answer, or they blame the lack of response on Him "moving in mysterious ways." I mean, seriously, if someone asked *you* for "finances" would you be able to help? Wouldn't you like a bit more information? God isn't a genie in a lamp; He is here to help the faithful, not the Fools. And, like any good Father, He wants His children to figure a few things out for themselves, and that's what we're doing here. *There is an art to praying for things you want.*

"That which is far off and exceeding deep, who can find it out?" – Ecclesiastes 7:24

So, let's put it all together and create your daily prayer. We are first going to create the most important document you will ever create, and I call it your "Freedom Promise." Take a quality piece of blank paper and a quality pen, and then simply write on it the following:

By (enter the deadline date) I wish to have made $(enter your freedom figure).

Simple, yet incredibly powerful and clarifying. Please write this out in ink and by hand, not from a computer—it means more that way. I want you to hang that document in a place you will be forced to look at it every day, and when you see it I want you to read it back to yourself; to make that *promise* to yourself as a basis for praying to God in a quiet and spiritual part of your home.

Great. Now we can work backwards and break down what we have to do in this timeframe, month by month, day by day. "What do I have to do today so that I "magically" end up at my goal come that date? Hmmm. Let's see what my calendar entry says…"

Get a calendar. That calendar is now a living and sacred thing. Work out all the little molehills that will add up to your freedom figure. On each day in your calendar make an entry that details "today's molehill."

Now, and this is the important part: under no circumstances do you go to bed that night unless you've honestly achieved today's molehill objective AND prayed for the accomplishment of tomorrow's molehill.

The first part of mastering the art of prayer is knowing exactly what to pray *for*, but not just for your Freedom Promise; *you need to be able to break it down into daily molehills so that you have a specific daily prayer to make for the successful completion of tomorrow's objective.*

Simply praying for your Freedom Promise isn't going to be heard that well. It's certainly better than simply praying for something vague like "finances," but your goal needs to be broken down into daily chunks. This way you don't get overwhelmed and most of all, your prayers get heard because we pray one day at a time *in the present moment.*

What would these smaller molehills look like? We've made a good start by breaking up your Freedom Promise into double-up steps—you simply focus on the next step in the double-up process. So if you've got $1,000, then you are no focusing *only* on accomplishing the next molehill of doubling that to make it into $2,000. That task can be broken down into daily tasks that you will learn as we move forward; the main thing is that you're only working on the next step in the process.

So there are *two* things you're focusing on and praying for each day, but with more focus and emphasis on the second one:

1. Your long-term goal—your Freedom Promise.
2. Your shorter-term goal—completing the next double-up step.

And I believe God wants you to convey to him precisely what the completion of your goal looks like and how you intend to achieve this. Remember, He is there to help you, not to wave a magic wand on demand! *And He is there to help the faithful, not the Fools, so you should PROVE your faith by <u>seeing</u> yourself receiving the thing you're asking Him for.*

This is simply the art of constantly seeing what you want to happen in your mind. I want you to close your eyes and see yourself achieving your objective on schedule, and exactly what you'll wish to be doing tomorrow that will take you a step closer to conquering the next molehill. Some people say they find it hard to visualize like this. If you're one of them, I want you to start reading a novel instead of watching a film because this will encourage you to visualize the images and characters in the story. Television is lazy because all the visualization is done for you! Another thing to practice is this: sit yourself down quietly in a room on your own and look around taking in as much of the surroundings as possible. Then, close your eyes and try to picture how the room looked in your mind. This is exactly the same principle as visualizing achieving your goal.

I'm often asked how I felt the day I was able to break free of the need to work ever again, and my response often surprises when I explain that I didn't really celebrate or anything. Does it surprise you? It wouldn't surprise high-achievers to hear this either because they know where I'm coming from:

Whenever I reach a landmark achievement I barely notice. Why? *Because I'd already seen it happening in my prayers a thousand times before, to the extent that the actual event seemed like déjà vu!*

Maybe that de-glamorizes the whole experience of achievement somewhat, but that's the reality I want you to take on board right here and now. You must not only know your goal, but also constantly visualize it so completely that it's a foregone conclusion.

I believe that when you do that in daily prayer you open the communication channel to God because you are forced to be *present* and to *believe.* That's how prayers get heard.

As The Bible says:

"Thy dream, and the visions of thy head upon thy bed are these... thy thoughts came into thy mind upon thy bed, what should come to pass hereafter." – **Daniel 2:28-29**

Here's how your daily prayer might read:

Dear Lord,

I pray to you for the successful completion of my Freedom Promise: to have made $(enter your freedom figure here) by (enter your deadline here).

(Now take sixty seconds clearly visualizing the successful completion of your Freedom Promise on schedule. See the money on your bank statement, see yourself living the WHY).

Thank you for the completion of today's step I took towards that Promise.

I now pray to you for the successful completion of tomorrow's goal, which is (enter tomorrow's goal).

(Now take a silent sixty seconds to clearly visualize yourself actually completing tomorrow's task).

Amen.

If you'd like a good Bible verse to add before saying "Amen," I suggest this one:

"For the Lord God shall help me; therefore shall I not be confounded: therefore have I set my face like a flint, and I

know that I shall not be ashamed." – Isaiah 50:7

Setting your "face like a flint" means having dogged determination to get to Point B, not Plan B...

Point B, Not Plan B

"If thou faint in the day of adversity, thy strength is small." – Proverbs 24:10

Do I bother with "Plan B's?" NO! Why? *Because failure simply isn't an option.* If things don't proceed as planned I just change course until they do, like an aircraft dodging bad weather. You must stay focused, courageous, and faithful, for your faith will be continually tested while on this journey.

"Let thine eyes look right on, and let thine eyelids look straight before thee. Ponder the path of thy feet, and let all thy ways be established." – Proverbs 4:25-26.

Negativity, doubt, laziness, slack-handedness, these are your enemies now. Those are the dark voices of old demons that are now nagging at you to turn back, telling you that you have no hope in achieving this, that you're wasting your time.

You must not let those demons win. You must prevail and focus on the light at the end of this passage to freedom. Your life is literally at stake in this battle between good and evil.

Once upon a time, I believed that becoming wealthy was something for other people. I must have been one of those "unlucky" types that just didn't get there. I assumed that the most I could expect was a decent job, an average car and the ability to retire with a modest pension at 60. Debt was just something that I had to accept. In short, although I didn't realize at the time, I didn't think I was worth the best things in life. I didn't think I deserved them.

I tried all the "positive thinking" books but they did nothing. These books are usually incredibly shallow in that they expect the reader to effectively paint a mask on their face. There's no point in nourishing the leaves of a tree if the roots are dying! The "core" of many of us is rotten. Before we start thinking positively, we need to mend it or we are wasting our time. Once, my core was rotten. I had a mediocre enough existence only, for some reason, each month I seemed poorer than the last one. Anyway, I was at a party one night and heard that one of the guests there was a self-made millionaire. Back then, I believed that they had some sort of special skill or advantage that I hadn't been "lucky" enough to have as well. I felt compelled to ask this guy what his particular secret was. What was his special "gift" that gave him such a "privileged" position over me? His reply was a little strange: **"Look at the *lens* through which you view the world if you want a part of it!"**

What you have running in the programming of your mind eventually manifests itself in the outer world. So if you want to change the life around you, you must first change your mental programming. When you try to change the life around you without changing what's going on inside your mind, you fail. Someone can believe totally that they deserve wealth but that they lack the *ability* to achieve it. This leaves them equally likely to fail as someone who didn't believe in themselves. If you don't think you are capable of something you will certainly not achieve it.

You have now calculated your freedom figure and are possibly a little intimidated by the size of it. Does it seem unachievable to you? If it does, then you doubt your abilities and we must address this situation before we go any further. *How can you expect to achieve something if you don't believe in your abilities to get it?*

Excuses are classic signs of someone not believing in themselves. You may now be saying, "It's alright for him, I wasn't given an education/I'm the wrong age/sex/race.... the government should do something...etc..." I used to think this way until I realized that external forces have nothing to do with the position I am in. The truths behind the excuses given above are unmasked as, "I **choose** to allow my education/age/sex/race to hold me back." Every time you are in a conversation and you feel a negative remark about your abilities coming on, STOP YOURSELF. Your demons are clever; they hide their sabotage with smoke-screens like these.

Take responsibility for your own life starting right now. Until you do, you will never get anywhere near your freedom figure. Just look at that word "responsibility" for a second. It is derived from "response-ability." In other words, you have the *ability* to *respond* to a situation as an advanced being rather than be trampled on like some apathetic creature.

There are thousands of millionaires in the world and the vast majority of them are no more talented than you are. All those people had was belief and determination.

Those people who succeeded weren't frightened of failure, and they never gave up. If at times on this journey you feel like giving up, say this verse to yourself:

"Our heart is not turned back, neither have our steps declined from thy way; Though thou hast sore broken us in the place of dragons, and covered us with the shadow of death." – Psalms 44:18-19

People have remarkably short memories when it comes to their failures. We bury our failures instead of learning from them. Learn from the Texans and their Alamo. The Alamo was obviously a huge defeat, but what do they do in Texas? They turn it into a monument and a tourist attraction!

That's what we should all do. Build a monument to our failures in our minds. Learn the lesson they taught you.

And if other people want to rub your defeats in your face, let them. Those people are clearly the ones who think failure is bad, who want to bury failures, and they will pay the price for that mentality. Understand: The difference between successful people and mediocre people is that successful people do the things that mediocre people don't want to do. And one of those things is learning to appreciate and remember failure so we don't lose the lesson it gave us.

Chapter 4: The Sea of Money

Let the Journey Begin...

*"For wisdom is a defence, and money is a defence: but the
excellency of knowledge is that wisdom giveth life to them that
have it." – Ecclesiastes 7:12*

That's the beauty of knowledge; it's a priceless gift that
never stops giving. *Wisdom* is something different
to knowledge but equally as valuable; wisdom is
something the first two lessons were filled with as you saw
through all the big lies "they" have fed you, as you threw off the
financial shackles and false values that were holding you back
and weighing you down. You cleared the path to freedom and
cast off the dead weight. But before you could take that first step
from Point A, we needed to know Point B, and so we've worked
through that and given ourselves a map to follow—you envision
a precise amount of money you need to retire and an exact date
by which you intend to have acquired it by.

But now is where your feet hit the street, now is where
knowledge is going to come into play more and more. The
reason I needed to give you wisdom before this knowledge is
summarized in that quote I began with:

*"For wisdom is a defence, and money is a defence: but the
excellency of knowledge is that wisdom giveth life to them that
have it." – Ecclesiastes 7:12*

In other words, you need to be wise in order to *act* on the
knowledge given, hence no knowledge should be given to The
Fools.

But we can't sit around and prepare forever, we have

to actually put our plan into practice! I know people who love to plan but never actually use their plan. They spend forever "getting their ducks in a row" and resultantly never take a single step forward, usually for fear of what will happen along the way if things don't go according to plan.

Listen my friend, *things never go exactly according to plan*! But we set off anyway, and we expect to adjust course as we go, dealing with anything as and when we come to it. You now know how much importance I place on "The 5 Ps" (Perfect Preparation Prevents Poor Performance), but I will also now tell you that even a Fool who actually takes steps towards a goal is going to have more success than those who don't act upon their plan!

So let the journey now begin. You're now in a powerful position because you should now hold in your hand a sacred document: your Freedom Promise. You should now know precisely how much money you need to retire and when you wish to have made it by. If you don't have that document I strongly urge you to go back to the last chapter and create it.

I make no apology for continuing to show you this chart, because this is why we're here:

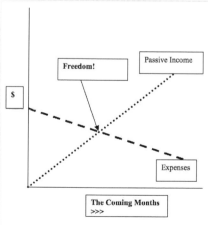

You've reduced your expenses (or are working on reducing them), thus lowering that line on the chart.

Now we're going to raise that line of passive income by creating streams of income for you that fill your bank account with enough money to cover your expenses with virtually no effort on your part. How are we going to do that? By *making money*. And then we're going to put that money to work as efficiently as possible, but it all starts with making money, plain and simple. How much money? You tell me; you have a precise number on your Freedom Promise.

If you want to make that amount of money, how are you going to do it? One reason why so many people never get started is that they're simply overwhelmed by not knowing where to begin. So let me clarify things by stating the simple fact that there are only 5 *legal* ways to make the amount of money you need to retire by the deadline you made in your Freedom Promise (and being employed or self-employed isn't one of them!):

1. Win the lottery.
2. Receive a large inheritance or gift.
3. **Stock market.**
4. **Real estate.**
5. **Your own business (but not self-employed).**

Winning the lottery and receiving an inheritance are out of your control, so that only leaves 3 (in bold). *That's it, that's all there is, just those 3 moneymaking methods, like it or not.* And I suggest you use all 3. If you own a home, then you believe in real estate. If you pay into a pension fund, then you already believe in the stock market (yep, all that money goes there!). If you rely on a paycheck then you already believe in business, but it's not *your* business! So you're *already* invested in the only 3 paths available to you, *but not in a way that will lead to completion of your Freedom Promise on schedule!*

I know you have preconceived and prejudiced ideas about all 3 of those areas, and I also know that those ideas and prejudices you harbor are entirely false because you've been told lies about them, and that has led to you having a bad experience with them.

But that is all about to change, because you are now going to bust all those myths you believe as we uncover the truth and secrets that will set you free. I'm going to begin by asking you a simple question:

It's a coin-toss. Heads you make $60, tails you lose $10. Will you play? And if so, for how many coin-tosses?

Think very carefully before answering...

Why do I ask that question? *Because getting that question right is the key to succeeding in business, real estate, and especially the stock market.*

I'll let you think on it more before giving you the right answer. Obviously, it would be great if we could have the coin land on "heads" all the time, and that's the objective behind the brand new secret we're about to move on to...

The 3rd Secret

"A prudent man forseeth the evil, and hideth himself: but the simple pass on, and are punished." - Proverbs 22:3

"The evil" is the shenanigans of big banks. You know the effects of this all too well, but you probably don't know how and why it happens, and how you can engineer their actions into your favor.

On the surface it seems obvious, but in a financial context there's a lot more to this verse than meets the untrained eye. *Ignorance of this secret is what will deny you the retirement you deserve and keep you a slave to the banking establishment your whole life!* If you'd have known this secret in May of 2008 you'd have not only escaped the brutal financial crisis that followed, you'd also have made an absolute fortune from it, perfectly legally and ethically.

Here's how the big-banks use this "evil" secret against you in 1-2-3 steps:

1. Entice you into sending them checks each month for some sort of investment/retirement account. You've seen the glossy brochures with happy retired couples walking down the beach at sunset; you know what I'm referring to.

2. Just in case you don't write them those checks, they lobby (read: bribe) the government to make it mandatory under law and to give you tax-breaks for doing so.

3. The banks then tell you that the investment is a *long-term* proposition, and you have to just stick to it, keep paying those checks in, if you want to look like that happy retired couple on the brochure, that is. In other words, *do not take the money out.*

4. The banks then take those monthly checks of yours and trade with it in the stock market. So the stock market rises with all that cash coming into it—and they call that a "bull market." When the stock market eventually gets too high, the banks then need an exit strategy— they need someone to buy all this now-overpriced stock from them. So they promote it to the public and they support prices up by continuing to buy stocks at tactical times. Only when they've offloaded all their stocks on the unsuspecting public do the banks stop buying, and the market crashes (after the banks have made special kinds of trades that profit from a crash). Note: it's only the banks" money that was saved, not yours. Your money goes up in smoke, and all those little checks you sent them are now worth half what they were. Sorry, you'll have to work a bit harder and a bit longer to be like that couple on the brochure—read the small print.

5. But the government is happy because the banks have paid huge amounts of tax to them for all that money they just made. The politicians are obliged to make some noise and even make a few arrests for the cameras, but the party must go on or they'd lose all that tax (to buy votes with) as well as those political contributions (read:

bribes).

6. The government charges you tax at the rate of around a third of all you earn, as you well know. They then give some of that money to the banks...

7. So, because the politicians are in the banks" pockets, the government lends the banks money at virtually zero interest—and the banks can borrow all this cheap money (your money) at seven times the cash reserves they have. If a bank has a million dollars, it can now borrow another seven million dollars from the government (read: YOU) at let's say 1%. So it now has 8 million dollars to lend YOU and is only paying 1% for it. It lends YOU and everybody else that eight million dollars at anywhere from 5-20%. Nice work.

8. But then the banks get greedy with all that cheap and easy money and start lending million-dollar mortgages to car valets who earn $20k a year. This causes demand for a lot more properties to be built. When the inevitable happens and the car valet can't pay his mortgage and defaults on the loan, foreclosures hit the market and the property market crashes. But not before the banks have secretly realized this would happen and have packaged up all this "toxic debt" into an investment product that they sell to someone else through the stock market. Eventually both the stock market and the property market crashes, and then the whole cycle starts over.

This goes on all the time, it will never stop going on, and the banks will get richer and richer while you get poorer and poorer.

The trick is to be able to see these cycles taking place, to see what the banks are doing and when. If you can accomplish this, then you will be the one getting rich by riding on the back of the banks, 100% legally and ethically.

"A prudent man forseeth the evil, and hideth himself: but the simple pass on, and are punished." You need to be that "prudent man."

Learn this secret and I promise you, you will NEVER again be blindsided by an event like the 2008 financial crisis— you will expect it, and you will profit by it.

But it all begins and ends with that coin-toss question...

The Big Question...

Heads you make $60, tails you lose $10. Will you play? And if so, for how many coin-tosses?

Is it possible to "forseeth the evil" of that coin landing on "tails?" Yes it is to a large degree, and I'm going to show you how simple it is to do precisely that, *but you need to be willing to play, and yes, to risk losing that $10 as a result.*

So will you play this game? If not, you simply cannot reach retirement because you will be unable to make the money you need on your Freedom Promise. Remember, there are only 3 ways to do it, and each of them will require you to play a game similar to this coin toss because each of them have an element of risk...

The trick is to make the downside as small as possible

and the upside as large as possible, just like that coin-toss game.

If you're still reading then I'll assume you've decided to play. Good for you! And now, *how long* would you like to play this game for?

To answer correctly, let's quite literally consider both sides of the coin. Obviously, a coin-toss is a 50/50 deal: there is a 50% chance the coin lands on heads, and a 50% chance the coin lands on tails. This is also known as a 1 in 2 chance of success.

Now, playing games of 50/50 odds like this isn't something I would do or would ask you to do. Games like this are nothing more than gambling and rightfully belong in a casino. BUT, and this is the key, although this coin toss may have an equal chance of going against you as it does going for you, *the reward for each of the two outcomes is drastically different: $60 win and $10 loss.*

And that's why we play. Most importantly, we ONLY play if we can find coin-tosses with rewards like this one: with a much smaller downside than the upside.

Now, if we accept that there's as much chance of the coin landing on heads as landing on tails, we can make an intelligent guess that ten coin tosses would get a result similar to 5 tosses on heads, and 5 tosses on tails, right? I know that's just the theory, but it's a very sound one. Though the actual number would vary from one set of ten tosses to another, on balance it would end up being a 50/50 split as bad luck and good luck eventually cancel each other out. So here's how ten coin tosses might look, with the result shown next to each one:

1. Tails $-10
2. Tails $-10
3. Tails $-10
4. Heads $60
5. Tails -$10
6. Heads $60
7. Tails -$10
8. Heads $60
9. Heads $60
10. Heads $60

Result: $300 win (5x$60), $50 loss (5x$10), so net win is $250.

Looks good, right? But take a look back at that demonstration. Ask yourself honestly by putting yourself in that actual situation: how would you have *felt* after the first three coin tosses where you *lost* $10 for three straight tosses? Would you have given up? Many people would have, but you would have been foolish to do so if you understood what's going on here—the upside outweighs the downside by a factor of 6 to 1!

So how long would you play this game? A game that pays you $60 if the coin lands on heads, and you lose $10 if the coin lands on tails?

Forever? Sounds fine to me, but *how about we say that we play this game at least until you've reached your Freedom Promise figure?* If you want to reach your Point B, the correct answer to the question is that yes, you would play, and you would play this until you attained enough money to retire.

Still unsure about playing this game? Think about it another way: you LOST the coin toss for 50% of the time and yet you ended up with a *profit* of $250! How is this magic trick possible? *Simply because the downside was small and limited, and the upside was large.*

The question should NOT be whether you'd love to play this game over and over or not. The question should be *how you could find such an incredible opportunity*; where the upside outweighs the downside by such a margin. And upon finding such an opportunity, you would play it without hesitation because you know what you're sitting on: fantastic odds.

You need to get into that mindset or remain in servitude to the system forever. Business, stock market, real estate, those are your only 3 guys and each one requires this mindset I'm explaining. Make friends with those 3 guys, wipe the slate clean, cast aside your old (incorrect knowledge), and let me explain the little-known secrets to make them work for you.

So what do you choose? Embrace those 3 paths or stay in financial shackles? Don't worry, with the powerful and simple secrets I'm teaching you none of those 3 paths to freedom will scare you, as long as you forsake your past experiences with them and vow to learn the proper way to harness their power. I promise you it's way simpler than anything you previously thought about those 3 paths!

And if you're thinking this sounds a bit too much like gambling, then you're mistaken to a degree because of misinterpretation of the word "gambling." You see, there is gambling and there is gambling. In a casino there are games of chance and games of skill. A game of chance is a game where you have zero control over the outcome, like roulette. A game of skill is a game where you have the opportunity to weigh up the downside against the upside and play the odds, like blackjack (the basic principle of winning at blackjack is that most cards are worth 10 and the dealer has set rules about when to hit or not). Blackjack still has poor odds, but you can win at it with enough patience and discipline—the methods I'll be teaching you won't require anything like that much patience! My point is that what we are doing is not gambling in the sense it's relying on pure chance; *we are playing a game of skill, not chance.*

The Bible makes reference to weighing up the downside in relation to the upside with this verse during the famous story of Sodom:

"And the Lord said, If I find in Sodom fifty righteous within the city, then I will spare the place for all their sakes." – Genesis 18:26

So we now should agree then that you would play such a game if only we could find it, for that would surely be the ticket to our freedom. So how would we find it? Let's consider the third secret, and even better; let's consult the man who was behind it...

Your Mentor: The Wealthiest Man in History
"And King Solomon passed all the kings of the earth in riches and wisdom." – Chronicles 2 9:22

King Solomon is known by most people as someone who possessed wisdom, the story that instantly comes to mind being that of two women subjects who came before him over a dispute about who would have the child. When Solomon took a sword and said he would cut the baby in half unless the women could agree, one of the women said she would rather give up the child than see it slain. So Solomon gave her the child, as she was clearly the most loving. So he was the quintessential wise old man, and he was clearly not averse to taking a risk when the downside was small compared to the upside! But what most people don't also appreciate is that Solomon was also the richest man in history, and he claimed the reason for it was that he received his knowledge direct from God.

King Solomon was and is still considered the wealthiest and wisest man in history, so who better to be our guide as I interpret his words for you and apply them to our task? The books of Proverbs and Ecclesiastes in The Bible were mostly his contribution, which is why we will be referring to those two books a great deal as we uncover this third secret which is taken from Solomon himself in Proverbs:

"A prudent man forseeth the evil, and hideth himself: but the simple pass on, and are punished." – Proverbs 22:3

And here's what he would have said about not playing that coin toss game from earlier:

"The sluggard will not plow by reason of the cold; therefore shall he beg in harvest, and have nothing." – Proverbs 20:4

Here's what Solomon would have said about harboring prejudiced and false beliefs about the only 3 paths to wealth:
"The way of a fool is right in his own eyes: but he that hearkeneth

unto counsel is wise." – Proverbs 12:15

It's decision time. You're about to set off from Point A towards Point B, and to do so you will be involved in this ongoing coin toss, using those 3 paths. But you will also be equipped with the simplest and most powerful secrets to do so, passed on through the most famous mentor you could wish for, written in the world's most famous book. What do you say? Make the choice now, and whichever way you choose, don't look back.

The Sea of Money

Let's begin with overcoming any preconceived ideas about the stock market. Firstly, it's pointless to be skeptical about the stock market because you're already investing in it! Your pension fund is the obvious example. You can't be skeptical of the stock market on one hand and with the other hand write a check to Wall Street every month and hope for the best—that's hypocritical nonsense.

You already agreed that you would play that coin toss game if you could find an opportunity where the upside was $60 and the downside was just $10. *So what if we could find you such an opportunity in the stock market? If your logic follows, then you must surely play, right?*

The Bible points to such opportunities, and these secrets have been proven over many years.

The stock market is a sea of money, and your Point B lies on the shore on the other side of it. If you know the secret of this sea, it will effortlessly carry you to retirement. If you don't, it will drown you and swallow you up without a second thought. Most peoples" experience with the stock market is a bad one, where this sea of money drowned them, and those people then vow never again to return… and so they angrily stay on the shore of Point A.

But those people failed because they didn't know the simple secret of this sea of money, the secret I will teach you, and the secret of Solomon. Most peoples" experience of the stock market is in one or both of these two categories:

1. They tried investing in some stocks directly with their own account, and usually lost money.
2. They pay into some kind of investment fund like a pension.

When most people try investing in stocks themselves, their coin toss is more like a reverse of the one I showed you earlier. For them it's a $60 loss for heads and a $10 gain for tails! Sound familiar? And when most people pay into an investment fund, all they can do is hope for the best and trust in Wall Street. Then events like the 2008 financial crisis happen and those same people are bitterly disappointed as their retirement gets put back by decades. Sound familiar?

That nonsense is all over for you now, for I am about to expose what is perhaps the biggest cover-up in the world, and from this truth shall come the kind of "coin-toss" opportunity that we seek…

The Biggest Cover-Up <u>in the World</u>

"And you will know the truth, and the truth will make you free." – John 8:32.

As I've said, western governments" biggest tax revenues come from the banks that sell you investments. We're talking vast percentages, like 40%. If governments lost this revenue they would go broke overnight, so extremely powerful interests need you to keep paying into the investment plans that banks sell you, and governments even give you tax incentives to do so, and in some countries, they actually make it law. Trouble for you is that those investment plans aren't going to get you to retirement by the date you wrote in your Freedom Promise.

But there's a dark truth that governments and the banks simply cannot afford you to uncover, and I'm about to explain it to you.

Listen carefully. Most investment plans currently are budgeting on getting you around 4% to 6% growth a year from investing in the stock market—this is most peoples" plan for retirement. But read the small print because in a year like 2008 those plans would suffer heavy losses, and you can forget that 4% to 6%! And what you get back is of course after their deductions for management fees, which can be significant. But what's the alternative? After all, the stock market is complicated and risky (so they tell you), so you should leave it to the professionals. I mean, you can't possibly do better than the professionals… can you?

Yes, you most certainly can. Would you like to know how to beat those Wall Street investment professionals and avoid their management fees? I can teach you how in four words:

Buy the S+P 500.

As you probably know, the S+P 500 is the benchmark stock index that is a big basket of the top-quality company stocks—you'll regularly see this quoted on news channels and investment websites. You're able to buy a share of this S+P 500 index as if you were buying shares in any company, and simply doing this with your monthly check instead of giving it to Wall Street would allow you to beat over 70% of professionals! And with no management fees.

The vast majority of investment professionals do NOT "beat the market." That's to say, they do not do any better than the S+P 500. *But both them and the government make a nice living from your monthly checks, monthly checks that you could be directly buying the S+P 500 with.*

That's why I call this the biggest cover-up in the world; because western civilization would be in severe crisis if everyone just bought the S+P 500 for their retirement instead of giving that money to the banks who in turn give taxes to the government who in turn ensure the country functions. Everyone needs you to buy into this lie, literally.

Why doesn't the media report this cover-up? Because they're owned by banks, controlled by governments, and most of all because they make a large part of their revenue from selling advertising space to banks.

The banking industry is built on very shaky foundations— the fact is that they rely on the public being kept in the dark and being too lazy to be otherwise. Fortunately for them (and us, because we don't want the government to collapse!), there are plenty of Fools that are all too willing to oblige. If you read between the lines of all banks" marketing material, there is a common message, "Don't bother trying to educate yourself on financial matters. Allow us to make enormous amounts of money from you by selling you poorly performing financial products instead."

Let's take a look at how well this strategy of simply buying the S+P 500 would have done for you in 2012 through 2014:

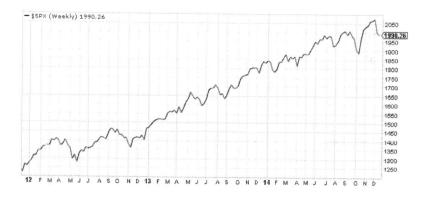

So there's the proof already that little old you can belly up to the bar with anyone of those Wall Street professionals, thanks to this one simple secret (and we're nowhere near done yet). By using this simple secret you would have *smoked* 70% of the big players on Wall Street...

Your Strength is Your Size

"And David put his hand in his bag, and took thence a stone, and slang it, and smote the Philistine in his forehead, that the stone sunk into his forehead; and he fell upon his face to the earth." – Samuel 17:49

King Solomon admired spiders because they are small and helpless creatures, and yet they live amongst royalty:

"The spider taketh hold with her hands, and is in kings" palaces." – Proverbs 30:28

You are the spider, and Wall Street is the king's palace. Let's not break open the champagne just yet though. You're in a *much* stronger position than you were at the start of this lesson, but although just blindly buying the S+P 500 will beat 70% of professionals, it still isn't going to get you to your freedom figure on schedule, and it's subject to downturns like in 2008. So let's dig deeper into The Establishment's dirt and give you more background information before we apply the wisdom of Solomon.

The banks" insecurity over their house of cards doesn't end with that S+P 500 cover up I just explained. Once you've handed over your money to them they need you to swallow two more lies so that you don't withdraw the money, and so that you accept their poor performance and high fees.

Here are those two lies:

LIE #1: Buy and Hold

"You just have to ride the bad times like 2008. Ups and downs are inevitable, but long term is what matters. Leave your money with us."

LIE #2: Diversify

"By diversifying the funds over different types of stocks we reduce risk. Oh, and by the way, this is quite complicated so you should leave it to us professionals…"

"Buy and hold" and "diversify." I bet you've had those two "pearls of wisdom" thrown at you plenty of times, right? You would be forgiven for admitting that you thought those two "rules" were the only keys to making money from the stock market. After all, this propaganda is widely spread because it's so crucial for the survival of the banks, and hence governments.

Let me now show you why these two widely accepted axioms are lies. Here's how the S+P 500 did from 2006 through 2008:

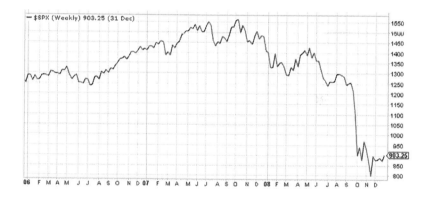

That chart above is why "buy and hold" is nonsense. A more appropriate phrase would be "buy and pray." The S+P 500 starts this chart at the 1,250 level, and ends it at 903, thus *losing* around 25%—three years of investment for that. You'd have been better off with cash.

But I will be showing you a simple way of avoiding such crashes, of "foreseeing the evil" and only sailing on the sea of money when the tide is in your favor. So we raise the upside and lower the downside!

Now let's look at why the necessity for diversification is a lie. On the surface it sounds clever to "hedge your bets" by spreading the money between different types of stocks. In this example, here's what happened over the last three years if you spread your money between retail stocks and coal mining stocks; in other words if you "bought and held" and "diversified."

First, here's the three-year chart for retail stocks:

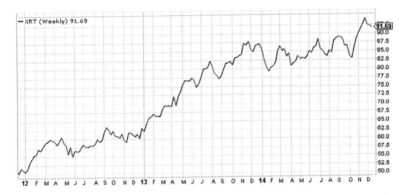

Great- a gain of 78%. And now let's look at our equal investment in coal mining stocks…

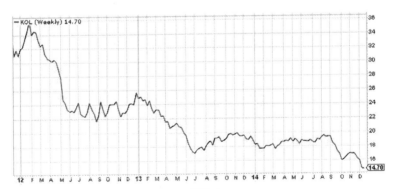

A LOSS of 61%, so that almost cancels out the good performance of the retail stocks investment. 78% - 61% = a lousy 17% over three years. You see the trouble with diversifying and buying and holding?

"Buy and hold" doesn't work because the stock market moves in distinct cycles that the trained eye can spot (and I will train your eyes). Diversification doesn't work because stocks and industries move in distinct cycles that the trained eye can spot, and one stock moving up while the other moves down is a net effect of *zero profit.*

By the way, the S+P 500 gained 60% in this same three-year period as those charts, so you'd have been better off just buying that, going to sleep, and saving all the fuss. Remember, investment professionals are simply trying to "beat the market"... and mostly failing. But they can't just go and buy the S+P 500 or how would they justify their existence? They have to look busy by analyzing things like retail stocks and coal mining stocks.

But there's something more sinister to these two lies of "buy and hold" and "diversify" than the simple fact that they just don't work. What the banks are also doing here is hiding their biggest weakness *and your biggest strength:* their big size and your small size. Their weakness is your strength. Let me explain...

The banks" problem is their size. Specifically, their problem is the vast sums of money that they trade with (all those monthly checks they receive from The Fools). They have so much money invested in the stock market at any given time that the simple act of them buying or selling too much stock at once actually affects the price of that stock. I'll simplify...

Consider that the price of any stock (or anything actually) is derived from the forces of *supply and demand*. If supply goes up, price goes down. If demand goes up, price goes up. And vice versa. Sound familiar?

Now add a bank to this supply and demand scenario, a bank that is buying or selling *hundreds of millions of dollars"* worth of stock. Let's say a bank wants to sell all its shares of XYZ. If they suddenly dumped all that stock on the open market by selling it, this simple act causes a greater *supply* of stock XYZ, and so XYZ price goes down. This means that the bank gets a lower price for its stock of XYZ and has shot itself in the foot. The same thing applies when the bank wants to buy a hundred million dollars" worth of stock XYZ—if they put that whole buy order in at once the price of XYZ would skyrocket and so the bank would end up paying a higher price, possibly too high a price.

Make sense? But *you* have no such worries. The trades you'll make would be so small that it wouldn't affect the price of any stock one bit.

So how is this their weakness and your strength? In a word, *agility.* After enjoying all the profits of an up-cycle like the one from 2012-2014 you can swiftly jump out of the market when a down-cycle is looming like that one in 2008—you can foresee the evil and hide:

"A prudent man forseeth the evil, and hideth himself: but the simple pass on, and are punished." – Proverbs 22:3

You can hop in and out of the stock market without affecting prices, the banks can't. If they were to attempt to do so, that simple act of dumping all their stocks would crash prices even harder. *This is a massive edge you have over them, but they can never let you know this, so they tell you to buy and hold (because they have to).*

Because of this reality most banks must stay fully invested at all times; they can never switch all that money just to cash. Why? Because selling so much stock all at once depresses prices (by raising the supply), and because how would they justify their existence if they weren't investing your money in something? The banks generally have to simply buy other stocks when they sell others, or switch into more defensive or aggressive stocks as and when the stock market cycles change, *but they generally must always be invested in something.*

But you do not have to do any such thing, and that is your edge. In 2008, cash would have beaten the market by a wide margin.

Your relative agility over the banks also allows you to do the most important thing of all: minimize downside and maximize upside. By only selecting opportunities in the stock market that allow us to bail out with a small loss if it goes wrong, we create the kind of coin-toss scenario we wanted. The banks cannot bail out on anything quickly because of their lack of agility, and so their downside is much greater than yours (and therefore so are your checks you write to them).

Therefore, if the banks can't protect themselves from the "evil" because of their large size, how can they minimize downside risk? Diversification is really all they have—spreading the funds between different types of industries. That's why they concocted the idea of diversification and then sold it to you as being a smart thing to do!

"Buy and hold" and "diversify" are the banks" key messages to you because the banks have *no choice* but to use those lousy strategies, because of the banks" size. You *do* have a choice!

David beat Goliath because of agility and brains. Banks cannot move swiftly in and out of the stock market cycles like you can, and it's *all* about cycles; cycles of the tide in this sea of money.

Turning the Tide

So the stock market is one of the 3 paths that will take you to your freedom figure, and it is a sea of money. Most of the money in this sea is that of the big banks, their size now explained to you.

So it's fair to say then that the buying and selling actions of the big banks are like the "tides" of this sea of money, pushing the tide up and down on a cyclical basis, and causing up cycles and down cycles in the stock market, and also within certain industry groups thanks to their diversifying. By the way, the better-known names for these up and down cycles are "bull markets" for up cycles, and "bear markets" for down cycles.

Here's how Solomon spoke of cycles and how they should be used:

"To everything there is a season, and a time to every purpose under the heaven: A time to be born, and a time to die; a time to plant, and a time to pluck up that which is planted." – *Ecclesiastes 3:1-2*

"He that gathereth in summer is a wise son: but he that sleepeth in harvest is a son that causeth shame." – Proverbs 10:5

If you try to sail against this tide you will fail. Sail with it and you will succeed. It's that simple. So the key is to identify which cycle we are currently in and to effortlessly sail with it. Is this a time to be born or a time to die?

To recap, we now know that by simply buying the S+P 500 we would beat 70% of investment professionals. But if all we did was "buy and hold" the S+P 500 we would be subject to brutal bear cycles as well as lucrative bull cycles, and that would severely damage our gains.

We want to be heavily IN stocks when we get a bull cycle like this one from 2012 through 2014 (a time for birth)

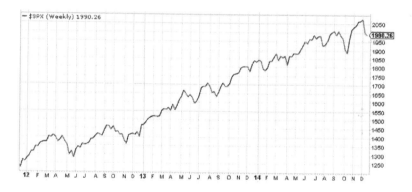

But we want to be totally OUT of stocks when we get a bear cycle like this one from 2006 through 2008 (a time for death)...

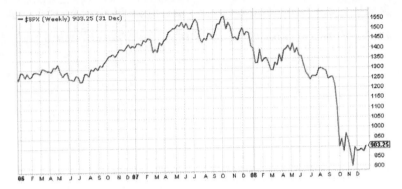

(Even better, we want to *profit* from bear cycles, and I'll show you how to do this too).

By the way, if you've ever bought a stock in a bear cycle and lost money, now you know why...

You must always be sailing with the tide, not against it.

Most investors don't even know whether they're in a bear cycle or a bull cycle until it's too late, in fact most people do the wrong thing at precisely the wrong time. They buy when they should be selling, and they sell when they should be buying, simply acting on what "feels" right at the time and what most other people are doing and what the TV and Internet "experts" are saying (I refer to this as "noise").

But does history reliably repeat like this? Don't people remember how it went last time and prevent themselves making the same mistakes? Thankfully, no, or this huge opportunity wouldn't exist! Solomon asks and answers this very question as follows:

"Is there any thing whereof it may be said, See this is new?

It hath been already of old time, which was before us." – *Ecclesiastes 1:10*

Nothing is new in the stock market, history continually repeats (even though we always say, "it's different this time"). Take a look at this chart from 1995 through 1997 and compare it to the chart of 2012 through 2014 below it:

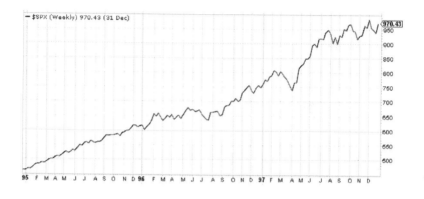

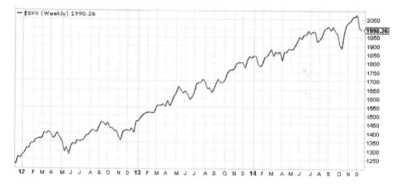

Pretty similar, right? And now look at this chart from 1999 through 2002 and compare it to the chart of 2006 through 2008 below it:

History doesn't exactly repeat, but it does "rhyme." These cycles repeat over and over again, and everybody seems to have amnesia when it comes to remembering this fact, despite Solomon's warning:

"There is no remembrance of former things; neither shall there be any remembrance of things that are to come with those that shall come after." – Ecclesiastes 1:11

Knowledge of these cycles, how to spot them, and how to exploit them to maximum value with minimum downside will make you all the money you will ever need, come bull or bear, because it will be the equivalent of the coin-toss game we seek. One cycle could be all it takes to take you to freedom.

And how to spot the cycles and exploit them is what I'll teach you next chapter...

I know it's a shocking revelation to learn what you've learned here; that little old "you can effortlessly beat the professionals," but the facts are plain. And if you ever feel doubt about this, remember:

Professionals built the Titanic, and amateurs built The Ark. What vessel will successfully cross the sea of money?

And if you're *still* reluctant to even leave your Point A and stay on the shore, then we need to talk; there's something I haven't yet told you...

You think you're safe not venturing on this sea of money? Think you're safe simply standing on the dockside? Well, that "safe" dockside you're standing on is made of wood, and it's on fire. Now, doesn't that sea suddenly look a lot more appealing? *Point A is burning.* It's burning from the fires of *inflation*, and governments are fanning those flames with reckless money printing. But the stock market (the S+P 500) has beaten inflation throughout history, as well as being one of the only 3 ways you will retire on schedule.

Sitting tight through life without taking a *calculated and relatively small* risk as I will teach you to, and just waiting for someone to enforce their will upon you and seize the opportunity for wealth that you turned away is madness. In other words, you must be pro-active with your life and finances if you want to win freedom.

Play this game or hand your money over to the banks (although now I trust you will not!), but doing nothing will be most costly of all because your Point A is burning. On that note, I'll leave you with this parable from The Bible (underlining and certain translations mine): ·

"For it will be like a man going on a journey, who called his servants and entrusted to them his property. To one he gave five talents, to another two, to another one, to each according to his ability. Then he went away. He who had received the five talents went at once and traded with them, and he made five talents more. So also he who had the two talents made two talents more. But he who had received the one talent went and dug in the ground and hid his master's money. Now after a long time the master of those servants came and settled accounts with them. And he who had received the five talents came forward, bringing five talents more, saying, "Master, you delivered to me five talents; here I have made five talents more." His master said to him, "Well done, good and faithful servant. You have been faithful over a little; I will set you over much. Enter into the joy of your master." And he also who had the two talents came forward, saying, "Master, you delivered to me two talents; here I have made two talents more." His master said to him, "Well done, good and faithful servant. You have been faithful over a little; I will set you over much. Enter into the joy of your master." He also who had received the one talent came forward, saying, "Master, I knew you to be a hard man, reaping where you did not sow, and gathering where you scattered no seed, so I was afraid, and I went and hid your talent in the ground. Here you have what is yours." But his master answered him, "You wicked and slothful servant! You knew that I reap where I have not sown and gather where I scattered no seed? Then you ought to have invested my money with the bankers, and at my coming I should have received what was my own with

interest. So take the talent from him and give it to him who has the ten talents. <u>For to everyone who has will more be given, and he will have an abundance. But from the one who has not, even what he has will be taken away.</u> *And cast the worthless servant into the outer darkness. In that place there will be weeping and gnashing of teeth."" Matthew 25:14-30*

Don't get cast into that "outer darkness," it sounds scary. Remember, God wants you to be wealthy—the proof is in the bible. Once you're able to truly believe this, the sea of money will be under your sails.

Chapter 5: The Power of Seventy

In the sea of money, we *always, always* swim with the tide—the trick, as King Solomon pointed out, is to calculate WHEN those times are so we can act accordingly. And that's what this lesson is about.

Now, one thing I can still hear you wondering is how you could possibly make money from the stock market when you have no experience. So let's remedy that right away, shall we? How would you like me to give you an instant stock market experience transplant? I'd say 37 years should be enough; that's about the length of a stock market professional's entire career. Over 37 years you'll pretty much have seen all there is to see.

Instant Experience Transplant

So you can see what I'm talking about regarding these tides, take a look at these simple charts of what happened in the stock market from 1980 through to 2017. As you go through them…

- Observe the constant bear and bull cycles we've been speaking about.
- Think about how much trouble a "buy and hold" strategy would have got you in.
- Consider Solomon's observations about continually repeating cycles, and, if you can, remember how you felt at significant stock market dates you'll see in there, try to recall those (fear and greed) feelings and how unproductive they may have been at the time.
- Notice how the downswings often happen faster than the upswings and last a shorter time.
- And think about how amazing it would be if you could be invested in the market for the big upswings

and completely out of the market for those painful downswings.

Okay, let the 37-year career transplant begin…

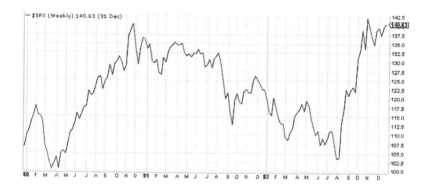

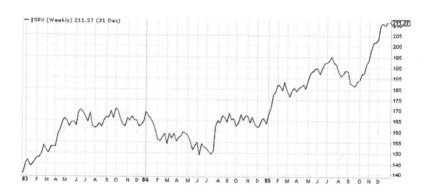

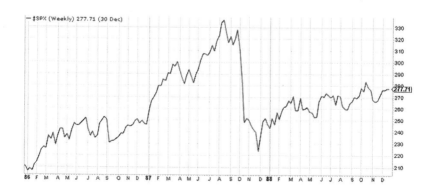

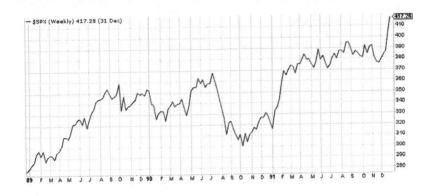

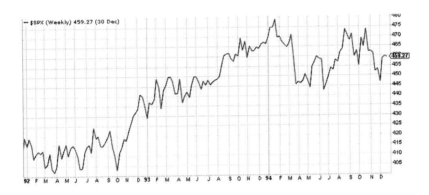

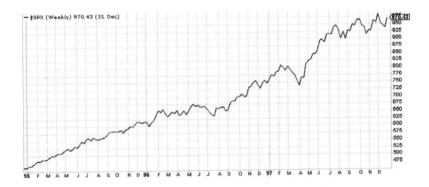

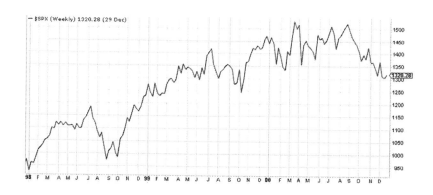

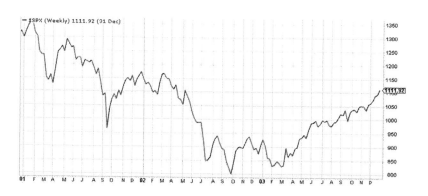

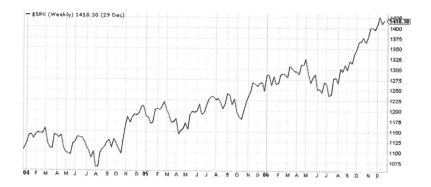

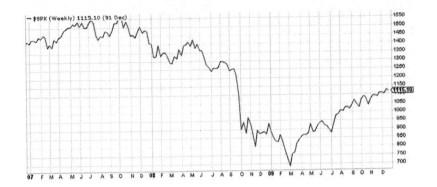

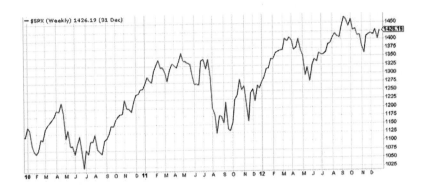

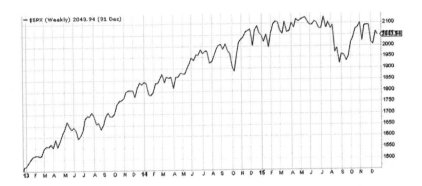

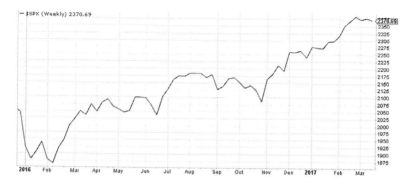

Now you have an entire career's worth of experience, let's see how to master it...

The Law of Averages

You've now seen the bulls and bears in action—you've seen how much money could be made by being on the right side of those swings, and how much could be lost by being on the wrong side. But how could you possibly guess which way the market will turn next?

The law of averages can help us. Stocks often return to their average price over time. In fact, most things in life return to their average baseline, also known as "reverting to the mean." Don't worry, this is nothing complicated, as I'll explain in a second. Here's what Solomon said regarding this law of averages:

"A false balance is abomination to the Lord: but a just weight is His delight." – Proverbs 11:1

What we look at is an *average* of stock market prices for a past period. Simple enough. Only, because time is constantly ticking along, we want that average to be constantly updated, right? The average price of XYZ over the last 50 days, for example, will only be any good to us if that average price is constantly refreshed every day.

So, the average price of the past however many days is updated every day—the average price over a certain period is therefore constantly changing, up and down. Considering this, it's called a *moving average, or "MA" for short.*

Now, the good news for us is that we don't have to constantly get our calculators out to log the latest moving average every day! Computers do it for us. Even better, the moving average of your choice is available as an overlay on those charts I showed you. Each day, the latest moving average is plotted on a chart so you can see that in relation to today's price.

Therefore, you'll be able to see if today's price is *above or below* the average price of the last however many days. You'll also be able to see which way the moving average is pointing, *up or down*, as a clue to where the stock market is headed next.

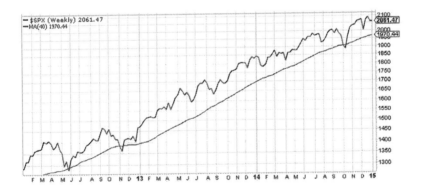

For example, in the above chart you saw just now for 2012, 2013, and 2014, I've added that smoother, long line you can see there. That particular line represents the average price of the S+P 500 for the last 40 weeks; the most commonly used long term average. It's useful in that it's telling us (in January, 2015) that the stock market's long term trend is decisively UP (because the line is pointing up), and the price of the S+P 500 is literally "above average"—it's above that moving average line. Because that's the 40-week moving average, it's abbreviated to "40-wma" (40-Week Moving Average).

Can you see how the price of the S+P 500 doesn't get too far from that line before it's pulled back towards it, as if the moving average line was a magnet? That's reversion to the mean, or returning to the average, as Solomon puts it:

"A false balance is abomination to the Lord: but a just weight is His delight." – Proverbs 11:1

Moving averages, if used correctly, can predict when to be IN the stock market and when to be OUT of it.

But which moving average should you use to help predict this? 40-week? 20-week? 152-week?? There are so many to choose from (any number you can think of), so how do we know which one can help us? Maybe we should consider which number King Solomon would use...

Sacred Seventy

There could only be *one number* Solomon would have used: the most sacred of all numbers: *seventy*.

Seventy has an especially sacred meaning in the Bible. It is born of the multiplication of two perfect numbers, seven (representing perfection) and ten (representing completeness and God's law). As such, seventy symbolizes perfect spiritual order carried out with all power (such as reversion to the mean). It can also represent a period of judgment (such as a key turning point in the stock market between bulls and bears).

Here's just a few examples of many in The Bible:

70 elders were appointed by Moses (Numbers 11:16). After reading the covenant God gave him to read to the people, Moses took 70 elders, along with Aaron and his sons, up Mount Sinai to have a special meal with God himself (Exodus 24:9 - 11). Ancient Israel spent a total number of 70 years in captivity in Babylon (Jeremiah 29:10). Seventy is also specially connected with Jerusalem. The city kept 70 years of Sabbaths while Judah was in Babylonian captivity (Jeremiah 25:11). Seventy sevens (490 years) were determined upon Jerusalem for it to complete its transgressions, to make an end for sins and for everlasting righteousness to enter into it (Daniel 9:24). In Midrash Alpha Beita we are told "on the festival of Sukkot, seventy sacrifices were offered for the sake of the seventy nations of the world who have seventy representatives among the heavenly angels." It is said that seventy languages emerged from the tower of Babel.

This number appears quite often in The Bible, more often than one might think, and not in an ambiguous way either, I might add. This number is often connected to prophetic events, and I'm now going to show you a series of prophetic events in stock market history.

If King Solomon were alive today, how would he trade the stock market? How would he apply his legendary wisdom? Based on Solomon's own precious writings, I guessed that he would want to tick all these boxes:

- ✔ He would make it 99.9% immune to market crashes.
- ✔ He would take a simple, "big picture" view, and thus avoid trading constantly.
- ✔ He would take advantage of history constantly repeating.
- ✔ He would take the emotion (worry of tomorrow) out of it.
- ✔ He would ensure it carried the least amount of risk and the most amount of certainty.
- ✔ He would use a strategy to get the most amount of bang for his buck.
- ✔ He would use the most logical path, without ego getting in the way.

And he would accomplish all that through the use of Sacred Seventy. Or for our purposes, the *70-week moving average*.

Now let's look at those 37 years again, only this time with the 70-wma line (70-week moving average) overlaid on each chart that you saw earlier. As you go through this again, imagine if you had bought the S+P 500 every time the price of it went above the 70-wma, and if you had sold the S+P 500 every time the price of it went below the 70-wma.

I'm not telling you to do this in real life; I don't need to. All I need to do is show you what is public record, and you can make your own mind up.

Okay, so let's run the instant experience transplant again, only this time imagine BUYING (entering the market) each time the S+P 500 goes ABOVE the 70-wma line, and imagine SELLING (exiting the market) each time the S+P 500 goes

BELOW the-70 wma line.

Let's see how well you do in this 37-year career, only this time with the help of Sacred Seventy and my footnotes as we go...

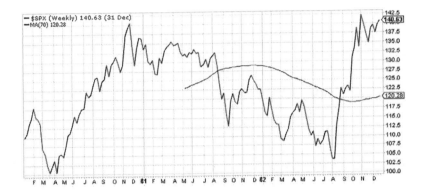

In summer 1981, the S+P 500 drops below the 70-wma, and if you had sold it then you'd have escaped the bear market of 81/82. Then you'd have bought it in September 1982, and profited from the bull market that followed into 1983:

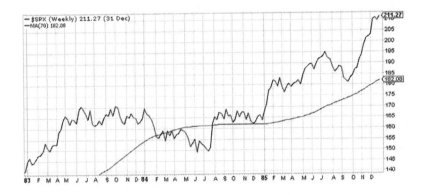

In February 1984, the S+P 500 dips below the 70-wma again, and if you had bailed out then you'd have escaped that brief fall that followed. It didn't go down very far in the end, but you didn't know this at the time, and you were safe from any deeper falls. Notice how a volatile period comes before a new bull? We will see this pattern a lot. In August 1984, you buy the S+P 500 at $165, and you enjoy the raging bull market that follows through into 1986 and beyond...

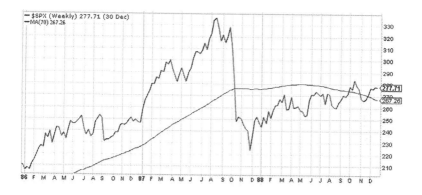

You enter this chart invested in the stock market, and by 1987 you're in profit by over 60%. Then, in 1987 the stock market gets heavily above the 70-wma by an unsustainable level, and in a crash that many will recall, the S+P 500 makes a dramatic fall. You escape this at around the $270 mark, thus keeping all of your profits and escaping the brutal bear market that followed into 1988. In October 1988, you buy back in—later on in this lesson I'm going to explain why you wouldn't have been affected by how it briefly dips below the 70-wma before you buy back in again at $275 to enjoy even more profit in 1989:

A short but profitable bull market (for you) in 1989 eventually turns into a SELL in summer 1990, and you walk away with profits and escape the sell off. After avoiding all the trauma, you buy the S+P 500 in early 1991 for about the same level you sold at, and then enjoy yet another bull market that soars into 1992 and beyond…

You may recall that 1991 and 1992 were years of a severe recession, but look how the stock market is climbing during that time. The stock market is always looking *ahead*. You enter this chart invested in the stock market after buying around $340 in 1991, so you enjoy a powerful bull market right through 1993. By the time the sell signal comes in 1994 you're well in profit. But then we see a very volatile patch as the S+P 500 oscillates above and below the 70-wma, resulting in one of the few small losses you'd have suffered. The key point though is that your losses would have been strictly controlled to ultra-small amounts, thus not eating much out of your previous gains. And what happens next more than makes up for 1994 anyway:

Remember what I said about how a volatile patch usually comes before a powerful bull market? The long bull market above is a classic example. My friend, charts like this one above will make you rich, they are why we are bothering with all of this! The stock market doubled.

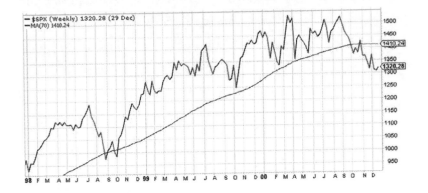

And, apart from that brief blip in 1998, the fun continues as you ride this bull market into 1999 and 2000. As you can see, there were a lot of violent ups and downs as we entered the new millennia, but none of it would have bothered us as it was all happening *above* the 70-wma. We didn't need to worry about all the arguing "experts" on TV, we just obeyed the system. In late 2000 we exit the market with enormous profits. The poor souls who stayed behind suffered this:

You sat it out while the long and painful bear market of 2000/2001/2002 took place. Notice how the stock market was *already* in bad shape before the 9/11 attacks? In summer

2003 the 70-wma says it's safe to go back in, and you buy the S+P 500 at $1,000; down about one-third since its peak in 2000. People who didn't sell back then were sitting on that loss and despondent about the stock market, right at the point they should have been *buying*...

"The wicked flee when no man pursuit: but the righteous are bold as a lion." – Proverbs 28:1

Because you're sticking to this system, you once again enjoy a powerful bull market as the S+P 500 bounces along the 70-wma as if it somehow knew it was there. All the action is above the 70-wma, so you just leave your investment alone. By the end of 2006 you're up almost 50%.

You probably remember this time well, but notice how you're given a sell signal in late 2007. That's long before the crisis of late 2008—once again, the stock market is looking *ahead*. You bail out in December 2007 with a fat profit, then you sit it out, invested in cash, as the painful trauma of 2008 unfolds for everyone else. The stock market has lost over half its value by the time the crash is over, but this 70-wma system got you out long before. In September 2009, you buy back in at $1050.

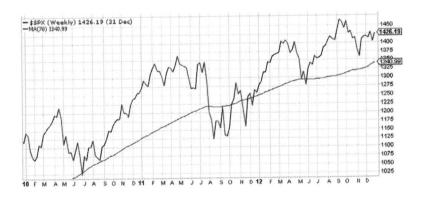

You ride a brief bull market through 2010, and then you take a nice profit as the sell signal is given in summer 2011 (sovereign debt crisis). Then, in 2011, we get bounced around again as the S+P 500 oscillates above and below the 70-wma, resulting in a small and controlled loss. You finally buy in late 2012 for $1,250. And do you remember what seems to happen right after such a time of volatility like that in 2011?

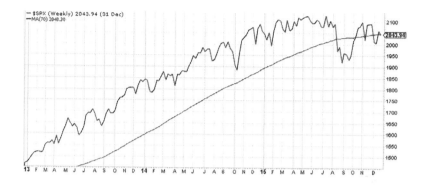

Our faith in the system was tested in 2011, and by sticking to it we enjoyed a massive bull market in 2012/2013/2014/mid-2015.

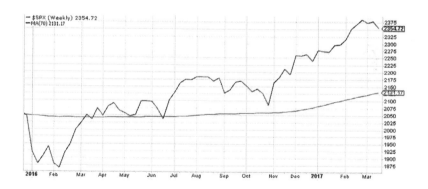

Mid-2015 to mid-2016 saw some indecisive patterns, but we got back in the market around March, 2016, and have stayed *in* ever since. What happens next as I write in early 2017 is unknown, but I don't need to *know*, I just need to do what the system tells me to.

Now let's take this even further…

The Treasure Trigger

Now I'm going to give you a bit more detail so you have the option of using a system like this with surgical precision!

Up until now we've used charts of the stock market where the price of the S+P 500 was shown by a solid line, moving up and down. Now we're going to graduate onto a different and more precise way of looking at the price of the stock market because we need to know at what point *exactly* the price of the S+P 500 goes above or below the 70-wma.

Why? Because we want to SELL as quickly as possible if a sell signal is triggered (price goes below 70-wma) so we avoid as much of the drop as possible, and we want to BUY as quickly as possible if a buy signal is triggered (price goes above 70-wma) so we reap as much of the upside as possible. Make sense? *We must not be late or early when the signal is given.*

So instead of using a solid line, we're going to use "HLC" bars like these below that show us the exact price that the S+P 500 closes at each week. That closing price of the week will be what we base the buy/sell trigger on. Here's what HLC bars look like:

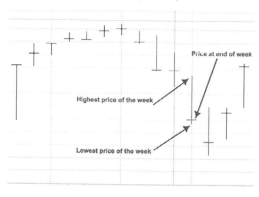

As you can see, you also get two other pieces of information as well as the closing price of the week: you also see the highest price of the week and the lowest.

That's why they're called "H.L.C." bars: it stands for the three pieces of information they give you—HIGH, LOW, CLOSE. The highest price of the week, the lowest, and the closing price. What we are concerned with is the CLOSING PRICE, shown by the small horizontal bar.

When you put HLC bars on a chart instead of that solid line we had before, it looks like this:

If you zoom in to the sell trigger in December 2007 here on the left, you can see the trigger as the first little horizontal bar to go below the 70-wma. See it?

 Same for this zoom in on the left for when the buy trigger was given in August, 2009. See it?

So, those are your more precise buy and sell triggers: if the closing price for the week is BELOW the 70-wma, you would SELL the following Monday morning. If the closing price for the week is ABOVE the 70-wma, you would BUY the following Monday morning.

Now I'm going to add one more simple refinement to improve accuracy even more.

Make Double Sure

I've come up with a way of adding a bit more certainty to the buy and sell trigger, and this often helps avoid unnecessary buys and sells at times when the price is oscillating above and below the 70-wma.

This is an additional requirement needed for a buy or sell trigger.

It comes in the form of an additional piece of information we can overlay on the stock market chart: The Relative Strength Indicator (RSI). Here's what it looks like:

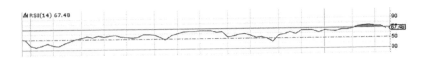

It's a simple percentage scale, 0-100%. Look on the right side and you'll see the percentages shown from 30 to 90. That zig-zagging line moves up and down on this scale to represent how strong the stock market is at any given time.

Now look closely and you'll see that the 50% mark is shown with a dashed line across the middle of the scale. See it?

That's going to be our secondary requirement for a buy or sell trigger—this is *in addition* to the price being above or below the 70 wma:

In order to have a BUY trigger, the RSI must be CLEARLY ABOVE 50%.

In order to have a SELL trigger, the RSI must be CLEARLY BELOW 50%

Let's run through those 37 years again, this time with our new refinements and specific buy and sell triggers in mind.

The RSI is shown separately above the price chart. In each case of a BUY or SELL I've drawn an arrow to point at the exact trigger price for each, and above it I've drawn an arrow to show the double confirmation made by the RSI being above or below 50%. These first two charts (1980 through 1985) are very clear...

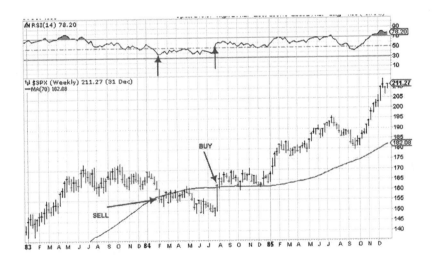

This chart is the first example of the RSI refinement stopping a needless SELL trigger. In November, 1988, you can see the price dip below the 70-wma, BUT the RSI does not *clearly* go below 50%, so no sell trigger is given. When I say "clearly" above or below the 50% mark on the RSI, I mean that I want to see some space between the line and the 50% mark. November, 1988, would not qualify.

Here's that volatile patch in 1994 again, only this time we avoid two false triggers thanks to the RSI refinement.

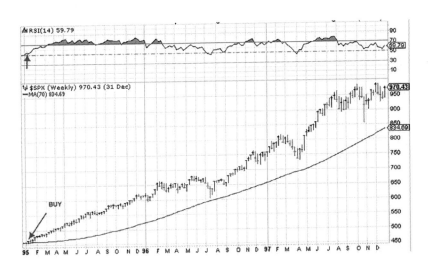

More false buy triggers avoided in September, 1998, and October, 2000.

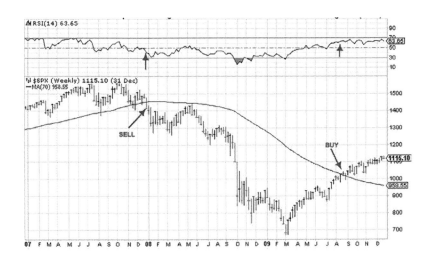

The above chart shows that not even the RSI refinement is infallible. But if you strictly obey a simple system it will still pay off in the end purely because you are in at the right time and out at the wrong time. King Solomon himself couldn't wish for more than this...

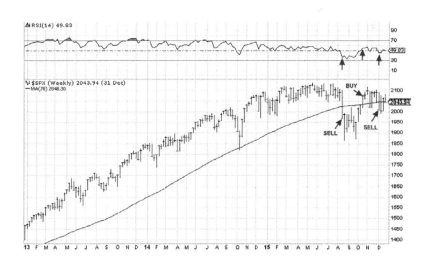

Congratulations. Have you any idea how powerful you just became?

You were invested in the stock market whenever it was rising, and you were in cash whenever it was falling. What's more, your downside risk was very small indeed because of your buy point being so close to the sell point (either side of the 70-wma). These are the simple yet elusive keys to wealth from the stock market.

You will recall that simply buying the S+P 500 and sticking with it, with no buying and selling like we just did, beat 70% of investment professionals. By doing that you did not "beat the market," you did as well as the market (and most professionals cannot beat the market). But what you just did by avoiding the bears and riding the bulls allowed you to *beat the market by approximately 100%. You did double what the market did.*

Now, having said all that, would you like to know the biggest weakness of this system?

You. You are the problem...

Unless, that is, you can master your emotions. The weakness is human interference, specifically lack of *patience* and *discipline*. Go back through those charts and really put yourself in those positions, feel the fear and greed as you would have instinctively wanted to take profits too early (greed) and take losses too late. Would you have the patience and discipline to actually do it? Or would you listen to your gut/the TV/"experts"/ friends/etc.? Most often your actions will be counterintuitive to the news at the time, the December, 2007, sell signal being a good example.

If you look back over those 37 years with this in mind you'll notice that not very much action is required of you—it's the laziest money you could ever make! In fact, triggers only come along on average 0.5 times each year (each of those charts represented 3 years). This will test your patience and discipline, which is why I give you this warning.

"He that hasteth to be rich hath an evil eye, and considereth not that poverty shall come upon him." – Proverbs 28:22

But I don't expect you to wait 37 years to reach your goal; nothing like that long. The length of the demonstration was purely to show you almost every situation you'll come across as well as how reliable the 70-wma is. For most people, just one long bull market like the recent one that started in 2012 is enough to make all the money they will need.

But let's now rewind and consider your Freedom Promise, specifically the amount of money you calculated you would need to retire.

The 7 Secrets Bring Freedom Closer

If you recall from Chapter 3 of this course ("Mountains into Molehills"), to calculate your Freedom Figure I asked you to add up all your required living expenses and then to multiply that number by 5.88. You probably wondered why the number was 5.88, and you probably also wondered why the amount of money needed to retire would be so low? Now I can explain.

Let's say that your expenses, with a simple and debt-free retirement lifestyle, came to $50,000 a year. You would have multiplied that by 5.88 to get a Freedom Figure of $294,000. That's a cheap retirement! Here's how that's possible…

Using a special enhancement I'm going to show you next chapter, that system we just covered using the 70-wma buy and sell triggers generated an average annual profit of 24% (*with* those few and small losses included!). If you invested that $294,000 at an annual rate of 24% you would get approximately $70,000 a year. That's your $50,000 you needed to retire, plus a safety margin of $20,000 to allow for inflation or whatever. Multiplying expenses by 5.88 is the formula that calculates this.

So, that's how you would retire on such a relatively small amount. The typical rate of return large pension funds budget for is around 5%. At 5% it would take a nest egg of $1 MILLION to retire on $50,000 a year! Can you see those golden goalposts of retirement suddenly thrusting a heck of a lot closer?

But even $294,000 isn't exactly pocket change. If you already have your Freedom Figure (perhaps through real estate or an existing pension fund), then that's great, but what if you don't? How are you going to raise even that low amount to retire? I'll show you…

Chapter 6:
The Biblical
Money Code

Moving Forward

"He that observed the wind shall not sow; and he that regardeth the clouds shall not reap." – Ecclesiastes 11:4

O ur journey to freedom is gathering pace. If you don't yet feel as though you're making much progress I suggest re-reading the past chapters and digesting them—you have to actually do something to exact change, not just be a spectator "observing the wind" and "regarding the clouds" (see above quote from King Solomon). Are you going to be someone who merely dreams or someone who actually *does*? This is a key difference between life's winners and losers.

If you look back on the lessons, you'll see how far you've come *if* you've taken the steps required, especially the step of creating your Freedom Figure—the amount of money needed for you to retire based on the special formula I explained last time:

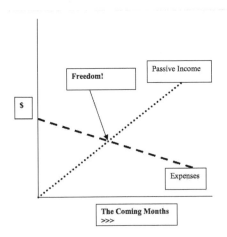

When your expenses are as low as possible by eliminating debt and seeing through how the system constantly milks you, the amount required to retire falls. When we create a large enough stream of passive income with the least amount of capital, and that income matches your expenses, you're retired. If you recall from Chapter 3 ("Mountains into Molehills"), to calculate your Freedom Figure, I asked you to add up all your required living expenses and then to multiply that number by 5.88. You probably wondered why the number was 5.88, and you probably also wondered why the amount of money needed to retire would be so low. Now you know why, thanks to the Secret of Seventy I started to explain last chapter.

But not only has the Secret of Seventy given you a proven way to retire on such a low amount; it's also made you master the most basic and most important part of success in the stock market: being able to identify which way the tide is running: bear market or bull market. And we are going to build on that with the introduction of a brand-new secret later on. First, let's fully equip you to use the Secret of Seventy…

Ride the Tide (Conclusion)

Last chapter you learned the criteria for buying into the stock market and when to exit it. But what do we mean by *buying into it?* How do you simply buy or sell the stock market? Please read carefully and pay close attention as I explain this in simple terms.

We can do this through a special type of investment called an Exchange Traded Fund, or "ETF" for short. What these

ETFs allow us to do is buy and sell certain things, like entire stock markets, as if they were regular shares of companies. For example, you already know that you can go and buy a share in Apple, Coca-Cola, Amazon, or whatever. And you probably know that all those large company shares are listed in large stock indexes like the S+P 500, Dow Jones, and Nasdaq. But instead of picking individual shares in a company like Apple or whatever, ETFs give us the ability to buy one share of the entire stock index, like the S+P 500 or the Dow Jones, etc. (as well as a great many other things). An ETF is like a proxy for something. Some would call it a "derivative" because it's derived from something else, as orange juice is derived from oranges, and ketchup is derived from tomatoes. It's the same principle, nothing complicated.

So, when we've been speaking about buying or selling the stock market, as shown on those charts last time, we've been speaking about buying or selling shares in the ETF for the S+P 500 (this is considered the benchmark stock index).

This particular ETF that represents the S+P 500, and the one used on the charts last time, is called "SPX." SPX is our reference point for our buy and sell triggers we saw last time.

Based on that 37-year study, using that system, you'd have made 12% a year—double what you'd have made from simply buying and holding SPX (but even doing that would have beaten over 70% of the investment professionals).

But, if you recall from last chapter, to retire on the small amount of capital your Freedom Figure represents, we needed an annual return of 24%, not 12%. Multiplying your annual retirement expenses by 5.88 is based on that amount of return (factoring in extra for inflation and a margin of safety).

So how are we going to magically turn a 12% return on SPX into a 24% return?

More Bang for Less Buck

"In the day that thy walls are to be built, in that day shall the decree be far removed." – Micah 7:11.

As the quote above alludes to, if you're going to do something anyway, may as well make it count. In other words, if you're going to buy the S+P 500, then let's really buy the thing. But I don't mean by investing more money in it (that would raise your Freedom Figure), I mean by getting more bang for our buck. So how can we turn a 12% return into a 24% return?

The answer comes once again from the use of ETFs. As well as there being an ETF as a direct proxy of the S+P 500 (called SPX), there are also ETFs that are *leveraged* on the SPX. These leveraged ETFs are based on double or even triple whatever the SPX does.

So if the S+P 500 goes up 10%, then the regular SPX ETF goes up 10% too. If you'd have bought one share of SPX for $100, then your share of SPX would now be worth $110—a gain of 10%. Make sense?

But, if instead of buying one share of SPX, you had bought one share of a double leveraged version of SPX, your gain would be doubled. If the S+P 500 (SPX) rose 10%, your one share of a double leveraged ETF would not have risen 10%, but 20%. You make double whatever the SPX makes. Simple.

So, what's the catch? There's always a catch, right?

The catch is that if the S+P 500 goes *down* 10% then your double leveraged share goes down double the amount. A drop of 10% on the S+P 500 would represent a drop of 20% on your share in a double leveraged ETF. But this catch doesn't apply to us as much as it would to everyone else.

Why doesn't this catch apply to us so much? Think about our strategy for a second. We buy the SPX as soon as it rises above the 70-week moving average, *but we bail out as soon as the SPX so much as flinches below that 70-week moving average.* What this means is that our risk is ultra-low anyway. It means that we protect ourselves from the deep falls that would make a double-leveraged ETF such a danger AND we still enjoy double the upside. That's the best of both worlds! As King Solomon said:

"A prudent man forseeth the evil, and hideth himself: but the simple pass on, and are punished." – Proverbs 22:3

And this is why we must not hesitate or break the rules regarding the buy and sell triggers. Do not buy too early or sell too late. Act without question, regardless of what your emotions are saying to the contrary. *"For we walk by faith, not by sight." – Corinthians 5:7*

This is how you turn a 12% gain with SPX into the required 24% gain with SPX: by buying a double leveraged ETF of the S+P 500. This particular double-leveraged ETF is called the Pros hares Ultra S+P 500, and its symbol is "SSO."

So you use the SPX as a reference point for the buy and sell triggers discussed last time. But when you actually make the investment you are using "SSO" as the vehicle.

But how would you like a 12% annual gain to become a *36%* annual gain, to *triple* the gain (and potential loss)? In this case, you can use a *triple*-leveraged ETF for the S+P 500 called, Proshares Ultra**PRO** S+P 500, and its symbol is "UPRO."

There you have it. If you *strictly and correctly* use the system we discussed last time that produced 12% a year on average for 37 years, and you use the SSO or UPRO ETFs as the investment vehicle, then, if you had the same performance as shown historically, that would equate to an average annual gain of 24% or 36% respectively. I promised you 24%, but you could even have 36%. I always try to exceed your expectations!

So, to summarize:

- The S+P 500 is the world's benchmark stock index; it's a collection of shares listed for the world's biggest companies. When I refer to "the market" and "beating the market," I'm referring to the S+P 500.

- An Exchange Traded Fund (ETF) is a proxy investment for something—it allows you to buy shares in something other than individual companies. The ETF that is a direct representation of the S+P 500 is called, "SPX." Owning a share in SPX is like owning a share of the entire S+P 500. So, if you wanted to beat 70% of pros simply by buying the stock market, you could buy a share of SPX with your monthly pension fund check instead. SPX mirrors the S+P 500 for gains and losses.

- Double or triple leveraged ETFs do double or triple whatever the S+P 500 does. They are called SSO and UPRO respectively. They allow you to have double or triple whatever the gain or loss of the S+P 500 is.

- For our Secret of Seventy system, we use SPX for our buy/sell triggers explained last time, but the asset we actually buy is a double- or triple-leveraged ETF to get the most bang for our buck.

So now let me show you where to get the information I gave you last time: those charts that you're basing your SPX buy and sell triggers on.

Free Treasure Maps Here

If you go **www.StockCharts.com** you'll find everything you need, completely free of charge (at time of writing). Go to that website and I'll walk you through the whole thing, screen by screen.

When you arrive at the website, go to the top left and click on "FREE CHARTS":

On the next screen, look midway down on the left side for the "sharpcharts" box. Don't enter anything in the box, just click on "Go":

SharpCharts

Candlestick, Line, Renko, Kagi, Ichimoku, ai

Create a SharpChart:

[ ] [Go]

User-Created SharpCharts:
Public ChartLists | SharpCharts Voyeur

Then you'll see this screen. This won't seem familiar to you based on what we saw in the previous lesson, but don't worry because we're going to change that with the click of a few buttons.

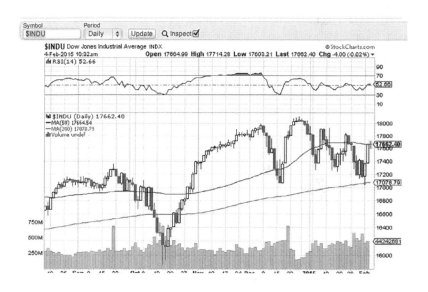

On the top left of the chart, locate these boxes and change them to "SPX" and "Weekly," like so:

Next, stay on that same page and scroll down to where all these settings are below. Don't panic, we're going to just click a few things to get what we need. Compare this one below to the changed ones after it...

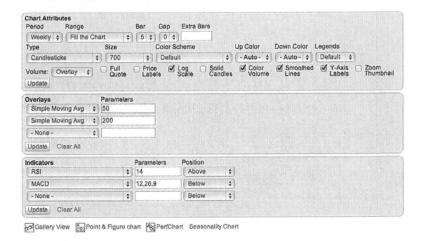

In the "Chart Attributes" section at the top, in the "Type" drop down menu, select "HLC Bars." And in the "Volume" drop down menu, select "Off," so it looks like this:

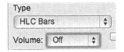

In the next section down, "Overlays," enter "70" in the top "Parameters" box. In the second down "Overlay" drop down menu, select "None," so it looks like this:

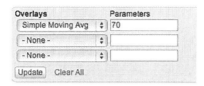

In the next section down, "Indicators," in the second drop down menu, select "None" so it looks like this:

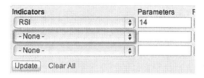

Finally, click on any of the several "Update" buttons to enter all those new settings you just made:

And then your chart will look like this one below—like the ones we were using in the previous lesson:

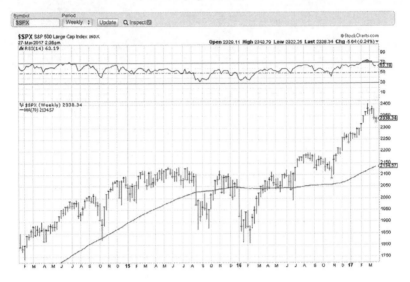

And you now know how to interpret this chart, and how to spot the buy and sell triggers. Check it every Friday after the market closes at 5pm New York time, and then make any necessary actions first thing the following Monday, without hesitation. Test yourself: look at that drop in June 2016. Was that a sell trigger or not? When was the very first buy trigger on this chart? A revision of the previous chapter will tell you.

So now you know how to turn your relatively small freedom figure into a very simple retirement plan—your passive income you will make from these annual gains will meet your retired living expenses, and you rarely have to do anything to manage this. Simply check the S+P 500 weekly chart once a week, and act according to the strategy. Most of the time you're simply doing nothing.

You have become more powerful than you may realize, especially when compared to the majority of people…

- You now understand The System—the rigged game. You will no longer allow the "pharaohs," the "money-changers," and the "talebearers" to take advantage of you.

- You have a precise and relatively small financial goal to retire, and you know *why* you want retirement. You have a Point A and a Point B.

- You know how to turn that financial sum into a comfortable and easy retirement.

- You know how to spot and take advantage of stock market cycles.

So now we can build on what you've learned and actually start creating wealth; let's begin actually *creating your freedom figure*. Now you know how to manage money, let's go about making some.

The Platform to Profits

As a recap, there are only three legal and controllable paths to get to your freedom figure: stock market, real estate, and business. You can and should take all three—do whatever it takes. Obviously, the first path we've focused on is the stock market, as much as anything so you understand how to manage your pot of gold when you get it. But we can also use the stock market as a way to actually *create* that pot of gold, and that's where the fourth secret comes in.

What you've learned about the stock market so far is also the perfect platform for moving on to trading individual stocks (such as Apple, IBM, Coca-Cola, etc.), because *any stock trades you make should be synchronized with the market.*

As a reminder: *The big institutions buying and selling are like powerful "tides" in this "sea of money." These tides are known as bull markets (for upswings) and bear markets (for downswings). We want to be IN the stock market for the bull markets and OUT of the market for bear markets.*

You only want to be *buying* individual stocks when the market is in one of these upswings.

That perhaps sounds obvious to you now because of your training here, but do you have any idea how many professionals do NOT know this? Most of them! I can tell you that the biggest revelation for me in trading stocks has been to appreciate just how much the effect of the market has on success. The quote below from one of the most respected economists in history is not biblical, but he's simply echoing the wisdom of Solomon that is repeated throughout the book of Ecclesiastes:

"An important part of investing is the game of knowing which way the crowd will swing rather than assessing the objective merits of individual shares." - J.M. Keynes.

You've already mastered that to a large extent. With this in mind—that you only buy stocks in a bull market—let's now see how to trade individual stocks as a way to get to your freedom figure.

Doubling Your Money

A quick recap from Chapter 3: An essential skill of highly successful people (whether they are aware of it or not) is their trick of breaking large tasks into smaller ones. They see a goal to be achieved sometime in the future, but they don't look at the size of it and go and cry in a corner! No, they divide it into "bite-size chunks."

Let's say your mountain is $300,000 and you make that your goal. Great, your mind gets to work on making it happen… and then it fails because of indigestion; that amount is simply too big to swallow in one goal, so your mind gets overwhelmed, and things "mysteriously" don't work out.

If you're faced with an objective that appears to be "far off and exceeding deep" then "who can find it out?"

So what we must do then is change our *perception* of it. We do this by turning mountains into molehills—we break up this objective into smaller, more "digestible" chunks.

Transform your mountain into several molehills. We are going to break this down into *daily* tasks so that you arrive at retirement as quickly as possible. And here's how we're going to do that…

We're going to aim to double our money 3 times a year. Here is a table of what it looks like to double your money, starting with just $100 and going all the way to $1.63 million in just 14 steps:

1. $200
2. $400
3. $800
4. $1,600
5. $3,200
6. $6,400
7. $12,800
8. $25,600
9. $51,200
10. $102,400
11. $204,800
12. $409,600
13. $819,200
14. $1,638,400

In this example, the *mountain* of $1,638,400 was broken into 14 *molehills* that began with just $100! That's the power of doubling your money, of *compounding your gains*. Now we're going to calculate, based on this table, how many steps you are from retirement:

Amount of starting capital: $_____

Now keep doubling that amount until it reaches your freedom figure.

Number of steps required to reach your freedom figure: _____ steps to freedom.

How many steps away from retirement are you? Whatever freedom figure your mountain is, you've just broken that mountain up into that many molehills. So, you can see how powerful it is to double your money; it makes $100 just 14 steps away from becoming $1.63 million! But how could we consistently double our money?

First of all, let's remind ourselves of what a bull market looks like, and you'll see how doubling your money is possible simply from using our Secret of Seventy system at the birth of a big bull market, and buying the UPRO ETF:

You'd have bought UPRO in July 2012 for about $30, and in 2015 it would be worth $129, with the trade still open. Your money would have *quadrupled* in 2.5 years. So, that's one way of doubling your money if your timing is right, and this is certainly an easy way of getting your Freedom Figure, just over a longer time frame. So, don't rule out this method of getting to your goal if your timing is right!

But trading individual stocks the right way can get you there a lot faster because there are more and faster opportunities to double your money and use the power of compounding that I showed you with that 14-step table.

The trick, as before, is to bail out early if things don't go right, and to keep riding the profits until you double your money or the sell trigger is given. ***So why not use our 70-week moving***

average line as the buy trigger, just like we did last time with
SPX?

Here are just a *few* examples of big-name stocks that
doubled in value based on you buying a stock this way. For each
one consider what your buy price was and see how fast you'd
have doubled your money (stock ticker code is top left):

You could've doubled your money on all of those stocks within a year. Okay, you clearly have a good buy/sell trigger here, but how do you know *which* stocks to use it with? How can you know which ones, when triggered as a buy, will go on to double in value? Well, of course, you can't possibly *know* anything for certain. *But* we can certainly make a very intelligent guess.

It's really very simple. The stocks that rise the fastest are the stocks that are *perceived* to be exciting *game-changers* with increasing earnings to match. A "game-changer" company is one with a product or service that looks as though it will forever change the way things are done. When I tell you the names of the stocks that these were the charts of, you will see what I mean.

The names of these stocks are (in order of appearance): **Green Mountain Coffee Roasters (GMCR), Apple (AAPL), Netflix (NFLX), Tesla (TSLA), and Linkedin (LNKD).**

GMCR: The company behind the Keurig coffee machine in many peoples' homes now.

AAPL: Apple is a continual game-changer, as you must surely know.

NFLX: Internet TV channel with worldwide distribution and low-cost monthly plans.

TSLA: World's first all-electric luxury sports car, American-built success story.

LNKD: Changes the way networking and recruitment is done.

How can you find out when new game-changers are entering the scene? By staying alert for announcements about them. A quality investment publication like Wall Street Journal,

Barons, Forbes, or Financial Times often writes stories on such emerging technologies and companies.

But there's also an even simpler way to spot companies like this. Look again at those five companies I gave as an example. You're probably already a customer of some of those companies! You drank coffee you made at home with your Keurig machine while you watched a show on Netflix… then your iPhone beeped with a job offer from someone on Linkedin. Then (perhaps in your fantasy!) you unplugged your Tesla and drove to work.

You didn't need to be an insider to see these companies were changing the way we live our lives. You witnessed these product revolutions in real time, and you as a consumer were impressed. Lines of people waiting outside your local Apple store at dawn just so they could buy the new iPhone even though they had one already—it was all there for you to see, you just needed to look for it!

Whether you believed in or used these products or not isn't the point; the point is that they were causing a stir and *capturing peoples" imaginations and visions of the future*, especially *the imaginations of the big investment bankers that drive stock prices with their massive purchases.*

So, to summarize this method of trading stocks:

1. Be sure you're in the first two years of a new bull market—this is when the most money is made from stocks. You need the price of the SPX to be above the 70-week moving average recently AND then wait for that average line to be pointed decidedly upwards. Based on the bull market that began in 2012 (see earlier chart of

SPX), it was about February 2013 before this condition was in place (notice how those 5 examples weren't triggered as a buy until then anyway).

2. Then find stocks of companies that appear to be game-changers, as already explained, and buy them when triggered by the Secret of Seventy system (criteria for this explained in the previous chapter).

3. Sell them when you've doubled your money OR if the Secret of Seventy sell-trigger is activated, whichever happens first.

I've just given you two unique ways of doubling your money so you can ride those compounding steps to your freedom figure—one very simple method (Secret of Seventy) and the less simple method I've just shown you. It's like anything in life, the more you're prepared to put in, the more you get back. For our purposes, it's a case of the more you're prepared to put in, the *faster and greater* your gains can be.

With that in mind, let me give you a third method for doubling your money with stocks… and with this system you could double your money *once a month and therefore possibly even get to your freedom figure within a few months!*

The 4th Secret

It's time for a brand new biblical wealth secret, the fourth of seven:

As you can see, this secret isn't an actual quote from The Bible, *but these numbers are quoted throughout The Bible with such consistency and in so many ways, to say this was some kind of fluke seems nonsensical. The Bible is trying to tell us something here.*

I'll tell you a little about the symbolic meaning of these numbers in biblical terms (except the number 70 as we covered that in detail last time), and then I'll explain how the meaning of these numbers and the numbers themselves create a powerful stock trading system.

The Number 4: Completion (of a cycle).

The number 4 derives its meaning from creation. On the **fourth** day of what is called "creation week" came the existence of our sun, the moon, and all the stars (Genesis 1:14 - 19). Their purpose was not only to give off light, but also to divide the day from the night on earth, thus becoming a basic demarcation of time. They were also made to be a type of signal that would mark off the days, years and *seasons (more on this in a second)*. Interestingly, the Hebrew word for "seasons" in Genesis 1:14 is *mode*, which literally translated is "appointed times" (divine appointments) in reference to religious festivals. This is the earliest known allusion to what would later be called the Holy (or Feast) days (periods) of worship, which are seven in number. There are **four** gospel accounts of Jesus" life and ministry. Each of these emphasizes a unique aspect of his sacrifice and ministry. Matthew's focus is on Christ being the son of David and a King.

"Also, thou son of man, thus saith the Lord God unto the land of Israel; an end, the end is come upon the four corners of the earth." The earth of course doesn't have four corners, but this is to show all **four** compass directions (North, East, South, West). When Jesus is said to have raised Lazarus from the dead, we were given a picturing of the resurrection wherein we all would be made alive, and thus complete a *cycle*. John 11:17: "Then when Jesus came, he found that he had lain in the grave **four** days already." *4 = completion of a cycle.*

The Number 50: Freedom from burden

Fifty can be found 154 times in the Bible. It symbolizes freedom from a prior burden. After Jesus appeared to Mary Magdalene on Sunday morning, April 9 in 30 A.D., he ascended to the Father in heaven (John 20:17). His ascension occurred on the day God told the Israelites they were to wave a sheaf composed of the first fruits of their harvest (Leviticus 23:9 - 11). It is on this day that the count of **50** days to the Feast of Pentecost begins. God promised Abraham that if he found only **50** righteous people in Sodom and Gomorrah he would not destroy both cities (Genesis 18:23 - 26). God commanded ancient Israel that every **50**th year, on the Day of *Atonement*, that a Jubilee was to be declared with the sound of a trumpet (Leviticus 25). During the Jubilee year, ALL debts were settled in favor of the debtor and inheritances were returned to their rightful owners. Also, those who worked as slave laborers in order to repay a debt were granted their freedom to return home to their families and land. *50 = freedom from burden.*

The Number 100: Promise of a large return.

This number appears to represent the number of the children of promise. Abraham was **100** years old when he had Yitz'chak, the son of promise. It is the children of promise who are to be blessed, and this blessing is also associated with these children in the number one hundred. The number one hundred indicates fullness especially when it comes to age. Since one hundred equals ten tens, the number is a round figure that conveys completeness. Israel's soldiers normally appeared in groups of a hundred. Obadiah hid one hundred prophets from Jezebel. A hundred denotes not only what is full; but also the principle of return. "And other seed fell upon the good earth and having sprung up it brought forth fruit a hundredfold." (Luke 8:8; Matthew 13:8; and Mark 4:20). Another good example of the significance of one hundred is in the parable of the lost sheep. We can see the emphasis on completeness and return. When one sheep out of a hundred wanders off and is lost, the number remaining seems lacking and incomplete by comparison. The shepherd is not satisfied until after he has found his lost sheep bringing his total back to exactly one hundred. "What do you think? If a man has a hundred sheep, and one of them goes astray, does he not leave the ninety-nine and go to the mountains to seek the one that is straying?" (Matthew 18:12) The number one hundred is a round, complete number. It suggests a large return: "The one who receives the seed of the word of God and keeps it will produce a hundredfold crop." (Luke 8:15). *100 = promise of a large return.*

4-50-70-100. When we bring these numbers together in

the context of stocks, the results can be incredibly powerful.

Translating The Biblical Money Code

4:

Four seasons make up the cycle. Stocks (and stock markets) go through a 4-stage cycle that's like the four seasons. The stock in the "summer" phase is rising rapidly. Look at the earlier examples of those individual stocks, here's the LNKD example broken down into "seasons":

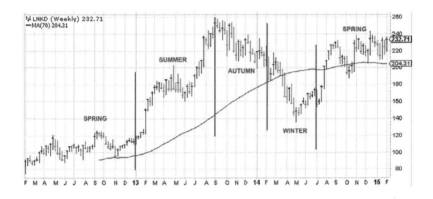

IMPORTANT NOTE: these "seasons" are metaphors; they are not to be taken literally. In other words, when I talk about buying a stock only in its summer phase I am NOT talking about buying a stock only during the actual summer months of the year! I'm referring to that phase in its cycle where it is rapidly rising. Spring is a flat, consolidating period after a destructive winter phase, but it soon gives birth to a "summer" phase where the stock shoots up again. "Autumn" is a leveling off period after the boom of the "summer" phase, a transition into "winter," where the stock falls below the 70-week average, and then the whole cycle starts over.

50:

Stocks that have just hit a new high price for the last 50 weeks (52 weeks in a year) are breaking into new ground and headed upwards. These stocks are now *free from burden* because a year has passed, and anyone who had previously bought that stock at too high price (usually during the stock's "winter" phase) and then looked to "get out even" by selling it at the first opportunity has now done all their selling. This constant selling by people who don't know what they're doing and then looking to "get out even" depresses a stock price until all that selling has been exhausted. So a new annual high in price indicates that a stock is *free of the burden* of all that selling pressure and has clear blue skies ahead of it. So stocks that have just hit a new 50-week high in price are usually set to climb higher.

70:

On the Relative Strength Indicator (RSI) explained in the last chapter, when a reading higher than **70%** shows up as in the shaded area, this represents extreme upward momentum, indicating that buying from big banks has entered a frenzied "euphoric" stage:

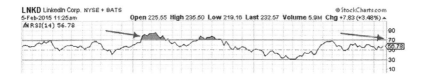

100:

Stocks that have just passed the $100 price mark per share have a psychological effect on buyers that often propels the price higher still (the *promise of a large return* seems evident).

Now let's put it all together…

Stocks that meet the following FOUR criteria (4 = completion) are often set to make a very strong move higher in the days or weeks ahead:

1. **In its "summer" phase of the 4 seasons cycle.**
2. **Just hit a new high price for the last 50 days.**
3. **Have an RSI reading of over 70.**
4. **Have just crossed the $100 price mark for the first time.**

Here's an actual example of one such trade I did recently that doubled my investment:

As you can see above, Gilead Sciences (GILD) was in its "summer" phase. Then, *all at the same time*, the other 3 criteria were met: new high in price for last 50 weeks, the $100 mark exceeded for the first time, and RSI went above 70%. You only make the trade when ALL FOUR criteria are in play at the same time. The chart above is the type of chart we've been using all along—it's a long-term chart called a "weekly" chart because each of those little vertical bars represents one week of trading (remember?). But now let me show you another type of chart...

This chart below is called a "daily" chart, and it's more of a short-term chart that's zooming in closer on the weekly chart you just saw. It's exactly the same as the one you're used to apart from two key differences: each of those tiny vertical bars now represents one DAY of trading as opposed to one week, and the period covered is 6 months as opposed to 3 years:

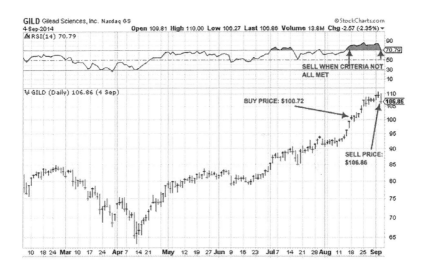

The weekly (long term) chart gives us more of a "big picture" view so we can check the stock is in the right "season." Once we've established that the stock is clearly in its "summer" phase we can zoom in and use a daily (short term) chart like this one for better clarity—we want to act the very same DAY that any stock meets all four of the buying criteria. NOTE: we want

BOTH the weekly *and* daily charts to have an RSI in excess of 70%.

As you can see, on 18th August 2014, GILD met the four criteria, and the buy trigger came in that day with a buy at $100.72. NOTE: go by the price at the *close* of the trading day (4pm New York time) NOT the price *during* the trading day. The trade was closed when all the criteria stopped being met; in this case when the RSI dropped below 70% on September 4th, with a closing price of $106.86. A gain of $6.14 or just over 6%.

Now, a 6% gain is hardly doubling your money though, is it? Well, no it isn't, *if* you're buying stocks the usual way. But in the next chapter I'm going to show you the special way to trade stocks that turned that tiny 6% gain into a huge 100% gain that doubled my money!

We'll also look at a couple more refinements I've developed for this stock trading system that will increase the chances of success even more. Before then though, let's answer the question I'm sure you're asking: where do you find stocks that are likely to meet the four criteria?

There are many websites and apps that will give you a shortlist of stocks that meet the criteria if you know what to enter. The website I use is **www.Chartmill.com.** As usual, I'll walk you through this one screen at a time. Here's what you see when you arrive at this website:

Click on the "Stock Screener" tab and you'll see this page next:

On that page, enter "Price above 100" in the "Price" dropdown menu, and enter "US Only" in the "Exchange/Fund" dropdown menu, as shown above. Then click on the "Technical" tab in that screen, and you'll see this page:

In this screen enter as follows, and as shown above:
Signal: "New 52 week high today"
SMA1: "200 SMA Rising"
SMA2: "Price Above 200 SMA"
SMA3: "SMA 50 Above SMA 200"

When you've entered all that, scroll down and you'll see your shortlist with the stock codes on the left-hand side, ready for you to enter into your charts on StockCharts.com. They are listed in order of relative strength, so the best ones come first. An historical example below:

Ticker	Name
RETL	Direxion Daily Retail Bull 3X Shares
CNC	Centene Corp.
MNK	Mallinckrodt Plc Ordinary Share

Results: Table View, Sorted by Relative Strength (DES

Remember, this list it gives you doesn't guarantee that all the criteria are met; this is just a *shortlist* for you to enter into a chart, and then it's down to you to see if the criteria are met. Chartmill gives you 3 stocks on this list for free, and any more than that costs a nominal fee each month.

If you want a free (but less accurate) way of finding a shortlist to check out, simply do an Internet search for "stocks making 52-week highs today," and you will get a good selection to look at.

Before moving on to the next chapter, consider that of the three stock trading systems I've explained this lesson that you don't have to just pick one; you might divide your capital between the three of them.

So you now know how crucial it is to only buy stocks in a bull market, and you know how to spot a bull market. But what if you're reading this at a time when we aren't in a bull market?

Remember, the stock market is just one of three paths to freedom, so if that path isn't looking good for you at this time there's another two to consider, and I'll give you the big secrets of those. Next time we will move onto yet another new secret...

This uncannily accurate secret will make or break you, it's that simple. Time your plans according to this consistently correct prophecy and *this secret alone will make you free* with what I'll be teaching you here (this was how I first became financially independent). But be on the *wrong* side of this prophecy and the path to freedom will become so long that you won't have enough years left to make it to the end—your dreams will die with you. Let's *not* allow that to happen!

Chapter 7:
Time for Riches

Believe...

"A scorner seeketh wisdom and findeth it not: but knowledge is easy to him that understandeth." – Proverbs 14:6

Some of what you've been learning here may have surprised you, perhaps even made you *suspicious* about how simple a lot of this information may seem... and yet the facts are all there before your eyes. Look at the quote above and consider this for a second.

That's why we spent that time preparing you in the first two chapters; to banish the "scorner" in you, the skeptic. It's weird, but some people will simply refuse to believe something that could help them greatly, even when faced with solid proof. Belief is crucial if you want to succeed: belief in yourself, and belief in what you can clearly see as beneficial, *even if doing so may conflict with what you previously thought was true.*

This discipline of not being a "scorner" is also a vital part of trading stocks successfully, as you'll see shortly. Most peoples" beliefs, both short and long term, are often nothing more than an emotional basket of prejudices, coping mechanisms, and urban legends. And, as you'll see later on, *emotions and biases will make you poor.*

Starting immediately, if you hadn't done so already, I want you to give yourself completely to what I'm explaining here, however uncanny and mystical it may seem, and however much it may conflict with what you thought to be true.

There are just some things in the universe that can't be explained (like the persistent appearance of the number 7 in events), and, however much humans get frustrated by not having an answer for every little thing, that little thing will continue to be so. Maybe some things simply aren't meant to be explained; they just *are.*

So let's begin…

Timing the Currents and Waves
"He that gathereth in summer is a wise son: but he that sleepeth in harvest is a son that causeth shame." – Proverbs 10:5

As we conclude your stock market training, there are a few more refinements I'd like to give you before we move on to something new. We've compared the stock market to a *sea of money*, and that the prevailing *tide* in this sea of money is either a bull market or bear market; a condition often predicted by the Secret of Seventy that I revealed in chapter 5.

This tide is powered by the prevailing mood of the big banks as they constantly buy and sell the market with trillions of (your) dollars. So your journey across this sea of money as you place your own trades is greatly affected by this tide, which is why you now know only to buy stocks in a bull market.

But if you consider a real sea journey, there are other factors that will influence your success or failure: the *"current"* and the *"waves."* Assuming you've judged the tide correctly and that you're riding *with* the tide, not against it, you must then consider the current and the waves. As we continue the comparison with the sea, here's what I mean by "current" and "waves":

CURRENT:

The short-term fluctuations of the stock market within a long-term bull market.

WAVES:

The type of companies in favor with the big institutional buyers (banks) at any given time.

Let me start by explaining the "current"…

Above is a chart with a format you should now be familiar with. You should know by looking at this that the TIDE is bullish, as shown by the long arrow I drew running alongside that upwards-pointing 70-week moving average.

But it's not a one-way street. Sadly, stocks and stock markets do not go up in straight lines! As you can see from those little weekly price vertical bars, *within that bull market* there are short-term fluctuations, up *and down*, within the prevailing longer-term upwards trend. The TIDE may be rising, but within that rise the CURRENT is moving both UP *and DOWN*.

It's important to appreciate that if the current goes against you with a short-term drop in the market, it could ruin your trades. BUT, by the same token, if the current goes *for* you, it will make your trades even more profitable and even faster.

So we want to be synchronized with BOTH the current (short term situation) and the tide (long term situation) in this sea of money when we place a trade. Here's a guide on how to judge the current.

Below is a DAILY chart of the S+P 500. Remember, the daily chart is how we zoom-in on the weekly chart shown on the previous page. The daily chart gives us more clarity, and each little vertical price bar is a single *day* of price movement, not a week. You should also remember from last time that additional indicator called, Relative Strength Indicator (RSI), which is shown as a separate chart above the price chart:

Notice the dashed line on the RSI section that represents the 50% mark? This is a good way to judge the direction of the current—over 50% is good, and below 50% is bad.

- **Only open new trades as the RSI rises above 50.**
- **Don't open a new trade if the RSI goes below 50, and if practical, close any existing trades if the RSI goes below 50.**

I've drawn in examples on the chart above—as you can see, this is a very accurate guide of what the current is doing. Notice how those price drops in the SPX that you can see in August, October, and December are predicted by the RSI going below 50?

Timing is everything in life, and stock trading is the purest example. You can use *time for riches*.

And remember that when you use the Biblical Money Code we talked about last time, the trades aren't open very long—those upswings you can see in the current are usually long enough to put enough wind in the sails of your short-term trades to really make them fly.

But there's one final thing to consider on this sea voyage: the *waves*. So, what do I mean by *waves*? I'm talking about something we touched on earlier: *sectors*. Stocks are grouped into industrial sectors such as technology, healthcare, industrial goods, etc. Now here's the important thing:

At any given time, there will usually be one or two sectors that are in particular favor with the big buying institutions, and this of course has an effect on the prices of stocks in those sectors.

Wouldn't it be a useful thing if we could figure out which

are the hot sectors at any time? If we could be synchronized with the big trend of the market (tide), plus the short-term fluctuations (current), plus the hot sectors (waves), especially when we use the Biblical Money Code, we would have a LOT going for us! So, let's look at how we might deduce which are the hottest industrial sectors.

Let's revisit ChartMill.com. When you get there, click on the "More" tab, over to the right:

And then, in the dropdown menu underneath the "More" tab, select "sectors" as shown:

Then you'll be presented with this table of words and numbers below, but don't panic, it's going to be very simple to extract what we need from it. On the left-hand side column, you can see all the different industrial sectors of stocks listed:

▲ Name	Stocks	ARS	Today	Best	Worst	Advancing	1w	2w	1m	3m	6m	VI	PP	NH	NL	3DER	6DER
Basic Materials	279	92	-0.21%	11.30%	-15.09%	46.93%	2.11%	10.57%	14.33%	-9.76%	-22.46%	-7.57%	2.55%	0.38%	2.51%	-0.2%	-0.8%
Conglomerates	9	61.75	0.56%	5.59%	-0.83%	53.56%	2.9%	6.59%	6.11%	3.95%	4.21%	15.87%	8.57%	33.35%	0%	0.76%	0.58%
Consumer Goods	195	57.46	0.36%	11.35%	-3.26%	58.49%	1.56%	5.17%	4.86%	3.11%	5.50%	7.29%	4%	19.97%	3.39%	0.2%	-0.06%
Financial	547	52.1	0.03%	7.84%	-4.97%	50.46%	0.57%	3.98%	3.86%	1.22%	2.56%	-12.15%	4.08%	7.86%	1.65%	0.06%	-0.34%
Healthcare	266	61.26	1.17%	36.93%	-19.62%	67.67%	3.16%	4.85%	7.76%	14%	15.11%	15.65%	3.81%	11.25%	2.26%	0.13%	-0.22%
Industrial Goods	173	46.89	-0.17%	4.86%	-16.6%	43.93%	3.02%	7.75%	8.96%	0.3%	6.16%	-1.66%	5.2%	17.34%	1.73%	-0.35%	-0.45%
Services	466	57.67	0.17%	12.59%	-5.8%	53.04%	2.02%	6.11%	6.07%	4.56%	8.56%	3.57%	5.43%	18.3%	1.32%	0.06%	-0.2%
Technology	394	36.3	2.61%	356.67%	-6.86%	48.18%	2.54%	6.73%	7.29%	5.65%	8.71%	4.52%	5.26%	17.77%	1.27%	-0.07%	-0.45%
Utilities	79	57.50	-0.24%	4.17%	-2.66%	36.71%	-1.74%	-2.86%	-3.53%	-0.74%	2.66%	29.61%	1.51%	8.3%	3.06%	-0.22%	0.15%

Along the top of the table, locate the heading "6m" and click on it twice, until the little black arrow to the left of it points *down*, as shown below. IMPORTANT: it's vital that the little arrow is pointed DOWN:

▼ 6m

Then look to the left-hand side column, and write down the top 3 sectors. In this historical example, as you can see below, the top 3 sectors were Healthcare, Technology, and Services:

Name

Healthcare

Technology

Services

Next, do the same with the "NH" heading, so it looks like this below:

▼ NH

Now look to the left-hand column again, and write down what the top 3 sectors now show (they will probably be somewhat different). In this historical example, the top 3 sectors showed up as Conglomerates, Consumer Goods, and Technology:

| Conglomerates |
| Consumer Goods |
| Technology |

Now compare your two lists of what the top 3 sectors were from each of the two selections. Look for any sectors that appear in *both* lists. In this historical example, you can see that the Technology sector was the hot sector to be in at that time (remember: these are historical examples and will be different at the time you read this!).

(If you're interested in knowing what's going on here, what you selected just then was a ranking of the sectors with the best six-month performance (6m) that also had new highs in price for the last five days (NH). This way you're seeing sectors that have a long trend of good performance already established, but that they're also *still* performing well because they're reaching new highs in the last five days.)

And that's it!

What do you do if there are no sectors that appear on both lists? Well in that case it's probably best not to trade and check this again the next day.

Being in time with the "tide" as well as the "current" and "waves" is extremely powerful! Use the Biblical Money Code with this in mind and it will be very hard to lose.

Get all these factors working for you at the same time and The Sea of Money will practically part for you!

And if you have to wait for all these factors to align all at once for you, *then wait*. If this means that you only trade a few times a year, *then only trade a few times a year.*

The objective is to make money, not lose it, and you

make money when the odds are most in your favor. And you lose money when you're being impatient and reckless!

So when those opportune times do come along, you really need to make the most of it. Here's how...

Time is Money

"And when thy herds and thy flocks multiply, and thy silver and thy gold is multiplied, and all that thou hast is multiplied; Then thine heart be lifted up." – Deuteronomy 8:13

Now I'm going to show you how I turned that small gain I showed you last time into a big gain. A quick recap...

The weekly (long-term) chart gives us more of a "big picture" view so we can check the stock is in the right "season." Once we've established that the stock is clearly in its "summer" phase we can zoom in and use a daily (short-term) chart like this one for better clarity—we want to act the very same DAY that any stock meets all four of the buying criteria. NOTE: we want BOTH the weekly *and* daily charts to have an RSI in excess of 70%.

As you can see, on 18th August 2014, GILD met the four criteria, and the buy trigger came in that day with a buy at $100.72. NOTE: go by the price at the *close* of the trading day (4pm New York time), NOT the price *during* the trading day. The trade was closed when all the criteria stopped being met; in this case when the RSI dropped below 70% on September 4th, with a closing price of $106.86. A gain of $6.14 or just over 6%.

Now, a 6% gain is hardly doubling your money though, is it? Well, no it isn't, *if* you're buying stocks the usual way. But now I'm going to show you the special way to trade stocks that turned that tiny 6% gain into a huge 100% gain that doubled my money.

The secret is to harness the power of *time*. When you're trading stocks the way I'm about to show you, *time literally is money*.

Let me explain this with a simple example of something you've probably heard of before. Please pay close attention, and you may need to re-read this section. As you know, you can buy a piece of land. But, you can also buy an *option* to buy that piece of land. Here's how it works:

Let's say the land is priced at $100,000. Instead of buying it, you say to the owner, "I'd like the exclusive option to buy this piece of land for $100,000 at some time within the next six months, and I'll pay you for that option. If I don't buy the land for that price within the six months, then you keep the money I paid for this option."

Now, why would someone offer this?

The reason why someone would offer this is so he didn't have to part with $100,000. Instead he would just make a token payment, maybe a few grand in this case, to pay for the option of being able to buy this land within a certain time frame.

But the real angle here is that this buyer of the option then has six months to try and sell this piece of land for a price *higher* than $100,000, and thus make a profit on something he didn't own; he didn't own it, he merely *controlled* it. You see, even if that piece of land became worth $150,000 sometime in the following six months, the owner would still have to sell it to this options buyer for the agreed $100,000 because the land owner and the options buyer had a *contract.*

So it's all about what happens to land prices in that six-month period that followed the signing of that contract. In other words, it's all about *time.* What that option buyer has actually purchased is a six-month period in which he hopes the price will rise. He's literally *buying time.*

If the buyer had wanted a longer period for the option to expire, he would obviously have paid more money, because he's got more *time* for things to go in his favor. Make sense?

So let's say that the price does in fact rise from $100,000 to $150,000 within the six months. And let's say that the option to buy this land at that agreed $100,000 price within six months cost him $5,000. So, the buyer happily buys the land for $100,000 when the market value is actually $150,000.

What's his profit? $50,000?

Wrong. The profit is actually $45,000!

How so? Because his only investment was the cost of the option: $5,000 in this example. So his profit was $50,000 less $5,000 = $45,000, or **900%!**

900% profit as opposed to what would have been 50% profit if he had simply bought the land. That's another reason why you might buy an option instead of just buying something the usual way. And the only risk was that $5,000, not $100,000. Remember though, no asset was purchased here; all that was purchased was an option contract.

The downside would be if the price of the land did not increase in value. The six months would expire, and the option to buy it at $100,000 would therefore be worthless, and the option would have lost all its value.

That's the catch. *So the trick is to have a good idea about where the price of something is headed next.* And when it comes to stocks, I think you may now have such an idea, no?

But before I bring this conversation around to stocks, let's first consider another couple of scenarios for the person who wants to buy an option on this piece of land currently priced at $100,000.

We already said that if the options buyer wanted the option to go on for longer than six months that he would pay more for it because there's more time for the price of the land to go up. Likewise, if he wanted the option to be for *less* than six months then the price of the option would be less. Make sense?

The other scenario is that this option buyer doesn't want the option to buy at the current price of $100,000—he wants the option to buy at a different price. He might ask for the option to buy the land at $110,000 (more) or $90,000 (less).

In that scenario, obviously, he would pay *less* for the option to buy at a higher price because the price has to go up $10,000 just for the option to be worth anything.

Likewise, he would pay *more* for the option to buy the

land at $90,000 because it's already worth $100,000. In this case the option has what you might call an *intrinsic value*, value that's already built-in, which in this case is $10,000.

It's all perfect common sense when you think about it, nothing complicated.

In a nutshell, the further out the expiration date of the option, the more you pay for it. And the lower the price there's an option to buy the asset at, compared to the current price, the more you pay for it.

So how does this apply to stocks and how I can turn a small gain like 6% into a large gain? The answer is from something that's simply called *options*. And when you reflect on our land owner example with that 900% gain from what was actually a 50% gain (land worth $100,00 sold for $150,000), I hope you can begin to see how this works.

You can do exactly the same thing with stocks (and stock markets) as that example of a man buying an option on that piece of land instead of actually buying the land. The trick, as in the land example, is to make a correct prediction about where the price is headed next. And now that you're armed with the powerful secrets I've given you, I trust you're excited about the possibility of using them with trading options.

As in our land example, trading options is all about *time*. You're buying time. Options are priced on a complex formula that you don't need to know, *only that this formula is based largely on the time factor.*

With stock options, because of this computerized formula that's in play, the sooner things go your way after you place the trade, the better. If you buy an option today, and the very next day the stock price it relates to shoots up in value, then your option will become dramatically more valuable *overnight*—disproportionately higher in value than the jump in the actual stock price.

Why does this happen? Because the unintelligent computer program makes the blind assumption that this rate of price increase will continue for the duration of this contract—until this option reaches the expiration date. The computer thinks, "Well, if the stock price immediately went up 10% after this contract came into effect, and there's still 6 months until expiration, then this stock could continue to rise at this daily rate and could be worth a great deal more than it is today. So, let's increase the price of the option accordingly."

If you look back at my example where I traded GILD options using the Biblical Money Code, you'll see that the price began moving upwards immediately after I placed that trade and it kept moving upwards. The options *time* pricing formula was working for me in this scenario.

That's another reason why the Biblical Money Code is so powerful; because the speed at which it performs (if executed correctly) "fools" the options pricing computer into pricing the option a lot higher very quickly, resulting in fast and disproportionately high gains.

When you buy an option on a stock it's called a "CALL" option. When you place this order with your broker you'll also need to tell him the expiration date of your option. You'll also need to tell him the price at which you'd like this option to buy the stock at—this price is referred to as the "STRIKE PRICE." In our land scenario, we discussed this when the option buyer could have had the option to buy the $100,000 piece of land at perhaps $90,000 or $110,000, and paid accordingly—$90,000 and $110,000 were "strike prices." By the way, you won't actually buy the stock at your strike price come expiration, it's purely theoretical for the purpose of making this trade.

Remember: The further out the expiration date, the more you pay for the option (the more time you're buying). The lower the strike price (the more built-in or intrinsic value you're buying), the more you pay for the option. And that's why there's so many numbers to choose from when you trade options—because of all these variables.

What expiration date and strike price should you use? That's up to you, but personally I pick a strike price that's as close to the current price as possible, and I pick an expiration date that's 6 months out.

So, let's say stock XYZ is currently priced at $100. You see a buy trigger because all the stars have aligned for this trade. Today's date is January 1st (hypothetically).

You would buy a CALL option on stock XYZ with a STRIKE PRICE of $100 and expiration in July. That's exactly how you'd place that order with your options broker. Actually, the order would sound like this: "Buy to open XYZ $100 July call."

There are many options brokers to choose from when you search for them online (I can't tell you which to pick). And you can also of course trade online. So, here's a full demonstration of how to trade an option, and in this example I'm using an OptionsXpress account.

Let's say I want to buy a call option for Apple stock (AAPL). The month is January and the price of AAPL is $127. So, going by what I explained before, I'm looking for a strike price at or close to $127 (the current price), and an expiration close to July (6 months from now). After you've opened an account and logged in, here's the process…

On the "Quotes" tab, from the dropdown menu select "Option Chains":

Then you'll be presented with a large table of numbers that are default set to the options for "SPY" (the S+P 500). Locate the "symbol" box where "SPY" is:

In place of "SPY" enter the code for the stock of your choice—in our example it's Apple. So, we enter AAPL as shown below. It will give you a dropdown menu of likely matches, be sure to choose the correct one:

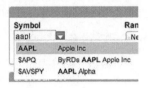

Then select more items in the boxes to the right of where you entered your stock code. In the "Range" box be sure it's set to "Near the Money" (this means you want a strike price close to the current price). In the "Type" box to the right of that select "Calls":

To the right of those boxes above, ignore the "Expiration" box, and simply click the "View Chain" button next to it:

Then you'll be presented with a big table of current month prices for Apple options, but directly above that table look for this section below that shows different expiration periods. Select the period you want. In our case, we want an expiration that's six months from January, so let's select July (shown as "Jul15"):

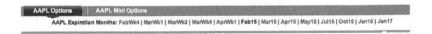

Then you'll be presented with the screen like the one below. The strike prices available are listed on the left-hand side under "strike":

▲ Strike ▼	Last	Chg	Bid	Ask Calls
July 2015				
120.00	12.65	0	12.60	12.75
125.00	9.70	0	9.70	9.85
130.00	7.25	0	7.25	7.35
135.00	5.35	0	5.25	5.40

Our current price for AAPL stock is $127, but you'll notice in the above that there's no strike price for $127, only $125 or $130. Given the choice, I'd select the slightly higher price. So, let's go for $130 strike price.

What we do then is follow our strike price line across the row until we reach the column shown as "Ask." Then we can see in the zoom-in below that the price of the AAPL call option with a $130 strike price and July expiration is $7.35 per option purchased. So click on the price that applies, in this case "7.35":

130.00	7.25	0	7.25	7.35

When you do that the next screen will show your "Trade Ticket" ready for you to check over:

All-In-One Trade Ticket

Let's look at this screen above. Now we need to check this is what we want. Reading across, we can see that it's a BUY, the month is July 2015 in this example (Jul15), Strike Price is $130 in this example, it's a CALL, and the price is 7.35 as we selected. The other box to check in the above screen is "Quantity," and that requires a quick explanation that you need to focus on carefully.

The price you were quoted in this example of $7.35 is the price of 1 option purchase. Now, the minimum number of options you can have per trade is 100. So, the cost of this would be 100 x $7.35, which equals $735 in this example.

100 options = 1 contract = minimum number of contracts.

What you see in the "Quantity" window on that screen above is 1 contract. If you want more contracts, select the number you want. If you selected 2 in the "Quantity" window (200 options) it would cost you $1,470 (200 x $7.35).

A "contract" is like the agreement with that land owner in our example; it's just another expression for a "deal" or opening a trade.

So if we're happy with 1 contract, let's go ahead and click on the "Preview" button in that screen, and we'll see this:

Check the top writing in green to ensure this is what you want. The broker adds their commission ($12.95 in this example—usually a set fee), and you see the total as expected. You click to execute the order if you're happy, and that's it. The clock is running.

Armed with all the stock trading secrets revealed in this book, I now trust you can see how it's perfectly possible to double your money a few times a year, and therefore create your Freedom Figure in a relatively short time. When you can double your money, and keep rolling up the profits, you're only ten steps from turning $1,000 into $1,000,000. As well as that, you now also know how to manage your Freedom Figure to give you an astonishingly high yield.

Before I conclude our discussion on the stock market though, there's one last crucial secret I *must* share with you.

Win from losing

"Riches profit not in the day of wrath: but righteousness delivereth from death." – Proverbs 11:4

Right now, you may feel as though you've been given the keys to the kingdom. And you have, but you need to prepare yourself for losing sometimes. How can that be? With all the clever tricks you've been shown, and you've witnessed working as proof, how can you possibly lose?

Just please understand that you can, and sometimes *will* lose, regardless of everything you've been taught, even when you do everything right. Remember, what we're doing here is improving your *odds*, nothing is guaranteed. *But you will still win overall if you're disciplined.*

And by disciplined, I mean this:

1. You find a strategy that works for you and *you stick to it through thick and thin.* If it works, stick to it. If it doesn't work for you, find a new one that will. The important thing is not to keep changing!

2. You ride your winners as long as possible, resisting the urge to take profits too early.

3. You cut your losses early at a predetermined level.

Easier said than done because this all runs completely counter to human nature! Let me elaborate:

When you see your trades tick into profit your emotions of greed will want to take the money, out of fear that the profit could disappear the next day.

When you see your trades tick into a loss your emotions of fear will want you to not close the trade, out of denial and pride.

On any given day you'll look at your trading account and see some trades running a profit, and others running a loss. That's normal, as things fluctuate. But what your temptation will be is to snatch those profits showing up and to leave the losses in place (hoping they too will be in profit soon). But that's often the exact OPPOSITE thing that you should do. Do NOT underestimate this warning I give you!

Understanding trading is relatively easy. The hardest part is being able to take correct actions that are counterintuitive!

Try to think of it this way: your trading account is like a garden that you lovingly tend to. In any garden there will be parasitic weeds and blooming flowers. The job of the gardener is to remove the weeds, and nurture the flowers, right? *So why would you do the opposite?* Cutting your winners and letting your losers ride is like ripping out blooming flowers and leaving the weeds in place!

But to go back to the main point, you will win overall even if you lose half the time. In fact, you can even win if you lose MORE times than you win! Let me demonstrate how. Here are ten fictional trades showing profit or loss, in chronological order at which the trade occurred, starting with a $10,000 account. Please put yourself in these shoes and experience all the *emotions* as we run this simulation:

1. 10% loss. Account balance $9,000.
2. 10% loss. Account balance $8,100.
3. 10% loss. Account balance $7,290.
4. 10% loss. Account balance $6,561.
5. 10% loss. Account balance $5,905.

Okay, let's pause before moving on to the next five trades. Your account is now *down* from $10,000 to $5,905. Wow, that was money well spent... not! Had enough yet? Still believe this can work? The overall market is UP—you'd have been better off just buying the market! *Do you have the discipline to sit this out?*

These are the questions that will mess with your mind and tempt you into doing something silly during times like this! And, thanks to Murphy's Law, I often find that it's soon after these times that the tide turns. It's often darkest before dawn. Here are the next five trades...

6. 60% gain. Account balance $9,448.
7. 70% gain. Account balance $16,061.
8. 20% gain. Account balance $19,273.
9. 10% loss. Account balance $17,345.
10. 30% gain. Account balance $22,548. UP over 125%!

Listen, this is very important:

Do not judge your success by any short-term outcome, judge it by the decision-process you went through. Go back and honestly ask yourself if you didn't miss anything that we've spoken about. If you're *truly* doing all the right things and getting lousy results, you're just having a run of bad luck (known as a "drawdown"). But the key word there is "truly."

So, in that simulation you lost 6 trades out of 10 and you were still UP 125%. And I wasn't being unrealistic on those gains, either, especially when you consider the power of options. It's like magic, isn't it? How is this possible? The answer to that question is in the percentages of gain and loss that you saw. *The losses were never allowed to be more than 10%.*

It's ONLY possible by letting your winners ride and cutting your losers early! If you cut your winners early and ride your losers late, the winners will NOT make up for the losers. Result: LOSS.

Try rerunning that ten-trade demonstration with the gain/ loss numbers *reversed* and see for yourself how the result turns out! My friend, please appreciate that *this is why most people lose money in the market. Because they are emotional creatures.*

And I'll tell you something else: the secrets I'm teaching you work precisely *because* of these human foibles that cause people to lose money in markets. If you are disciplined you will be the recipient of that lost money in the market. If you are not, then you will be the one losing it!

All most people think about when first coming into trading is what and when to buy, they never consider when to SELL. But now you understand how critical it is to sell at the right time! It could be the difference between success and failure!

You have very precise buy and sell triggers for the Secret of Seventy, the Biblical Money Code, and everything I've taught you, SO USE THEM PROPERLY OR NOT AT ALL.

It hurts to take losses, but the important thing is *preservation of capital* so you always live to fight another day.

As King Solomon said: ***"A living dog is better than a dead lion." - Ecclesiastes 9:4.***

That sobering but crucial note concludes our discussion on the stock market—you've come so far in such a short space of time. I wish you could truly appreciate what an edge you have over the rest of the world now, even the professionals. Well done—you have successfully navigated The Sea of Money as we make this journey to freedom.

So now let's continue our journey to freedom and move on to a brand-new subject and a brand-new secret—after all, we've only covered one of three paths to your Freedom Figure.

Timing the Great Cycle
"Pride goeth before destruction, and a haughty spirit before a fall." – Proverbs 16:18

Let me introduce this next secret and subject with this article I wrote at the depths of the real estate crash in 2009:

All too often, investors only look at the upside. They should always consider this too though: "What if I'm wrong?" I said that caveat to myself last week on my way to view a foreclosed property, and I wondered if I was wrong about property currently being a good investment.

Anyway, I parked the car and inspected the foreclosed home. It was in reasonable condition for a foreclosure: just superficial work (and that's good because if a home is foreclosed, the departing owner, understandably perhaps, sometimes lashes out at the property. And drywall is easy to put a fist through).

Then I walked onto the rear patio, and something hit me

between the eyes...

The home had all the usual remnants of broken dreams, nothing I wasn't used to, sad though it was. But what I saw on this occasion made me walk back to the car and gather my thoughts.

What I had seen on the patio was an abandoned child's tricycle. Its merry colors had faded from sun and rain, and I imagined what had happened the day the family had to leave, and I imagined the child on the tricycle crying. Call me soft if you like, but I'm a human being as well as an investor.

(Sidebar: There's nothing wrong with buying a foreclosed property, the damage has already been done by then and it's not my fault. If anything, I'm helping matters by getting the housing market moving.)

So why was I so fixated on the abandoned tricycle? Because I'd just seen a ghost, and a flashback from 20 years earlier crashed into my mind.

When I was 20 I'd landed a lucrative job as a regional sales manager for an automotive manufacturer. As my role drifted away from front line sales (to teach others to sell), my childhood dream to become an airline pilot caught up with me. So I saved, begged, borrowed, and sold. The training was going to be expensive as I was self-sponsored.

Anyway, I finally got my commercial pilot's license in 1993, but there was still a bad recession, so no airline jobs going. And I had NO money. And I really mean *none*. My pilot training had wiped me out and I had no income at all. I've never been so poor in my life; I literally didn't know where the next meal was coming from. So, I contacted an old friend who used to sell cars with me to see if he could get me a job selling for a while. It turned out he was now a realtor and he got me a job at the branch he was working at.

I wasn't happy. I was now a trained airline pilot, and here I was back in sales. Not only that, but I was selling something I had no clue about: houses. I would just bide my time and wait for the airlines to start recruiting.

But as it turned out, selling houses was a whole lot easier than selling cars. I didn't have to know a bunch of product knowledge, I didn't have to deliver anything, and if the house broke after the sale it wasn't my problem! There was just one teensy-weensy problem...

Nobody was buying any darn houses!

Being a realtor in 1993, I can tell you, you couldn't *give* houses away back then. Moreover, we would sometimes be required to be the first people to enter a foreclosed property after the owner had left. Sometimes the "owner" was still there, sitting in a pile of ashes. I had one man break down in tears in front of me, explaining how his wife had left him and taken the children because of the foreclosure, as he clutched one of his young daughter's drawings. Poor guy—I'll never forget his face.

I wasn't having fun.

And it was on that day, in a freshly foreclosed home on a rainy day back in 1993, that I saw an abandoned tricycle, and I imagined the conversation that had surrounded its abandonment. I saw that empty tricycle as a symbol of the low point of despair I felt in the economy then. It seemed property was doomed forever. Nobody was buying and everybody was saying they never would again. I wanted out.

I would stare into my prospecting diary on my desk and pray that Richard Branson would just walk in and save me by giving me a pilot job for Virgin. But at the other end of our premises there was a lot of activity, and that made me curious.

We may not have been selling any houses, but the rental department was going crazy. Hands were being shaken and jangling keys were palmed over all day long, and the rentals manager was a happy guy.

I asked him how much one-bedroom apartments rented for. The rental manager said around 500-600 a month, and that he couldn't get enough units to rent. It made sense as nobody was buying, and they had to live somewhere. As the rentals manager said, "People will never stop making tricycle motors, will they? Boom or bust, people will always need somewhere to live."

I asked the mortgage guy how much deposit I would need to buy a one bedroom apartment, and what the monthly payment would be. There was a reasonable profit there of a couple of hundred a month, but the deposit would be three grand. I didn't have a penny to invest, but I kept it in mind.

A week later one of the owners of a listed property called me and asked about any viewings. But instead of giving him the usual bad news, I had an idea. I asked if I could go and meet him at the property that night after work. He agreed.

When I met him later, I made my proposition: "Your home is listed at fifty grand, yes?"

"Yes," he said.

I said, "Well, would you accept forty-seven grand for it?"

"In this market? Of course!" he said.

"Well," I said, "What if I gave you fifty grand, but you paid my three-grand deposit?"

He thought about it for a second, then, as the light went on, he agreed.

A month later I walked into his property as the new owner, and I hadn't spent a penny. Better still, the bank that had provided the mortgage had given me a cash back bonus, so I was actually up already!

Then the nerves set in: "Will I get a tenant though?" I sweated for all of a week over this, but what would be the worst case when I hadn't invested any money in it?

Everyone thought I was crazy. Colleagues told me there were many more foreclosures still to hit the market, and that the property market was dead forever.

As the rental manager had promised though, a good tenant moved in a few weeks after closing. I was 23, a property investor, and feeling pleased with myself. So I did it again. And again.

A year later the economy had started to turn, and I got a flying job for a regional airline. But I had been bitten by the bug. My profession was a pilot, but my **business** was property. And we all know what happened to property prices after 1993.

Back to present day, 2009 and sunny Florida, I walked back to the patio and stared at that abandoned tricycle again, just like the one I'd seen in that foreclosed house in 1993, then muttered to myself, "We've been here before. When will we ever learn?"

How can we make sure we're on the right side of this cycle? The answer is the same answer we discussed earlier with options trading: it's all about *time*, or *timing* to be exact.

Little did I know back in 1993, but I had inadvertently caught a ride on what I refer to as The Great Cycle. You need to catch this ride, for it could catapult you to your Freedom Figure... OR it could tear you away from it if you get on the wrong side of it!

This uncannily accurate prophecy will make or break you, it's that simple.

Time your plans according to this consistently correct prophecy and *this secret alone will make you free* with what I'll be teaching you here (this was how I first became financially independent). But be on the *wrong* side of this prophecy and the path to freedom will become so long that you won't have enough years left to make it to the end—your dreams will die with you.

In the coming lessons I'll be explaining this secret a lot deeper, but more than that, I'll be passing on the 1-2-3 step systems that are supercharged by using it. When you combine this super-accurate secret with the clever tricks I've used in the past, this one secret could be all you need to retire. I really can't emphasize the power of this highly enough.

You must know the secret of The Great Cycle. It's time to introduce a brand-new secret, and none of the secrets I'm explaining in this course are as emphatic about the time factor as this one. **The 5th Secret:**

"Behold, there come seven years of great plenty throughout all the land of Egypt. And there shall arise after them seven years of famine." - Genesis 41:27

It's all about *time.* The message is clear: seven good years in the economy and real estate market, and seven bad years. You probably know this already because you've seen good times and bad times, *but did you see them coming?* Most people don't see these times coming. In fact, most people do precisely the wrong thing at the right time and do the wrong thing at the right time! Your stock market training is the perfect platform to build on because you now understand the importance of identifying cycles and riding them on the upside and getting out before the inevitable downside begins.

So this secret says there are seven good years and seven bad ones, but how do you know *when* the seven years begin and end? *How* will you see the next cycle coming? It's vital you know this secret for our next two paths to freedom: real estate and business. In the next chapter, I'll show you precisely how to see these seven-year cycles coming as we continue harnessing the power of *time* for riches...

Chapter 8:
The Secret of Kings

Choose One: a) Feast b) Famine

"Behold, there come seven years of great plenty throughout all the land of Egypt. And there shall arise after them seven years of famine." - Genesis 41:27

A s I mentioned, you *must* learn to be in time with The Great Cycle. This cycle is like a double-edged sword; it is make or break. And even when you do know how to see this "invisible" cycle coming, it will often be counterintuitive to act upon it. What I mean is that when The Great Cycle is telling you to sell everything and prepare for bad times, this warning often comes when everyone else is doing the opposite and buying like crazy. Likewise, when The Great Cycle is telling you to buy everything, this message comes at a time when everyone else is pessimistic and selling everything. As King Solomon cautions:

"There is a way which seemeth right to a man, but the end thereof are the ways of death." – Proverbs 14:12

It's all very well knowing this secret, but you have to ask yourself an important question to be able to actually *use* it:

Are you able to act independently of the herd mentality?

Think about situations in life where you've done things purely because of peer pressure or because you said to yourself, "If everyone's doing it then I should do it." Remember, the vast majority of people, sadly, are poor. The majority has no real wealth, and simply live month to month. With that in mind, why would you worry about what *most people* are doing/saying/

thinking?

I'm going to reveal an incredible secret now: The Great Cycle...

This is how The Great Cycle looked for the last 37 years in our three paths to freedom: stocks, real estate, and the economy (business). It's the same time frame that we looked at for the stock market—37 years is a good sample; about the entire career of a person, enough to see everything there is to see. Don't worry just yet about the right-hand column ('recession Gap"), as I'll explain that next. The STOCKS column reflects buy and sell triggers given by our Secret of Seventy system. Take a look through this, try to recall what you did and how you felt on certain years, and then I will reveal the code that's hidden in it...

	STOCKS	REAL ESTATE	THE ECONOMY	RECESSION GAP
1980			RECESSION	5.8
1981	SELL		RECESSION	
1982	BUY	BUY	RECESSION	
1983				
1984	SELL, BUY			
1985				
1986				
1987	SELL			
1988	BUY			
1989				
1990	SELL	SELL	RECESSION	7.7
1991	BUY		RECESSION	
1992				
1993				
1994				
1995	BUY			
1996				
1997				
1998	SELL,BUY	BUY		
1999				
2000	SELL			
2001			RECESSION	10
2002				
2003	BUY			
2004				
2005				
2006		SELL		
2007	SELL		RECESSION	6
2008			RECESSION	
2009	BUY		RECESSION	
2010	SELL,BUY			
2011				
2012	SELL,BUY			
2013				
2014		BUY		
2015				
2016	BUY			

I strongly suggest you tear out that page and keep it somewhere safe. Now, for those times that you can recall in those 37 years (or have you conveniently erased them from your memory?!), did you buy and sell at the right times? Or did you do the opposite? Were you braced for those recessions or did they blindside you?

Don't feel bad if you found yourself on the wrong side of The Great Cycle. The past is gone forever. What matters is the *now*, and that we trust in what the universe is telling us.

"A man's heart deviseth his way: but the Lord directeth his steps." – Proverbs 16:9

So, what's the hidden code within The Great Cycle? Look closely and you'll see it. The secret is a single number. This number is *the most referenced number in The Bible.*

Used 735 times (54 times in the book of Revelation alone—the final book that is a *reckoning*), the number 7 symbolizes the foundation of God's word. Seven is the number of completeness and perfection (both physical and spiritual). It derives much of its meaning from being tied directly to God's creation of all things. The word "created" is used 7 times describing God's creative work (Genesis 1:1, 21, 27 three times; 2:3; 2:4). There are 7 days in a week and God's Sabbath is on the 7th day. The Bible, as a whole, was originally divided into 7 major divisions. There are at least seven men in the Old Testament who are specifically mentioned as a man of God. They are Moses (Joshua 14:6), David (2Chronicles 8:14), Samuel (1Samuel 9:6, 14), Shemaiah (1Kings 12:22), Elijah (1Kings 17:18), Elisha (2Kings 5:8) and Igdaliah (Jeremiah 35:4). In the book of Hebrews, written by the apostle Paul, he uses seven titles to refer to Christ. In Matthew 13 Jesus is quoted as giving seven parables (Matthew 13:3 - 9, 24 - 30, 31 - 32, 33, 44, 45 - 46, 47). Seven Psalms are ascribed to David in the New Testament (Psalm 2, 16, 32, 41, 69, 95 and 109). In the book of Revelation there are seven churches, seven angels to the seven churches, seven seals, seven trumpet plagues, seven thunders and the seven last plagues. The first resurrection of the dead takes place at the 7th trumpet, completing salvation for the Church.

I could go on, but you get the message! Seven is the most powerful number in The Bible. Now let's look at each path to freedom in turn as we see the uncanny relevance of the number 7, and how this number unlocks the secret to The Great Cycle…

STOCKS:

You already know this one from The Secret of Seventy. Seventy is the product of 7 and 10, 10 being a "perfect" number. You already know the importance of being on the right side of this cycle.

THE ECONOMY:

Take a look at that right-hand column, "RECESSION GAP." The numbers shown are the number of years between recessions. When you calculate the average of those numbers it comes to 7. The average time between recessions seems to be 7 years. I believe that the unusually long gap of 10 years in the nineties was an anomaly caused by the Internet boom, but the average gap seems to come to 7 years.

You can't set your watch by it because it's an average, but it's very useful to know that when you find yourself in a recession that they don't usually last long and that an average of 7 good years are about to follow.

That's why starting a business after a year or two of recession is actually a smart thing to do, but not what most people would do; most people would start a business when things are booming—the time that usually comes right before the next recession. This is why I asked if you'd be able to mentally resist the power of herd thinking!

Whether you work for someone else, work for yourself, or you have your own business, you must be aware of this cycle and prepare accordingly. More about this one later.

REAL ESTATE:

Real estate seems to be something you *can* set your watch by in The Great Cycle. Those BUY and SELL entries on that table are based on what were the ideal times to buy and sell property. If you look carefully and reflect on past events, I'm sure you'll agree. For example, selling property in 2006 would obviously have been an excellent idea! But that was the precise year when *most people* were *buying*.

Now, here's where it gets interesting. *Count the number of years in between each BUY and SELL indicator on the REAL ESTATE column.* What is that number?

SEVEN. There are 7 years in between the ideal time to buy and sell real estate. Whether it's your personal residence or investment property, you *must* become synchronized with this real estate cycle! If you do, you will make a LOT of money.

If not, your plans for a swift retirement could suffer critical damage.

Combine this knowledge with all the clever tricks I will teach you about real estate, and you will have a solid path to your Freedom Figure.

So let's begin, starting with the basics...

I will be showing you proven methods of buying properties to provide you with passive income, using none or very little of your own money. Those by itself represent minimal risk, of course, but let's understand why real estate itself is a relatively safe investment of your time.

Would your bank manager give you a loan to buy some shares? Of course not! Would he give you a loan to buy property? Yes—and give you a much lower interest rate than any other type of loan! Why? Because property is considered a safe investment; if you default on the loan, the bank can easily get their money back by taking back the property. Plus, you get a tax-deduction on the interest you pay AND you're allowed to claim back depreciation (!). More about this at a later stage, but the advantages of property are endless!

PLUS, property increases with inflation but the borrowing on it stays the same. Say you buy a house for $200,000 with an $180,000 mortgage. In 20 years, the value of the property could very easily be $600,000, but the mortgage debt would be the same!

The greater the demand is, in relation to the supply of something available, the higher the prices become, right? So what is the overriding supply/demand factor in the property market?

First Time Buyers.

What's going on in these people's heads is the key to it all. Let's become clear about just why they're so important.

Firstly, without them, virtually the entire property sales market stagnates. To elaborate, if you own a property already and want to move, you need a buyer, and for them to sell their property they need a buyer and so on. Very obvious I know, but it's an important principle to always bear in mind. For the whole chain of buyers to start moving there needs to be someone at the bottom—a first time buyer.

So what makes them tick? Who are these upstarts that we have to pay so much consideration to? It stands to reason that they are younger people, aged 18 to 30 usually, and often childless couples. Probably in the early stages of their career, job security and relocation are key factors that dictate their buy/rent decision.

Clearly, if the economy is doing fine, they feel secure in their jobs and their postings, they will have surplus income to save up for deposits and furniture and generally feel confident enough to buy a property rather than rent. Check The Great Cycle regarding the economy.

As well as all that, there's a very simple question going through FTBs" (first time buyers) heads, "Can I afford the monthly payments?"

Notice something: the question they're asking isn't as much about whether the property is worth the money or how the mortgage will be paid off. Generally, as long as the monthly payment fits their budget, they're happy. And what determines affordability? Interest rates.

Is it cheaper to buy or rent? The levels of interest rates answer this question for the FTBs. But either way, you win. Here's how...

So, what's this win/win trick that will set you apart from the crowd and make you profit regardless of what's going on in the heads of FTBs?

Making sure that whatever property you buy is suitable for renting as well as selling!

Get it? People have to live somewhere! If FTBs are in a buying mood, you profit by selling them property; if they are unsure, then you profit by renting them property. As a rule anyway though, there is pretty much always a rental and purchasing market if you know what you're doing. **In any case, it's all about *creating value* in a property.**

So there now follows a list of possible modifications/ improvements to properties. We're going to play a little game now to get you thinking! What I want you to do is arrange these things in order of what you think offers the best return for money spent, i.e. which ones have the biggest effect on the value of a property in relation to what it cost to do them.

- ✓ **Converting the garage into another room**
- ✓ **Swimming pool**
- ✓ **Tasteful remodeling**
- ✓ **Landscaping/tidying the garden**
- ✓ **New kitchen**
- ✓ **New bathroom**
- ✓ **New carpets**
- ✓ **Creating a carport when there wasn't one before**

When you've finished, take a look at what follows to find the correct order.

1) **Creating a carport when there wasn't one before** (we'll talk about why in a second)
2) **Landscaping/tidying the garden** (presentation and convenience)
3) **Tasteful remodeling** (as above)
4) **New carpets** (as above)
5) **New kitchen**
6) **New bathroom**
7) **Swimming pool** (a bonus, nothing more)
8) **Converting the garage into another room** (this is likely to devalue the property)

Do you see? It all comes down to convenience and packaging. Now listen up, this is the essence of making money from buying and selling property: *The things that cost the least to-do are the things that put the most value on a property!*

I know people who make their living *just* from this simple piece of knowledge—I'm talking more than most people earn in a year.

Most people work harder than ever before—they have less time and more money as a result. People lack imagination and the foresight to picture how a property *could* look if they did all the work themselves. Presentation is everything. They want something they can just move into—a ready-made home. And convenience carries a price! That is where the shrewd property developer comes in.

A carport can be installed for as little as $1000 but will

increase the value of the property by as much as $10,000!

Let's think about this for a second. Say you buy a property for $100,000. Forget about arranging the finances and the down payment for now, because later I'll be showing you how to do all this, even if you have no down-payment and a lousy credit-rating.

You get the property with a $10,000 down payment, which you may have borrowed from the bank. Okay, so you then install a carport for $1000 and tidy up the yard and remodel and get the property refinanced at a new, increased value of $120,000. The bank then advances you 90% of the new value = $108,000 mortgage.

With that $108,000 you pay off the original $90,000 mortgage, leaving you with $18,000.

With that $18,000, you pay off the loan you took out for the $11,000 for the down payment and the carport, leaving you with $7,000. Closing costs would run at about $5,000. This leaves you with $2,000 AND a property that earns you a rental income of approximately $150 a month after expenses!

You didn't use a penny of your own money and you walked away with $2,000 in your pocket and a monthly income. Do enough of these and there's your Freedom Figure.

You think there would be too much competition to find a property without a carport? Just the opposite. Most people would turn away BECAUSE it doesn't have one.

Something else to consider when thinking about improving either your own home or a future investment property is this: 50% of buyers have made up their mind by the time they walk through the front door. The front of the house should look tidy. The hallways bright and new. You should always show potential buyers the best parts first in a viewing. Keep the colors fairly universal—creams and beiges work the best.

People aren't just buying your home though. They are buying your lifestyle. Strange as it may seem, buyers seem to forget that all the nice furniture, dishwasher and TV are not sold with the house. Pay careful attention to lighting. Set the dinner table. Put the yard furniture out. You get the idea. Simple, but this is very important. Obviously this doesn't apply in whole to investment property, but this demonstrates the classic trait of human nature that will make you a great deal of money— laziness!

I don't care what anyone tells you, bargains ARE out there. Too many people think if something sounds too good to be true, it must be. If that's what they choose to believe, every time you come across something that sounds too good to be true, (like a property worth $250,000 that's on the market for $200,000) you'll dismiss it as a hoax and move on to more "believable" deals.

Let me give you a few reasons why bargains that could make you $50,000 quickly are sitting in your own city today, just waiting for you:

1. Divorce.

Sadly, this is usually the most common reason properties are sold well below value. They just want "out" so the couple in question can get on with their lives.

2. Not getting an appraisal.

People think they're saving a buck or two by not bothering with an appraisal of their property. Very often, they may not appreciate how much their house is worth.

3. Foreclosure.

Banks aren't in the property business; they're in the lending business and they just want their money back quickly. This means a bargain price usually.

4. Realization of an inheritance.

A property may have been left in a will to a few children. They won't be greedy, as this is money they didn't have anyway. They'll just want the money out quickly.

There are many reasons, but they all come down to one thing: *A Motivated Seller*. These are the people you must home in on to find the bargains in your city. I'll be showing you how to uncover the bargains in your city, later on. Motivated sellers make up about 5% of all sellers, but they're quite easy to spot when you've had some practice. They are irrational and very flexible.

Previously, I explained why debt was a bad thing. But, in fact, debt is a double-edged sword; it can work for you or against you. It works against you when you borrow money to buy things which don't give you any income. However, if you borrow things that DO bring you income, debt is a GOOD thing. Make sense? Let me explain further…

How the "Money-Changers" can Make You Rich!

If you're a homeowner, you've already probably made money from buying property—your house is probably worth far more than you paid for it. Well, although what you say is true, any gain on the property you live in is in fact "paper money," because you don't have access to the capital, and if you sell the house, the next place you buy would eat up all your capital, unless you downsize. Let's take a typical example:

John bought a house for $100,000 with a 5% deposit of $5,000. He cosmetically improved the property for little expense and a few months later he sold it for $120,000.

After paying closing costs he was left with a profit of $14,000. Now a question: Please can you tell me the percentage net profit John made on this property?

Are you thinking the following? Profit = $14,000? 14,000 as a percentage of 100,000 (cost of home) = **14%?**

Well you're wrong! How does **280% profit** sound?

Absolutely true, and if you think back to our conversation about trading options you'll remember why. You see, John's investment was only the deposit of $5,000. If he proceeds to make a profit of $14,000 from it, that's a 280% return on investment.

This process is called gearing. It involves using other people's money (OPM) as leverage to get more "bang for your buck." **More fortunes have been built on borrowed money than any other way! And this is how you can gain financial freedom from a relatively small amount of money.**

Please note the difference between consumer and commercial credit. Consumer credit involves buying a load of depreciating assets such as stereos and TVs at ludicrous rates of interest. Commercial credit is good but consumer credit is bad and it is most important that you learn to distinguish the two if you want to grow wealthy.

9 Steps to a Million

In a previous lesson, I showed you the power of compounding. Now I'm going to show you what happens when you combine the power of compounding with the power of gearing.

Let me show you how compounding and gearing turn $5,000 into $1,000,000 in nine simple steps. If you don't have $5,000 right now, don't worry, as I'll be showing you how to start with absolutely nothing.

If you can make even a 100% return on your investment, once you can do it again, only by using the power of compounding, you can buy two properties or a bigger property and so your profits keep multiplying. Let me demonstrate your nine steps to a million starting with $5,000 doubling each time:

Property 1 profit = $5,000, so total capital is now $10,000. You buy a property twice as big now.

Property 2 profit = $10,000.

Now you do the same again by buying two properties. Then four properties, then eight, and so on.

Stage 3 profit = $20,000.

Stage 4 profit = $40,000.

Stage 5 profit = $80,000.

Stage 6 profit = $160,000.

Stage 7 profit = $320,000.

Stage 8 profit = $640,000.

Stage 9 profit = $1,280,000.

You won't even have to pay any tax on that, as I'll explain later!

Now let me tackle all the common objections most people have about property. By the way, MOST people will have a problem with investing in real estate and they will tell you as much. But remember once again, MOST people are also poor or hopelessly trapped, living from paycheck to paycheck! Is it worth listening to them about real estate? In fact, doing the OPPOSITE to them sounds like a great plan, as you've now seen. The secret of The Great Cycle is the secret of kings, not common people.

"It's not possible to get a 95% mortgage!"

There are banks that will do this. Check out the Internet. Even if you can only find an 80% mortgage, what's to stop you borrowing some of the equity on your existing home? I'll also be showing you how to construct deals where you don't part with a dime… and even walk away with cash in your pocket.

"What if I lose a tenant?"

You just get another. I'll be showing you how to get and keep the best tenants.

"I don't want calls from tenants in the middle of the night to go and fix a toilet!"

What makes you think I do? I don't know one end of a hammer from the other! I'll be explaining how to get a suitable management company to do all this for you while you take it easy.

Okay, now let's get started on how to actually do it!

More Biblical Numbers at Work

Perhaps you or someone you know has considered investing in real estate but decided against it, as there were no suitable properties to be found. This usually means they took an afternoon to look at a couple of local properties and then gave up...

Here's the rule: If you look at 100 properties, put offers in on 10 and try to arrange financing for 3, you MAY end up buying 1.

Amateurs ignore this principle which is why they always believe, "all the good ones have gone already." Don't worry though, it's not as much hard work as it sounds. By looking at 100, I don't mean actually physically seeing the property; you might just look at the details on paper after a realtor faxed them to you.

After you've seen around 20, you should be getting a good idea about what represents a bargain in your criteria. How are you supposed to find time for this? Come on, arrange it properly and you can easily see 15-20 properties in a day! You either want financial freedom or you don't. It may seem like hard work now, but it's all so you can take life easy in the future! Think about WHY you're doing it. Here's a neat idea if you're really pushed for time: Recruit a bunch of college students or teenagers. Tell them specifically what you're looking for and tell them you'll give them a hundred bucks if they find a suitable property that you end up buying.

So now let's see just what we're looking for and how to find it…

The Classified Ads can be Goldmines!

I'm talking about the small ads of just a few lines in local publications, notice boards, and on the Internet in places like Craig's List. These are prime nesting grounds for motivated sellers. These are people who are clearly not using a realtor. This means they quite often don't know the true value of their property. Sure, sometimes they'll want way over market value, but, by the same token, they will also be sometimes way under. Plus, they'll have less interest this way as opposed to having a realtor arrange viewings. *This means they'll be more open to offers.*

I Love Realtors And So Should You!

I want you to go and do something you never thought you could ever do—go out and hug a realtor today! Why do some people get offered ripe investment properties before others? Because they know how realtors think and work. Once upon a time, I was a realtor and I learned a great deal. When a new property comes on to the market, they will call the people who are the strongest prospects first—i.e. the people who are serious and can move fast.

You'll need to introduce yourself to the realtors in your chosen area and state your intentions. Befriend them. Take them out for a beer and a sandwich or whatever. Be professional; the knowledge in this book will enable you to talk like a pro. Realtors know that serious developers move fast and that way they get their commission guaranteed fast. Realtors love property developers.

Breaking the ice and making your first deal is the hardest part. Gain their trust by not wasting their time and by following through with all offers you make. Tell them that you will be at the property within twenty minutes of him phoning you with the details! And make sure you're there. Time is of the essence once a good development property comes on to the market. Plus, this lets the realtor know early on that you're not a time waster.

The only way to be able to make fast decisions is to know the local market back-to-front in terms of prices. Learn what prices properties are actually selling for rather than what they're on the market for—there's a big difference sometimes! A neat way of giving yourself a crash course in discovering what's what in the area is to pick a day and ask an agent to show you a dozen properties with the most development potential. When you make these viewings, ask as many questions as possible.

Don't spread your market knowledge thin by trying to deal in loads of different areas; select just one. Knowing your market is key.

Other Pointers for dealing with realtors:

- Never use just one, have several working for you.

- Work with realtors who are property investors themselves, if possible.

- Walk into a realtor's office and ask who the best person is to talk to regarding investment properties. IF someone comes forward, ask them what the best investment property they have on their books is. IF they give you one, ask them WHY they think so.

If you're really having trouble getting off first base, it's time to start fishing. Here's a good way to jolt yourself into action: ask the realtor to show you all properties that have been on the market for more than four months. This way, the very least you'll accomplish is to learn why these properties are not selling, but you may even stumble across a bargain that everyone else has missed—remember the owners of these properties might be getting desperate now and could be open to a low offer!

Pay close attention to this "bullet" guide:

- ✔ Area. You should aim to buy in a fairly established town— this way there will be some older properties that have renovation potential (= profit). There will also be established service and transport links.

✔ The area is more important than the actual property. A smaller property but in a better area will have more profit potential than a larger property in a poorer area. The poverty gap is widening and people will pay a premium for the "right" area.

✔ The standard of schools varies widely from one area to another and, as you know, children are generally only allowed to go to the schools within their area. If a family home is within the area of the good school in the area, it will sell quickly.

✔ Trying to spot an up and coming area is too risky, really. If you get it wrong you could be out of pocket, so keep it safe and simple by sticking to good quality areas that are already established. This way there will also be more renovation potential as discussed. A good way to spot an area that is just about to become quality is when a Starbucks (or similar) opens up there.

✔ Bear in mind the people you are trying to attract. People want to live in an area where there are other people like them.

✔ Visit the area/property at night, at the weekend and at a weekday to get a true picture—at different times of the week a street can become totally different. Facilities, shops, and good transport links should be reasonably close by.

✔ If possible avoid properties close to railway lines, pylons and telephone masts.

- Some streets can be deceptive. It may appear that it is dominated by houses when in fact they are all converted into apartments and this will result in parking problems because of the extra capacity of cars the road was not designed for. The trick here is to count the number of doorbells on each property.

- A little bonus that will serve you well is trying to get a property with just one special feature—particularly in an area where the houses are very similar. This gives the property an unquantifiable uniqueness that justifies a higher price than the others in the area.

I've told you how to get realtors on your side—having a network of reliable "bird dogs" is by far the easiest. But there are other ways to find the right investment property. Private ads and leaflet drops are other good ways—you have the advantage of offering no agent commission too.

Here's a sample letter and leaflet:

(Your address)
Date

Dear Sir/Madam,

I'm sorry for writing to you out of the blue like this, but I was passing your house today and realized that

it's just the thing I'm looking for. I didn't see a "For Sale" sign outside so I wondered if the property was for sale or if you are considering selling in the near future. The benefits of this for you are of course a saving on realtors" fees of around 8% of the purchase price!

Please let me assure you that I am not a realtor. I have the deposit and mortgage in place and am therefore in an excellent position to move quickly and have no chain beneath me.

If you have no intention of selling now, then I apologize for disturbing you, but can I ask that you keep this letter safely tucked away somewhere in case your future situation changes?

Thank you.

Get the idea? Don't make it too slick (= untrustworthy) and don't make it look like the sort of thing realtors put through doors (i.e. don't use headed paper).

Now here's an ad you can use…

Property Urgently Required!

Probate, repossessions, scruffy properties needed. No chain, quick sale. We will view anything in any condition. Save realtor fees and release the value of your asset.

Call 123 456 7890

This is the sort of thing you just leave everywhere and anywhere as often as possible. On cars, through mailboxes, in realtor's offices, etc. Even when you send a check off to pay a bill, stick one in—the person who opens it is a potential seller. People keep things like this for never knowing when they might need it. People inherit property all the time and just want a quick return on it.

If you put an advertisement like this around enough or even put it in a local newspaper, you can be prepared for some calls. Here are the questions you will need to ask people when they phone:

1. Is the property already listed with a realtor?

First question. The best ones are usually not listed, but if it is already listed, don't be put off—remember, the seller will be inclined to take a lower offer by saving on agent's commission. Plus, the fact that if the property is listed and the seller is phoning you, then he's getting desperate.

2. Where is the property?

Get the full address. If you don't recognize it, ask where it is. If the area is not a good one, don't let that rule a purchase out completely.

3. What is the asking price?

4. What is the condition?

5. Why are you selling?

It's unlikely that the seller will have prepared for the last question so you might catch them off guard and get an honest answer! We want to qualify each call thoroughly without scaring them away. Conclude the conversation by arranging to view the property.

Other Methods

✔ Keep a voice recorder (on most phones now) or notepad in your car and as you drive around, start to notice properties that are looking shabby and put a leaflet through their door, stating an interest in buying if at any time in the future they were interested.

✔ Visit your local planning department and ask about condemned properties.

✔ Get referrals. Whether people you come into contact with sell, buy, or don't do either, tell them that you will pay $200 cash for introducing you to a buyer or seller that results in a deal payable upon exchange of contracts.

Traps for the Unwary

You need to be able to tell the difference between cosmetic distress and serious problems with a property, and fortunately, with a little experience it's not that difficult. If the place has had all the doors ripped off, the décor is non-existent, the floor is saturated with pet urine, the kitchen is encrusted with grease and the garden resembles the Amazon jungle, that's absolutely perfect! IF the price reflects it of course—for this you need to compare similar properties but in good condition as a guide for profit potential.

1. However, if there are sloping floors, this suggests a problem with the foundation, for example.

2. Long cracks in the outside walls are a warning sign for subsidence.

3. Whenever you view a property, be sure to turn on all taps, flush all toilets and test the heating/ac system. Be sure to turn on the highest tap in the premises.

4. To test for wet rot, slide a pocket-knife into the wood suspected at a right-angle to the grain. If it penetrates easily, there is a wet rot problem.

5. Woodworm is easily visible (small holes) but the best place to look for it is under carpets and around toilets.

6. Dry rot is indicated by cube-shaped cracks in wood.

If in doubt, take a professional tradesman with you. We'll be covering renovation in detail.

Even though you now know the timing of The Great Cycle, you don't have to simply buy when property is at its cheapest and then sell it at a later time (7 years later). You can make more money by being active. *The point here is that your activity is simply aware of The Great Cycle so it doesn't affect your real estate operations!*

If you are reading this at a time when property prices have been knocked hard, perhaps because of recession, then great! But don't sit around waiting for it. The strategy of the players is to buy properties that are in need of cosmetic work because, if you recall, the things that cost the less to do to a property increase its value disproportionately.

But what happens if you can't sell it quickly? You'll be stuck paying the interest on it every month! That's why any property you buy for the purposes of resale should also be suitable for leasing!

And always remember here that the larger properties attract less rent as a percentage of their value, so it is probably a better strategy to buy several smaller properties than one or two big ones. Give yourself a deadline by which you will either have an offer on the property or a tenant installed—two months maybe.

Absolute fortunes are made from buying run-down property in recessions and then renting them out until the boom times return and then selling them.

Now I want to explain something called The Rule of Margin:

You need to achieve a 20% mark up after all costs on the resale of the property.

The reason for this is to discipline you into not buying property too expensive. If you can't make 20% then move on to the next one! Observe the two commandments and brand them into your forehead:

1. Anything you buy must be equally suited to both rental and resale.

2. You must always, always use the 20% rule!

How will you achieve freedom? Slash your expenses and raise your passive income, right? One of the ways to increase your passive income is through renting out property.

Many people can't get the deposit together or have a poor credit rating. Many are in a transient stage in their lives and don't want to be tied down. And many are in between houses, perhaps due to relocation or divorce. There will always be a large number of people that choose to rent rather than buy. Recession? Brilliant. Even more people will be renting than buying from fear of committing savings or losing their job.

Let's do some example figures:

One bedroom condo value = say $60,000
Deposit of 20% = $12,000
Monthly mortgage payments on balance (6%) = $240
Property Tax = $60
Monthly rent = $550
Monthly profit = $250 PLUS appreciation in property value

"That's all very well if you've got $12,000 to spare!" True, which is why over this course I'll be showing you how to buy a rental property with no deposit at all. Now though, I want to talk about the actual principles behind leasing.

Just think if you had ten of these properties! You could live off the rent for the good 7 years and then sell them at the right time and have made so much on the appreciation in value that you could retire very comfortably indeed. The very wealthy are acutely aware of this fact, which is why real estate is always at the core of their investment portfolio. Most of them made their money by running a business and pumping the proceeds into shares and real estate.

Let's now talk about expected rental yields (income) from different types of property. Don't make the mistake of thinking that the larger the property value, the larger the rent! It's actually the other way around. The reason being that there is a higher demand for smaller. Look at the following table:

Average rentals as a percentage of the property value

Furnished Rooms	**19.3%**
1 Bedroom Apartment	**12.5%**
2 Bedroom Apartment	**11.5%**
2 Bedroom House	**10%**
3 Bedroom House	**8.1%**
4 Bedroom House	**6.3%**

We'll talk more about furnished rooms later.

With apartments/condos, you do have to take into account community charges for maintenance of the communal block facilities (entrance hall painting, gardening etc.), which vary from one apartment to the next. Even so, one and two bedroom apartments are very good news in the right location (more on this another time). Small one and two bedroom houses are also worth considering and have the benefit of being free of any maintenance charges. Now have a look at this table to demonstrate the fact that smaller properties are better for rental:

Size of Property	Avg. number of vacant weeks per year
1 Bed/Studio	2
2 Beds	3
3 Beds	4
4 Beds	5
5 Beds	6

Now this is important. **There is an inverse relationship between properties for capital appreciation and properties for rental income.** That is to say, a one-bedroom apartment will give you a higher rental yield, but at the other end of the scale, a luxury four-bedroom house may give a lower rental yield, but the actual property will appreciate more in value each year. So it depends on what you want. The two ways to make money from properties are:

1. **Buying and selling for profit—larger properties.**

2. **Renting—smaller properties.**

There's no reason why you can't do both, but don't ever confuse the two!

You also need to allow for a leasing agent's management fees which are usually 10% of the annual rent. Please don't bother trying to do this for yourself—believe me, the fees are worth it as long as you find a good one. The thing is, that good ones are few and far between.

Their job is to find you a tenant ASAP and keep them there as long as possible. They should check the tenant's credit and stability of employment, write an inventory, document the condition of the property and move the tenant in. But make no mistake, all they are interested in, quite rightly, is their cut. If your property is vacant for a few months, they don't lose out— you do. If the tenant misses a month's rent, they don't lose out— you do because they get their fees in advance—they will collect one month's rent in advance and one month's rent as deposit from the tenant and deduct their annual fee from it.

With this in mind, it's important that you choose your agent very carefully indeed. The following tips on what to look for are extremely important:

- A prominent location that will attract potential tenants and regular advertisements in the local paper. If someone is offering low fees it's because they can afford to, by not having these things in place—don't be tempted!

- Conduct a "mystery shop" on them. Phone up pretending to be a potential tenant and judge their customer service skills. Ask yourself if you would be comfortable renting something from them.

- Check that they have indemnity insurance.

- It's a good sign if many of their clients are companies.

Companies use rental agents for relocating staff often and this is very good news indeed. You can charge more and the rent is always paid.

- Make sure it isn't just "bolted on" as a sideline for a realtor. Many of the best ones are affiliated with realtors but be sure that it is a totally separate and dedicated department.

- Ask them outright why you should use them as opposed to their competitors.

Your aim is to find a good agent and build a relationship with them that will last a long time. Explain to them that you plan to expand over the years and want someone to count on. They will offer you "full management" for an additional 5% a year. For this, you can basically leave everything down to them—they arrange all repairs and maintenance as and when it happens. Now, this depends on you and your situation, but I advise against it. I'll be showing you how to do a much better job yourself for little effort and it's a great way to learn more about this business anyway.

Now here's the most important thing to remember with leasing agents: they want you to charge as little as possible in monthly rent! The reason?

Well let's say you could get $600 a month in rent. If they can knock you down to $550 a month they'll be able to lease it easily and make their money quicker—they'll only be $5 down a month (10% of $550 as opposed to 10% of $600) but you'll be $50 down a month!

At the same time if your property is too expensive, it may remain vacant for a while and this is something you definitely don't want. Study prices and know your market. Combine this knowledge with how much you feel you can trust the agent and set a price that will pull tenants in. Of course, when the property is viewed, this will make the decision for them if it's right, and this is a whole new trick.

I bet your mind is filled with problems about this, isn't it? What if they don't pay the rent? What if they damage the place? What if they move out? Blah, blah. Excuse me, but this is nothing more than putting obstacles in the way! Your mind senses upheaval and is trying to protect you. Let me tell you something:

A real problem is having to be a wage slave for the rest of your life constantly depending on other people for the next pay-check!

Sure, you're going to run into problems occasionally, even with all the advice I will be giving you here. Deal with it—it only becomes a problem when you make it. Don't start cursing and blaming me for it— "I knew this was a bad idea!" That's the loser mind set.

Put yourself in the shoes of the type of people you want to attract. Your tenants are likely to be working people, possibly without a car and in a transient point in their lives. The following pointers will guide you to getting the right rental property:

- Make sure there are a few large companies around, especially big names—this is good news for relocation tenancies, which pay top dollar on time and are usually long term. What tends to happen is that the company leases the property indefinitely and puts various members of staff in as and when needed.

- As you've seen, apartments produce a higher yield than houses generally. A central as possible location is desirable with good access to public transportation, bars, and stores.

- The town itself should be sustaining growth, not declining. Take a look around—are new developments going up everywhere, or is the whole place generally deteriorating? What is the town's main source of employment? Is this industry in decline or growth?

- It shouldn't be out of easy reach for you. It doesn't have to be in the same town, but any more than two hours" drive would be undesirable from the point of keeping your finger on the pulse.

- Older properties tend to mean more maintenance; A/C, plumbing etc., you just don't want the trouble from the leasing point of view.
- When looking at apartments, ensure you check on payments to the management company for community charges and don't forget to factor this into your business plan.

Once you have found the right property, you need to make it suitable and attractive to tenants with the following advice:

- If the place is cosmetically scruffy, all the better, as you will increase the value drastically with remodeling. If you are going to replace a bathroom make it white and with a kitchen make it dark-colored with durable work surfaces.

- Use neutral or pastel colors when decorating. Carpets should be a medium shade, durable texture; preferably with a speckled pattern as this shows less dirt, stains, and marks. Apartments generally have quite small rooms so you can get good carpet from surplus shops.

- With apartments it is best to get it furnished—especially if you want company leases. This shouldn't cost much because the "minimalist" effect is very attractive and makes the place look bigger.

- Provide a firm double bed, a durable neutral cloth sofa, again, with a slight speckled pattern, a bedside table and perhaps a coffee table and a TV stand. The bed and sofa need to be compliant with modern fire regulations. A great place to get this stuff is shops that specialize in used hotel furniture.

- Use lamp shades and "soft tone" bulbs but make sure the place isn't too dark—apartments generally have few windows so you need to be creative with lighting to make the place look big.

- Always use rugs in the bedroom, bathroom, and lounge. This protects the carpets and adds a "homely" feel.

- Smoke detectors are a legal requirement and must be serviceable, so it's best to buy these new. Check all local regulations for leasing property also.

- You will also need to provide a washing machine, a stove, and a refrigerator. Again, these can be purchased very cheaply from a second-hand or reconditioning shop—but they must be checked electrically for fire hazards. Ensure the washing machine is fitted well to avoid problems down the line.

- Flea markets, yard sales, dollar stores, etc. are good places to get cheap items. Remember, don't sink too much time and pride into this—the aim is to keep costs down—you're not going to be living there!

- Try to bring your property on to the leasing market in January or August/September. These are the busiest times of the year for tenants. This way, with a one year contract, every time a tenant moves out your vacant weeks should be minimized.

- Use an agent that has an agreement whereby as one tenancy comes to an end, you have the right to have the agent show new prospective tenants the property before the existing tenants have moved out. Used successfully, this technique could reduce your vacant weeks to zero!

The information provided here must be adhered to exactly. You may think it's just my personal opinion or common sense, but believe me, this knowledge has taken years to acquire—the hard way! So if you have the right property equipped in the right way, you have gone a long way to ensuring that it is always rented out for top money with few problems.

Now let's look at some basic procedures for ensuring things stay that way, while building in a little more "safety margin" for ourselves in the process:

- It is well worth making the effort to actually meet tenants at the beginning of the tenancy. Be pleasant and subtly let them think that you've sunk every penny into the place. Tell them you hope they'll have a pleasant time there. If the tenant sees you as an actual honest-working person, they are less likely to abuse the property and get behind on rent. Don't get over-friendly though—this is a business relationship and in the future you need to not feel guilty about raising rents!

- Try to catch small problems before they build into big costly ones. Each time the tenancy is renewed, snatch a moment to give the place a thorough check.

- If maintenance is required don't get the agent to sort it out for you—they won't care how much other people charge you! And don't bother hiring out specialists such as plumbers, etc. —far better to get acquainted with a general handyman for much cheaper rates.

- From time to time, walk past and have a subtle look at the outside of the property. Do not enter though.

- Take photos of the property's inside and all the furniture, as a record.

If you follow all my instructions, you should find tenants quickly and have little problems. If the property is not let out within a week or two, approach the agent. You then either need to find another agent or reduce the price based on your gut feeling, always remembering that the agent wants you to knock the rent down as low as possible.

Finally, the (highly unlikely) problem of non-payment of rent. If you've taken all my advice, and especially if you have company lets, I would be surprised to find you in this situation. Nevertheless, here's what you should do:

- Don't jump to conclusions if the rent doesn't appear on time. Banks make mistakes and so do individuals and there could be a perfectly simple explanation. A belligerent attitude will lose you respect from the tenant. Make a simple enquiry through the agent; failing that, ask the actual tenant.

- Your next step depends on what the outcome of the last one was. Remember all rent is paid in advance, not arrears, and it <u>cannot</u> be allowed to pass—the tenant asking you to use the deposit or pay in arrears is not acceptable.

- If an immediate solution is not forthcoming, you must write a letter giving a deadline by which the outstanding rent must be paid before legal action is taken. Deliver this letter personally at 8:00 am on a Sunday Morning. This is not harassment, just a polite way of letting the tenant know that this will have an impact on their life and privacy. The second letter should repeat the message of the first with the addition of stating that within one week you will place an announcement in the local paper stating the tenants name and what they have done and refer the incident to a credit agency. If they don't pay up after all this, then you've done a lousy job of vetting them in the first place!

Don't be put off by all this talk of non-payment of rent. In all the time I've been doing this I've never even encountered it once so don't take it out of perspective. Like I say, if you do all your homework in the first place it shouldn't be a problem.

Why not start right now? Before you read the next chapter, prove to yourself bargains exist by searching your area using the methods I've given you. Choose a reasonable, quality area of your town. Become an expert on how much a 3 bedroom, 1-2 bath family home costs there. How? By seeing as many family homes as possible in your chosen area. This is the only way you'll be able to spot that bargain.

When you've done that, scour the classified ads. Call every single house for sale and verbally offer 20% below the advertised price and see what happens! Don't worry about actually buying the property; I just want you to realize there is money out there looking for a home and it may as well be yours.

Unlike trading the stock market, as you've now surely realized, the path of real estate involves interacting with other people and getting what you want from the interaction. And on that note the best advice I can give you (and for any networking situation) is from King Solomon again:

"Pleasant words are as an honeycomb, sweet to the soul, and health to the bones." – Proverbs 16:24

All the real estate secrets I'm giving you now are to be used within the right times of The Great Cycle, and next time I'll continue with those as well as move on to yet another brand-new secret, the sixth secret of the seven.

Make the choice, right here and now, to synchronize yourself and everything you do with The Great Cycle. The Great Cycle is correct; the opinions of most people are not. You need to make the right choice to succeed. The secret of The Great Cycle is the closely guarded secret of kings, not his subjects.

Chapter 9: Fortress of Freedom

It's More "When" than "What"

"Remove me far from vanity and lies: give me neither poverty nor riches; feed me with food convenient for me." – Proverbs 30:8

A s we complete our training on using the power of real estate in time with The Great Cycle, let's remind ourselves of why we're on this journey, because it's easy to lose sight of the destination when the journey itself becomes so engrossing.

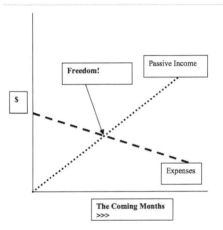

Once we have our expenses reduced as much as possible (without sacrificing the quality of life), our objective is twofold: to build capital, and then put it to work as efficiently as possible so that it gives you a passive income you can live on forever. A passive income is an income that you don't have to work hard for—it requires very little input on your part. When passive income equals your expenses, you're retired.

In previous chapters, we blew away the fog surrounding the stock market, and showed you a remarkably simple way to beat 90% of professionals and get a 36% annual return (based on extensive past performance). When it comes to using real estate as your weapon of choice (and you can use all weapons available, not just one), you need to look at it from two perspectives— two different types of real estate strategies for the two different objectives of building capital (to create your Freedom Figure) and creating a passive income (to live off your Freedom Figure).

To build capital in real estate, the best strategy is to buy LARGER properties, force appreciation in price on them, then sell them for a profit.

To create passive income from real estate, the best strategy is to buy SMALLER properties and then rent them out. If you can also force appreciation on them then all the better.

You need both, but at different stages of your journey. *But above all else, the little-known key to success with all of this is to be on the right side of The Great Cycle.*

It's more about "WHEN" than "WHAT."

Your previous training in the stock market should have made you clearly see that, and the same applies to real estate with that 7-year cycle I showed you last time. This big secret is given to us very clearly in The Bible. And only with that secret firmly in mind can we complete our real estate discussion.

Power Negotiating

If we're going to force appreciation on a property, it stands to reason that our first step is to buy it as cheaply as possible— the money is often made in the buying. So we need to be able to negotiate a good price.

Of course, when it comes to the part of making an offer on a property, no one likes it because haggling is involved and confrontation makes us uncomfortable. But it doesn't need to. Just bear in mind that this is a business transaction and you need to make a profit—it doesn't need to be awkward. There are some crucial techniques that you need to be aware of:

- Virtually everyone with a property to sell expects buyers to come in with an offer that is lower than the asking price. But, and this is the important part, they also expect to have to meet you halfway.

- NEVER say a number first. Whoever does, loses!

- I'll use a real-life example of my own here. The property was up for $98,000. Now amateurs wouldn't expect to get more than a few grand knocked off. After asking him what he realistically expected to get, I offered $89,000 knowing full well they wouldn't accept it. So why bother?

Because the point of meeting halfway has just been lowered—let the haggling commence!

Halfway between $98,000 and $89,000 is $93,500. I actually bought the property for $92,000. You see, they will probably go nuts when they hear your first offer, but your haggling position is starting from a favorable point now and, more importantly, their perception of the value of their property has been lowered. This is why $89,000 has more affect than $90,000—it sounds a great deal lower than the asking price *deliberately.*

- Staple a check to your low offer contract. This can work very well as money is hard to turn down. If they cash your check, they are obliged to accept your offer. This appeals to peoples' greed and they also see that you're serious. Money today is better than a promise of money tomorrow.

- If the seller won't play ball, ask them to justify their stance. Explain that there are properties around that are cheaper and that you are in business to make a profit. Politely!

- Reiterate your buying position—the purchase isn't contingent on your selling of another property, etc. They may not get another offer. Put some uncertainty in their mind because sellers only think what they want to think.

- If you're negotiating through the seller's realtor and they are insulted by your low offer, remind them that they are required *by law* to submit all offers to their clients. Also, dangle your custom in the face of that realtor as a reminder that you could bring them a LOT of business in the future.

- If you end up involved in a bidding match and all interested parties are requested to submit their final offers, here's a neat trick that could get you the property. Most people will offer in round numbers like $110,000. Your offer should always end in 111 e.g. $110,111. Those extra few bucks might just clinch it! The same principles apply to auctions especially.

- A wise seller will be trying not to look desperate even if they actually are. Look for clues in their conversation and around the house when you view the property. Ask probing questions. People won't look at you when they're lying. Watch their eyes—the eyes can't lie. If there are signs of financial difficulty, divorce, job relocation, death of the owner etc. these are the ingredients for a knock-down price (see previous chapter).

Now don't think you're cheating anyone here—they don't have to accept your offer! And you could be doing them a big favor.

Look, I know from personal experience that it can seem like you're taking advantage of people who may have fallen on hard times. I've actually had the dirty job of taking over foreclosed properties for the purpose of resale in my days as a realtor—I've had one owner literally crying on my shoulder as he gave me the keys. You don't need to tell me about how sad it is because I know more than most!

But look at this interesting fact. Only 10-20% of foreclosures involve the owners being evicted from their homes! Many foreclosures are due to fraud, money laundering, and a staggering 80% are due to the owners abandoning it! Anyway, even if it is a hard luck case, you can't help it and it wasn't your fault. Someone's going to make money from the situation so it may as well be you!

Flags to watch

You need to be able to tell the difference between cosmetic distress (=good) and serious problems (=bad) with a property, and fortunately, with a little experience, it's not that difficult.

If the place has had all the doors ripped off, the décor is non-existent, the floor is saturated with pet urine, the kitchen is encrusted with grease, and the garden resembles the Amazon jungle, that's absolutely perfect! IF the price reflects it of course—for this you need to compare similar properties but in good condition as a guide for profit potential.

1. However, if there are sloping floors, this suggests a problem with the foundations, for example.

2. Long cracks in the outside walls are a warning sign for subsidence.

3. Whenever you view a property, be sure to turn on all taps, flush all toilets, and test the AC. Be sure to turn on the highest tap in the premises.

4. To test for wet rot, slide a pocketknife into the wood suspected at a right angle to the grain. If it penetrates easily, there is a wet rot problem.
5. Woodworm is easily visible (small holes) but the best place to look for it is under carpets and around toilets.

6. Dry rot is indicated by cube-shaped cracks in wood.

    If in doubt, take a professional tradesman with you.

Raising the Cash

Remember what we said in the previous chapter about gearing before you start getting nervous about borrowing: More millionaires have been created with other people's money than any other way!

There's a massive difference between consumer and commercial debt—the latter is good and the former is bad. Buying a washing machine with your credit card is a lot different than using the power of gearing to make a 100% return on your investment! We discussed this in an earlier lesson.

Okay, we're going to construct a business plan for your property activities. There's no need to get a headache because there's nothing complicated about it and we need to impress those bank managers by showing we've done our homework (more later).

When buying a property to sell you need to be looking at a 20% mark-up after all costs (remember?) so you start at the price you intend to sell it for and work backwards.

You are able to calculate this by looking at similar properties in the area that are in excellent condition—the condition you will be presenting your property in.

Inside Secrets of Lenders

Does it fill you with dread having to see a banker? You're not alone, but why is it so many of us feel that way? I think it is mostly down to the fact that there is a certain air of mystique around banks and bankers. But the fact is that they are nothing more than money stores and <u>you</u> are the customer; you are going to get them to help you get to freedom!

I have to get you out of the private customer mindset and into the commercial customer mindset. Walk into a bank with your hat in hand for a $10,000 loan for a car and they'll try to hide their yawn as they hand you a form to complete. If you're a businessman, they get excited.

I realized this one day when my bank told me that I now had a personal banker and asked if he could arrange an appointment to see me... at my home! You'll see a different side of banks once they start to take you seriously, and you'll then realize that it is you that is doing them a favor, not the other way around!

Deposits are the lifeblood of banks. Bankers are paid bonuses for bringing them in. If they have your money on deposit for any longer than 24 hours they are making a profit on it. Of course, the other way banks make money is interest on loans, and that's what we're interested in.

When loans go bad, all eyes turn to the person that granted it. It is not only a banker's responsibility to bring in loan business, but to bring in **reliable** loan business.

So although you are the customer, bear in mind that sitting on the other side of the desk there is a nine-to-five worker trying to cover themselves at the same time.

You need to know the six "Cs" that bankers will use to assess your application. In order of importance they are:

1. **Character.** Number one on the list. You can have a solid gold credit score but if they think there's something not right about you, they'll decline the business. It's extremely naïve and idealistic to think that bankers aren't influenced by their

own prejudices and opinions about certain types of people. Generally speaking, bankers reject people far more than the actual loan application. Make sure that everything about you stacks up on paper, and seems consistent. Do an Internet search on yourself first, as well as check any social media, because these days you can bet they will look at all of this!

2. **Capacity.** Capacity to repay. This is based on your earnings and outgoings—your personal balance sheet and profit and loss, which we already covered in an earlier chapter.

3. **Collateral.** The security you have to offer. For our purposes, this is the deposit. If you need to show proof of this, you can always borrow the money temporarily from another source, but be advised that if the loan is from an official lender it will show up on your credit report, and that may mean that you can borrow less. But if you borrow money from another bank it won't show up on your credit search until a few weeks later!

4. **Conditions.** The economic climate at a national and local level and how it affects the type of project you're involved in.

5. **Credit.** Credit history. Notice how low down it is on the list! We'll talk about this in the following chapter.

6. **Capital.** Your net worth—assets and liabilities.

Are you aware that even millionaires get turned down for loans sometimes? It's true. The reason for this is banks are highly regulated in that they must have a balanced investment portfolio. That is to say, loans cannot be focused too highly in one area such as property or businesses in a certain industry. They will try to spread it around for different uses so that they are not exposed to any one area, should it be badly affected for some reason. Obviously, if they had too many property loans and that market went through a bad spell and people started defaulting on their repayments, they would be in difficulty. So you may get turned down for a loan simply because their portfolio is too heavy in that particular area right now, although the banker won't tell you this. Here is how to get what you want out of banks:

- Firstly, be professional. Always arrange an appointment and look the part—suit, tie, polished shoes—the whole deal. NOT because you're groveling but because you are projecting an image of a serious player who can be trusted.

- Put together an attractively presented business plan along with a brief resume about yourself and your intentions. Include your credit report along with explanations for any adverse entries and your assets and liabilities. Package the whole thing in a clear sleeve presentation folder. Little things like this are rarely done and bankers will tell you (off the record) that it goes a long way indeed.

- Do your homework fully about your project and think of what you will do if things go wrong—they won't generally if you follow all my advice, but this is how the banker will be thinking. An experienced banker will be able to tell in the first five minutes if you know your stuff.

- Bankers prefer it if you have a job. Very strange, but true. It's so they can see that you have something to fall back on and a regular income. If you're self-employed, give yourself a job by having actual pay slips.

- Never rely on just one bank. Mergers and takeovers mean that the person you developed a rapport with might not be there next week and their replacement might not be so sympathetic to your cause. You want as many credit lines as possible.

- It's not so much cash as cash *flow* that gets bankers excited. Your bottom line profit is of nowhere near as much interest as the amount of cash your business generates. More businesses go under as a result of lack of cash flow rather than lack of profit. Don't worry, I'll set you up in business in the next lesson!

Okay, let's look closely now at the type of finance you will need to support your property activities, because it's significantly different to the type of mortgage you would get to buy your own home. Let this bullet guide make this complicated area simple for you:

- They will usually require a 10-20% deposit for reasons you now know. But there are ways I will show you to get around this.

- Make sure there are no early redemption charges—if you plan to sell the property shortly after, this will cost you dearly.

- The interest rate can be expected to be about 1% above the personal mortgage rate.

- Some lenders offer fixed rate deals—this can be an excellent way of knowing exactly where you stand every month in terms of profit.

- Get a mortgage broker to do the shopping for you. One that charges a fixed fee rather than a commission from the lender—this way you'll get the best deal rather than the one that pays the broker the most commission!

- Get a broker who's on your side when it comes to getting the loan approved—one that doesn't mind bending the rules occasionally!

- Use the broker to assess your business plans—they'll have a good idea about the local market.
- If you are unable to raise the full amount of money you need, and the property needs renovation, you could argue that the work you will do will put extra value on the property so the bank would have that extra security.

I know that some people are a little anxious about all this because you have a poor credit rating, and we did discuss this in an earlier lesson.

It depends on the individual lending criteria of the bank in question—look at the six "Cs" and see how far down credit is on the list of priorities! Bankers know that many people have had some sort of credit problem in the past. Commercial banking is different—they can overlook things like this if you give an explanation before they discover it for themselves.

Anyway, before we look at the past, let's concentrate on the present. If you are currently having trouble paying any debts do not bury your head in the sand! Phone them up and tell them so and that the monthly repayments must be reduced—either that or consolidate your debts into one low cost loan and don't get into anymore consumer debt ever again.

You want as many credit lines as possible open so that when bargains float to the surface you can pounce without delay. You do this by applying for loans and then paying them off early.

Apply for a credit card and then spend up to the limit (only for things you would have bought anyway!) and then pay off the whole amount at the end of the month. I bet they write to you soon after and up your limit! Build relationships with bankers—go to see as many as possible and tell them you look forward to doing business with them. You are the customer and they are in business to make loans.

Get a secured loan. You give the bank $1,000 as security for a loan for the same amount.

This is an excellent way to build/rebuild your credit!

Okay, now it's time to drag out all those skeletons from your closet of the past—we're going to dress up your credit rating! Your credit file is there for all to see; you can't just wave a magic wand and change it, but you can make it look more favorable.

First, you need to know what you're dealing with, and bad news looks far more honest and professional coming from you than the banker finding out for himself. When you receive your credit report (from Experian), read about what all the codes mean and check the report for accuracy.

By far the most common query is someone with the same surname and possibly the same address that is on their file and affecting it adversely. If this applies to you then write a letter back disassociating yourself. Check thoroughly for accuracy throughout because you may find that things are there that shouldn't be.

Instant Freedom

I'm going to tell you how to achieve financial independence from a single property deal now, as promised. This is how Conrad Hilton (the founder of the Hilton hotel chain) started out! In the previous lesson, I gave you a table comparing different types of property to the percentage of value they return in rent. If you recall, there was one type of property that returned a massive 20% rental yield!

Remember? If you don't, the type of property I am referring to is rooming houses.

Now as you know, there are two ways to make money from property; renting and buying and selling for profit and the two should never be confused.

Larger properties produce the biggest profits for buying and selling and smaller properties produce the biggest profits for renting.

But somewhere in the middle is a compromise between the two.

And if you take two extreme examples from either camp; let's say a large, six-bedroom house and a one-bedroom apartment my point becomes more pronounced. The rental income you would get for the large house would barely even cover the mortgage—you may even make a small loss. However, this is fine because you sacrifice the monthly income in the knowledge that you are going for capital gain. Let's take the apartment now; the capital gain you make on the property won't be anything near as high as the large house, but the rental income will easily cover the mortgage payments twice over. So we have this classic dilemma of capital gain versus income.

But here's something that has the best of both worlds!

What if, timing it right with The Great Cycle, we took a large six-bedroom house and converted it into as many rooms as possible? You would have the benefit of a rental yield twice as high as a one-bedroom apartment, and when you wanted to sell at the end of the 7-year cycle, you simply convert the property into a fancy, single-family home for capital gain! If you're happy to take a longer-term path, this single property could be enough to get you your Freedom Figure with its capital gain, and while you're waiting for The Great Cycle to run its course you should make a nice monthly profit.

When we think of rooms for lease, the image is somewhat depressing and you would be forgiven for wondering what sort of low-life wants to rent such a place. But that perception is inaccurate. Young people in the early stages of a career, people in transitional stages in their life, elderly, students, and low-income earners among others all need somewhere to live but can't afford to pay a mortgage or the rent on an apartment. *But they can afford to pay $50-100 a week for a room.*

You need to convert it to as many rooms as possible for maximum income. Upstairs will be easy as they are already bedrooms. With the downstairs, you will need to keep one area as a "common room" for the tenants to eat, watch TV, and socialize in—preferably in the kitchen. The other rooms have to be converted into furnished rooms, nothing some dry wall and paint can't accomplish.

If there is an opportunity to convert *any* area into another room then take it; a conservatory, an attic, a basement, or a garage are all good examples. In many homes, there is needlessly wasted space that you don't even see—it's just empty space hidden behind dry wall, such as under stair cases. For the example we are using here, let's say we convert the garage into a fourth room for downstairs. Check the local planning regulations; you may find that a window for each room is mandatory but this is relatively cheap and easy to do (just knock a hole in the wall).

Each of the rooms needs to have a lockable door and a master key, held by you, that opens all of them. Tenants will expect to share bathrooms—one downstairs and one up. It's relatively easy for a builder to put a shower in the downstairs bathroom. The bathrooms must have good locks for privacy and you might need to install an extra capacity water heater. Something that will really attract tenants is having a basic satellite TV package installed with TV points to all rooms. Again, this represents minimal cost when shared amongst the tenants.

The rooms will need a basic lesson of furnishing;

1. A double bed

2. A bedside table

3. A chair

4. A wardrobe/dresser

5. In the common room a small TV and a phone

The furniture can be purchased second-hand but must comply with modern fire regulations (nearly new stuff will probably comply, but check everything). If you buy all this at once you should be able to negotiate good discounts. The ex-hotel furniture shops I mentioned in an earlier chapter are excellent for this sort of thing.

The amount of management is higher than with other types of rentals. You will need to advertise for and get tenants yourself, as leasing agents don't get involved with this end of the market generally (maybe a business opportunity?). Advertise in the local paper and have cards or leaflets in local supermarkets, newsagents, and any local industry notice boards or publications. Ads like this:

Comfortable Rooms to Let

Newly refurbished double rooms in Smithville. Color Satellite TV, all facilities. Close to public transportation, Main Street, and bars. $99 per week. Call 123 456 7890 to view.

When screening tenants, you can't expect them to be smartly dressed executives! The only requirement should be that they are in employment or have a provable form of income, they don't appear troublesome and have good personal hygiene. No one moves in without cleared funds of one week's rent plus $100 deposit as security, refundable on departure. Arrange to have all the rents due on a certain day—Friday is good because of weekly wages. If the tenant is able to pay monthly then all the better.

There are some particular requirements to bear in mind when selecting the property. First you must be located in a busy city—this won't work in rural or very suburban areas—I don't mean the middle of New York, but somewhere in between the center and the edge of town. Ideally, close to an industrial area like an airport or large industrial park. The area shouldn't be a poor one though, if you want to have a large capital gain upon re-conversion and sale. Public transportation must be excellent—your tenants are possibly unlikely to have their own cars—as must the vicinity to plenty of stores, bars, and leisure facilities. The actual property itself needs to have as many rooms, or the potential to have as many rooms, as possible, both upstairs and downstairs, preferably with a bathroom both upstairs and down.

How to Buy a Property with Zero Cash

I bought my very first investment property with zero cash. In fact, I walked away with cash in my pocket! Here are some ingenious ways of buying a property with no cash at all—I've used them myself when I was first starting. The first method is to get the seller to pay the deposit for you! Here's how it works:

- Let's say the property is up for sale at $60,000. The deposit you would need here can be 10% if you shop around = $6,000.

- So you ask the seller if they would accept an offer of $53,000, of which they are likely to accept if they are a motivated seller.

- Then you simply tell them that you will offer the full price of $60,000 if they pay your deposit. Same difference and the closing company can arrange the whole thing!

   Now, the second method:

- The second way is to get the seller to pay an allowance for renovation/decorating on closing.

- If the property is priced at $100,000 but it needs a lot of work, say you will offer full asking price on condition of a renovation allowance of $15,000 payable on closing.

- This can work well with repossessed or probate properties—anywhere the owners are looking for a quick sale.

Third method:

- Using the techniques I showed you, even if you have a poor credit rating, you get a bank loan for some capital (OR if you have a low rate/zero rate credit card with a reasonable credit limit, use that). Get this loan quickly, the same week that you apply for the mortgage.

- You get the property with a $10,000 down payment, which you may have borrowed from the bank. Okay, so you then install a carport for $1000 and tidy up the yard and re-decorate, and get the property refinanced at a new, increased value of $120,000. The bank then advances you 90% of the new value = $108,000 mortgage.

- With that $108,000 you pay off the original $90,000 mortgage, leaving you with $18,000.

- With that $18,000 you pay off the loan you took out for the $11,000 for the down payment and the carport, leaving you with $7,000. Closing costs would run at about $5,000.

- This leaves you with $2,000 AND a property that earns you a rental income!

Fourth Method:

How To Buy A House For Zero Cash And Walk Away With $10,000 More Than When You Started!

- Even IF you don't have a home to borrow against for some capital, you could ask the seller to carry 20-30% of the price.

- If the house costs $100,000 you'll be able to get a mortgage for about $80,000. You ask the seller to hold $30,000 of the mortgage they have already in the form of a note (an escrow company can arrange this and it is secured against the home).

- So you walk away with a rental property providing you passive income AND $10,000 of capital for your next deal! You're on your way.

And yes, it DOES happen, and yes, it IS legal! It's all about finding that motivated seller we talked about in the previous lesson and applying the 100-10-3-1 rule. The reason most people don't believe deals like this can happen is because they don't know how to, or can't be bothered to find the motivated sellers out there!

Okay, so no more excuses about not having the cash to buy a rental property to get you on the road to financial freedom. Now let's talk more about adding value to your investment properties by fixing them up...

How Home Improvements Can Lose You Money!

A classic mistake made by the public and amateurs is this: the nation has become obsessed with DIY programs on television—I dread to think how many people have blown half their house away with a gas explosion or gotten electrocuted as a result of the frenzy! I suppose it's far easier to fix up your existing home than take serious action with your life to move to a bigger and better home in the first place. But you know, there's a saying in the professional property world:

You can't polish dirt!

In my days as a young realtor in my early twenties, I

learned a lot about this principle. You would be invited around this guy's house to value it for him and he would enthusiastically whisk you around the place, showing you all the incredible home improvements he had done: the built in tropical fish tank set in marble, the $10,000 kitchen, the garage conversion etc. All very nice, it's just that the value it had put on his property was only a few thousand, if that. The reason? Because the house was, at the end of the day, in an attached block in a very run-down neighborhood. Do you get my drift?

There is only so much value you can add to a property in a particular situation.

It wouldn't have mattered if that guy had the finest interior money could buy, the type and location of his property would always hold the value back. I tried explaining this diplomatically, but of course he insisted that the value of the property should have increased by the amount he had spent on it, so I took it on at his asking price hoping that once people went inside they would be swayed by the palatial interior.

Never mind getting them inside, I couldn't even get anyone to view the darn place! Those customers that did overlook the exterior photo (which I took very carefully to hide the burnt-out car on one side of the house and the loaded dumpster on the other side), would turn up to view the property by prior arrangement but didn't even bother knocking on the door once they saw the exterior.

You must bear this in mind when fixing up your investment properties. The key principle is to find a property that is cosmetically distressed, and fix it up for resale, based on the fact that people neither have time or imagination to see the potential, and will pay a premium for convenience.

Let's say you find such a property. Perhaps a typical 3 bedroom, 2 bath in a reasonable neighborhood that is in a very poor condition cosmetically—needing a new kitchen, redecorating, and gardening. Fine…

But if you put a $10,000 kitchen in there you will only put about $5,000 on the value of the property. Tops. It may look fantastic but you won't be the beneficiary of it and more to the point, you will have just lost $5,000!

On the same note, the interior not only needs to fit the type of property it is in, but it needs to appeal to as many people as possible. For this reason, keep everything fairly neutral and simple. Kitchens and bathrooms should be white; the décor, pastille shades and creams. Large, executive homes have different rules here. Anything above four or five bedrooms in a good area will pay to hire an interior designer to arrange carpets, drapes, and wall color. This really will command a high premium in your mark-up.

Forcing Appreciation of Your Assets!

Décor, landscaping, and general tidying can be done by just about anyone. There's no need to get expensive contractors in when you can pay students, retired folk, and just about anyone else looking for casual work. Just ask around and you'll come across plenty of people looking for a bit of pocket money, and many of them—especially the retired—are very skilled and conscientious workers.

When it comes to bathrooms, plastering, demolition, and any other specialist work, you will have to use a professional tradesman. If you've been concentrating on what I've been telling you in these lessons you'll stay well clear of properties that need serious building work, but I appreciate the fact that there will be a need for tradesmen from time to time so here is my survival guide for dealing with them:

- The best way to get a reliable, quality tradesman is by positive recommendation from someone who has actually used them and you have inspected the work. Also, look at customer ratings on websites like AngiesList.com

- Do not attach any value to memberships of trade organizations or guilds. These bodies do not check on the quality of the builder in question.

- Do not employ a contractor to handle several different tradesmen (plumbers, electricians, plasterers, etc.) as their markup will be as much as 30%. Become your own contractor by booking the respective people yourself. Build reputations and negotiate discounts.

- Be very specific about quotes and get exact details about the requirements of the job in writing to avoid any quibbles further down the line. If they run over allowed time, what will the daily rate be? Who will supply the materials and what exact standard will they be? How long will it take? Will you use sub-contractors? What exactly does fully-tiled mean? How long have you been trading? Will you be doing this job full-time until it is finished? Don't be too aggressive though because a good builder can pick and choose their jobs and might be scared off.

- Tie them to a contract that penalizes them for running over schedule!

- As the job progresses, keep a journal of everything that is agreed and show to the builder. You want a fixed cost for the job—not a daily rate!

- Never, ever pay up front. A reputed company will have the necessary trade credit in place so there should generally be no need for this on the smaller jobs you'll be involved with. If the balance of financial power shifts in their favor they'll be tempted to go off on another job.

- Hold back 10% of the total bill for last minute snags you spot after they've left.

Other Renovation Points:

- Remember: TIME IS MONEY! You're paying interest on a loan so the faster they complete the job, the quicker you can get the place to earn its keep. Work on 4 to 8 weeks, depending on the amount of work involved.

- If the property is for rent, you want hard-wearing materials; things that are flimsy or wear easily should be avoided. Keep the garden low-maintenance too—preferably a patio.

- Priorities. Do the things that have the most visual impact for the least money first—see the previous chapters for details on this.

- Kitchens and bathrooms should always be in excellent condition; most of all though—90% of the time—the woman in the buying couple has the biggest say. There are ways to create immediate impact on a property: flooring and carpets, taps, walls, lighting, and a pleasant front door. Cleaning the carpet is obviously cheaper but only if the original carpet is in good condition.

- The same carpet running through all rooms gives the impression that the property is bigger than it actually is.

- Stick to your budget and time schedule! Spend no more than 10% of the intended final resale value on refurbishment. If you run over, make sure it's no more than a total of 15% maximum.

- A way to drastically increase the value of the property is by changing it! For example, converting a one-bedroom apartment into a two bedroom by carefully rearranging the rooms with a partition and using unnecessarily wasted space as discussed earlier. Houses are best for this—I recently converted a 3-bedroom house with a study into a 4-bedroom house simply by adding a closet to the study and calling it a bedroom. This raised the value and it took the property into a new class, and made it the cheapest 4-bedroom on the market, resulting in a fast sale. As long as you're careful what you sacrifice, this works well—nobody will miss a study if they need 4 bedrooms and they're on a tight budget.

- Consider the use of many mirrors in the smallest rooms to make it look bigger.

- Lighting is very important. Spotlights will appeal to your market; either embedded in the ceiling or on a rail. Especially in kitchens and bathrooms.

- The smell of new paint has a habit of lingering, especially in small rooms. But if you stir a couple of drops of vanilla essence into the paint before you actually start painting, the fumes should be neutralized! Another problem with paint is getting grit in it, which is often the case in properties that need renovating. To get around this, take an old pair of pantyhose and pour the paint through them into another container—this is a good filter.

Make the place look as beautiful and tidy as possible for minimal cost. This alone puts you streets ahead of other competing landlords!

Getting the Big Bucks

Now it's time to talk about selling the property. First of all, you should be selling in time with The Great Cycle, as the good seven years end. This is the biggest key, and with that firmly in mind let's concentrate on the actual sale. If you've done all I told you so far in terms of selecting and restoring the property, this bit is easy, but let's make it even easier and more profitable.

- Unless you're living in the property, it will look bare, but a few very simple homely touches can drastically change all that. Set up a transportable sales kit comprising of artificial flowers in vases, pictures, a coffee table, light shades, lamps, bulbs and anything else you can fit in your trunk. You need to give the imagination of your potential customer a little jolt.

- Always attend every viewing personally if you can. Some realtors don't have a clue and you know far more about the place, anyway. If the property is on a busy road or railway line avoid booking viewings during rush hour. Common sense applies.

- Get there in advance to turn on all the lights, have a quick vacuum and dust, squirt some air-freshener and open all the windows, unless it is very noisy outside.

- First impressions count for 50% of the decision process. Make sure the front of the property is tidy and attractive. You could put some artificial trees in pots on the front patio/path. Show the potential clients the best parts of the house first, even if it means taking an unusual route around the house.

- Tailor the presentation to your customer. What sort of person are they—married, single? What are they into? Sell the benefits of your property that suits them most. For example, what's the point in telling a young single man the fact that there is an excellent school a few blocks away?

- With apartments and small houses your market is likely to be first-time buyers. It is well worth furnishing the place with white goods, a sofa and a bed, and charging a premium for the convenience. Balance this with the fact that properties look more spacious with nothing in them.

- Don't oversell. The property will very often sell itself—it's far better to ask friendly questions about the actual customer than ramble on about the property. The relevant selling points will come naturally to you.

- Generate excitement with the property, but don't be too intense. People want what they can't have and you need to make them think you can pick and choose your buyer by asking about their position to buy. First-time buyers are best followed by people under offer, both of which must have deposits and mortgages in place and the sale is conditional on closing within 6 weeks. People whose house is not on the market are wasting your time.

- When pricing the property, pay attention to price brackets. Realtors can confirm these for you. Depending on the area, properties fit into certain price brackets and this can mean that buyer's price requirements can take large jumps. For example, a typical bracket is "Up to $100,000" and then "$125,000 to $175,000." Here, your property should ideally not be priced in between $100k and $125k; instead it should be either side. These price brackets apply to typical earnings of people in the area (for their mortgages) and for local and national laws regarding buying properties at certain prices as well as property taxes.

- Don't be greedy on the price—you want a quick sale to cover your costs and a property that's been on the market for too long looks bad.

I've mentioned that when showing an interested party around, it's good to turn all the lights on to make the place look bigger. But natural light is also worth a mention because it can make a massive difference. During renovation of the garden, be sure that all plants are cut away from windows—it's quite incredible how much natural light is kept out this way. With this in mind, look around the property inside for rooms that could be transformed by a window or skylight. You would need planning permission, depending on the location of the window, but this is an inexpensive improvement that really can put thousands on a property. The best example is adding a balcony or roof garden to an apartment or town house in urban areas.

How to Get Realtors <u>Really</u> Fighting in Your Corner

Once you've made the decision to sell, you need to move quickly because all the time the property is not earning you rent, you are paying interest on the loan. So like it or loathe it, you need to hire a realtor rather than try and sell it privately. Of course, the more established you become, the more likely realtors will offer you preferential rates as a regular customer. Indeed, a couple of months back and you might have bought the property from the very same realtor, so there is definitely room for discounts on the average fee.

There is a little-known trick though that will make the agent realize they are dealing with a pro. That is to propose a "split-fee." Here's how it works:

Normal fee method: Agent charges 6% of purchase price.
On a $120,000 house = $7200

The important point here is that if the buyer offers $110,000 the realtor only stands to lose $600 of the full $7200 commission so he couldn't really care less about taking a lowball offer, but you will have lost $10,000 from the price! He will be happy to get the sale and, whether you like it or not, in a case like this he will not have your best interests at heart like he should. To think otherwise is naïve and the mark of a rank amateur.

So your realtor sells it for $110,000 and gets a nice commission of $6,600, but you took $10,000 off the price.

Now here's the "split-fee" method:

You put your house up for the same price of $120,000. You propose a commission of 4% PLUS **10%** of any amount achieved over $110,000. Now the realtor has an incentive to get you a higher price!

House is sold for $115,000. Fees payable of 4% of $115,000 plus 10% of $5,000 = $5100.

Can you see? You've paid virtually the same amount of commission as before but your house has sold for $5,000 more!

The realtor doesn't like it? Why? Are they saying they are not good enough to achieve that price? Realtors generally claim to be brilliant—their sales pitch will focus on what great salespeople they are, so let them prove it. What are they afraid of? Of course, if the agent gets an amount higher than $115,000 they stand to make more money than if they were charging you the full 6%. Either way, you are better off.

There are, of course, other considerations though. You can get an agent to charge you a low fee but if your house is still sitting there, costing you interest next month, it won't be too good. In short, don't let fees be your sole focus. Best to find the right realtor and then negotiate on the fees. Now here are my top tips on selecting the right agent and the quick sale:

- A tactic often employed by realtors is to tempt you to go with them by being over-optimistic with the price they think they can get. Once you've agreed to sign up, a week or two later when the property hasn't sold, they'll ask you to lower the price. You don't have the time to play silly games so the moral here is to know your market, know about this tendency of agents to over-price and not to let greed get the better of you.

- Telling you that they have a buyer for the property on their books is another trick to get you to sign up. If the agent is that desperate for properties, why?

- Do your homework. Do they regularly advertise in the local property papers and what quality are they? Do they have many for sale boards up in the area? Do they sell many of your type of property—any previous examples of prices obtained?

- You should always opt to have a board outside your property. No excuses. The reason being that 25% of properties are sold by buyers driving around areas they like looking for sale boards. You should also give them a key so that they can do viewings when you're not around.

- Go for a realtor with a central location and branches in nearby towns that they share information with. You want as much exposure as possible. I particularly like it when realtors are all clustered together in one part of the town. Why? Well where would you go if you wanted some property details? It's the realtor that isn't located in this group that will lose out.

- Do a mystery-shop on the realtors in the area. Are they polite and professional? Did they get all your details and requirements including telephone number?

- Agree that if you sign up the realtor will advertise your property immediately with a large photo "house of the week" type promotion, complete with an "open day."

- In an earlier issue, when we discussed buying a property, I told you to look for clues to suggest that the seller was desperate. Now, the shoe is on the other foot, so make sure you aren't appearing desperate just to get a sale!

Wealth from Commercial Property

Commercial property (offices, retail space, apartment buildings, etc.) is even better than residential property, ONCE you have some inside-knowledge under your belt and perhaps a little experience. There's too much on this separate subject to go into detail here, but if you think you'd like to explore the benefits of commercial property check out our "One Deal to Freedom" course.

That concludes our discussion on real estate (apart from one last strategy I'll explain later on in this lesson). One way or another, whether it's your personal residence or investment property, real estate plays a big part in your plans to retire, so all this will be of great use to you, if for no other reason than understanding The Great Cycle! Now let's move on to a brand new secret...

Fortress of Freedom

"Be thou diligent to know the state of thy flocks, and look well to thy herds." – Proverbs 27:23.

You will not see the importance of this secret until you are well on your way to, or actually possess, your Freedom Figure, so I need you to use your imagination. I want you to "fast forward" your life to a few years from now. Close your eyes for a moment. Take yourself forward in time and vividly picture this scenario of a comfortable retirement. Feel the sun on your face and the release that comes from zero stress—zero stress that was brought about by your own skills and effort, no one else's...

Are you there? How does it feel? Fantastic? It should.

Now, how do you feel about a faceless "thief" depriving you of this life to benefit their own, because they couldn't be bothered to do what you did?

I know your main focus right now is on making money, that's why this secret was presented later in the course and why we won't spend much time on it, but we must give this some consideration *now*, not later. Why? Because you can get to your Freedom Figure a lot faster if you pay less tax, and especially if we protect your efforts from these thieves... or "extortioners" as The 6th Secret refers to them:

"Let the extortioner catch all that he hath; and let the strangers spoil his labor." - Psalms 109:11

To explain, the Romans placed a statue of Marsyas in the Forum, or law court, by which they signified that those who came into the hands of usurers would be skinned alive; and to show that usurers, as the most unjust litigants, deserved hanging, they placed a rope in the hand of the figure.

Personally, I translate this quote into a very simple idea that helps me think about protecting assets: *People who would attempt to take what's yours are only as effective as you allow them to be. If you fall into their trap then you are as bad as they are.* The Romans agreed, as does this advice from King Solomon:

"My son, despise not the chastening of the Lord; neither be weary of his correction: For whom the Lord loveth he correcteth; even as a father the son in whom he delighteth." – Proverbs 3:11-12

That's to say, all is fair in love and war, and that when something bad happens to you, it's actually a lesson that life is trying to teach you. But when it comes to money, these lessons can be expensive! One great benefit to learning from someone who's travelled down the path you're on is that they can spare you some costly mistakes, and I trust you've found that to be the case so far on this course.

So let's protect ourselves along the way, and bear some important things in mind for when that great day comes as we reach our Freedom Figure—let's build a fortress around ourselves to protect that freedom. I've talked at length in previous lessons about the "pharaohs," the "talebearers," and the "money-changers" (governments, mass media, and banks), so I'll ask you to remember those lessons rather than repeat myself, and now let's look at how to legally defend your hard-earned wealth from those and others.

Defend against Governments

Make no mistake, one way or another, by legal or rogue means, you will face no greater financial threat to your finances than governments. There are 3 threats that the government comes at you with: Taxation, Inflation, and Confiscation. Let's look at each in turn…

Taxation:
'render therefore unto Caesar the things which be Caesar's."
– Luke 20:25

"What about tax?" is an obstacle that people often put on their path to freedom! It's a worry that stops people getting started. The first thing I have to say about tax is this:

Tax is a nice problem to have!

If you owe the government money it means that you're

not being a lazy slob, and that you're actually *making money!* Well done. Now let's talk about defending that money...

There's no point in debating taxation and how much you should be taxed—the law is what it is in the place you choose to reside in, and *you must obey the law*. But there are some ways to legally reduce how much tax you pay. Understand: there is a big difference between tax *avoidance* and tax *evasion*. How much difference? About five years in jail...

Tax evasion is illegal and you should not, under any circumstances, evade taxes due. Regardless of what certain self-proclaimed "experts" tell you, there are no grey areas. If in doubt, check out the website of your government's tax collection agency and read all the regulations for yourself. For every "clever" little scheme you or your "expert" can come up with, I guarantee that the authorities have seen ten like it before you, and the confessions they coerced out of those ten offenders helped make their regulations even tighter. I obviously can't go into full detail here about the pages and pages of all tax regulations of all governments, but as a general rule, if you hear of a tax-saving scheme that seems too good to be true, check the actual regulations before you do it. Ignorance of these rules is no defense under law.

As I said, it's a total waste of breath to complain about taxation, but do NOT evade tax by breaking the law. Instead, *avoid* taxes legally.

Conversely, tax *avoidance* is not only legal, it's your legal *right* as a citizen to arrange your affairs in the most tax advantageous way possibly allowed within the regulations. So do not have any reservations about doing this!

The most powerful way you can evade tax is to simply vote with your feet and choose residency in a country that is kindest to you. There are many to choose from, and in an earlier lesson I gave you the example of Panama, where you can enjoy a tropical lifestyle without paying any tax at all! And moving to a tax haven doesn't mean you have to abandon your country completely. For example, you can live in the United States for 120 days a year without owing any US tax if you're a non-citizen. And you can live in the United Kingdom for 90 days a year without owing any UK tax. So, surprisingly, both those countries are tax havens *from a certain point of view that depends on your movements.* Don't forget that when you're retired and living off your freedom figure that you have freedom to move around. Note: US citizens have to file a return wherever they go, but you can earn up to $80,000 a year at time of writing, tax-free. Or if they get a passport in a new country such as Panama, they may elect to give up their US citizenship and be completely exempt from that requirement.

Failing expatriation, you can avoid tax in other ways, and the list is too long and constantly changing to go over here, but it's nothing a good accountant can't help you with. However, the best secret to avoiding tax in your home country is by using all the benefits of the seventh secret that I'll explain soon.

A couple of examples of tax avoidance follow, and I'm deliberately using international examples in this section to remind you that the world is your playground when you're retired—you don't have to do everything in one country—you can (and should) invest and reside where the government is kindest (if more people did this then governments would soon change their (socialist) stance on taxes!)

Two examples, then. With real estate in the USA, if you sell a property (personal residence or investment) and then immediately use the proceeds to buy another property, the capital gains are postponed for as long as you roll up the profits. In the UK, there is never any capital gains tax to pay on a personal residence, so you could keep fixing up houses for profit as long as you live in them while you do so and then never pay any tax. In the UK, you can also use tax-free spread-betting as a way to trade stocks. In the USA, certain local government bonds (Municipal Bonds) offer generous and tax-free annual yields. In both countries, capital gain taxes are reduced if you held the asset for more than a year before selling it. It's better to be an individual in the USA for tax-purposes than it is in the UK, but it's better to be a corporation for tax-purposes in the UK. In a place like Panama you *never* pay any tax! So weigh it all up, and arrange your affairs to best suit all systems available to you.

Remember: consider yourself as a citizen of the *planet*, not just a citizen of your comfortable little corner of it.

Important note about tax: do NOT make investment decisions based solely on tax advantages! Make investment decisions based on the sound principles I've taught you here, and *then* look for ways to offset the tax due! Remember: tax is a nice problem to have, and the priority is to actually *make some money* in the first place so that it *can* be taxed!

Final word on tax: *If you don't like the tax system where you are, don't whine about it, and don't break the law. If you don't like it then move somewhere else. And/or work on ways to legally avoid it.*

Inflation:

"And when money failed in the land of Egypt, and in the land of Canaan, all the Egyptians came unto Joseph, and said, Give us bread: for why should we die in thy presence? For the money faileth." – Genesis 47:15

A country is really no different than an individual. If it has debts to pay that it can't afford, something has to give. In these scenarios, a government only has four choices (and it MUST take one or a combination of them):

1. Default on the debt.

   If a country ever hopes to borrow again at reasonable rates, it had better not do this. Like with an individual, there's a consequence with credit agencies. The currency would plummet, and the economy would crumble.

2. Raise taxes.

   Taxes in most western countries are already high. And raising taxes doesn't get votes.

3. Lower expenses.

   Cut benefits even more? There would be riots. There have already been drastic cuts, and the people are at boiling point. And lowering benefits doesn't get votes.

4. **Print money to buy your own debt with.**

   But how about this option? This seems the best of a bad bunch, doesn't it? What would *you* do in the government's position? As The US Federal Reserve publicly stated, they have something called a printing press, and are prepared to use it. *And use it they have... and will even more...*

When money isn't backed by anything solid, only the promise of a power-hungry politician, it's called paper currency, or *fiat currency*. The US Dollar—the *world reserve currency*—is a fiat currency. Now let me say something that will shock you, something "they" aren't advertising:

No fiat currency has EVER survived in history.

Please read that again. It's *highly* significant. EVERY fiat currency that has EVER existed has ALWAYS eventually lost its ENTIRE value. I emphasize in the capitals above to show how absolute the statement is. There's no way out, no special cases, no exceptions.

It is a physical impossibility for governments to pay back all they've borrowed without them doing something drastic. The gorilla in the room is that they *won't pay it back as things stand. And that leaves printing money as the only option to buy the debt. And that means severe inflation, or even hyperinflation, by any historical measure.*

So how can you defend against this government-caused threat of inflation? Well, it depends on how bad inflation becomes...

High inflation scenario: Stocks will perform the best of all asset classes. Real estate and precious metals will also do well. By simply following our Secret of Seventy investment system you will be more than protected against inflation!

Hyperinflation scenario: I'd like to think that hyperinflation (out of control and rampant inflation) is something just for banana republics like Zimbabwe (where they recently had to print a trillion-dollar note!). Personally, I believe sensible governments will see this coming and aggressively respond by raising interest rates quickly. Either way, this will have a *negative effect* on the stock market, but once again our Secret of Seventy system will *automatically* bail you out of stocks probably months before this happens anyway. Due to rising interest rates, real estate prices would crash, but if you're in time with The Great Cycle, it's unlikely you'd still be in real estate at this time anyway. The greatest beneficiary of hyperinflation would be precious metals like gold.

In short, you should be covered against this threat if you're using our systems diligently!

Confiscation:
"Riches and honour are with me; yea, durable riches and righteousness." – Proverbs 8:18

As I explained, governments everywhere are desperately short of cash, so don't think they wouldn't just love to take all your money! But how?

Thankfully, if you're living in a civilized country, there are laws that protect you from rogue governments. In most cases, the only way they could confiscate your wealth is if you broke the law (see earlier section on tax!). But what if your government goes "rogue"?

The beautiful island of Cyprus in The Mediterranean Sea is a westernized financial center in the European Union—far from being a banana republic. And yet, in March 2013, anyone who held cash in an account worth more than 100,000 Euros in

Cyprus had most of it *confiscated* to help pay off Greece's debts!

Do you think people with less than 100,000 Euros (most people) complained about those "evil" rich people having their money taken away? On the contrary—it was a vote winner! It was a win-win for the government—they successfully confiscated money from innocent people, and at the same time got a cheer from the voters for punishing those "evil" rich people (an image you can thank the media for).

With that successful test case in mind, and under these unprecedented government debt levels, do you think the same thing can't happen in *your* country… to *your* wealth?

Remember, governments must respond to the cries of the bleating masses (The Fools) less they have a revolt on their hands, as this passage from The Bible reminds us:

"Pilate therefore, willing to release Jesus, spake again to them. But they cried, saying, Crucify him, crucify him… And the voices of them and of the chief priests prevailed. And Pilate gave sentence that it should be as they required." – Luke 23:20-24.

So how can you defend against confiscation by governments, apart from not breaking the law? Here's how below, and none of what follows is intended to assist you in breaking any laws!

- Hold as little cash or CDs as possible with your bank, while still having enough cash to live on for a few months. It's unlikely that the government would confiscate paper assets such as stocks or bonds as that would be bad for financial markets. In the 2013 Cyprus incident, I had previously advised clients there to only hold paper assets and no cash or CDs, and as a result their assets were completely unaffected by the EU government theft.

- Spread your money into different asset classes such as stocks, real estate, cash, and precious metals.

- *A government simply cannot confiscate what it can't physically access.* Remember that a government has an incredible advantage in that it makes the laws, and can change the laws overnight to suit its current agenda. There is nothing it can't touch *unless that thing is untouchable.* Precious coins in a bank safe are an example (check out our free report on buying gold)—these coins are also easily transferable should you wish someone else to own them. Any government that demands to confiscate *all its citizens'* gold may be considered by you as an unlawful "rogue" government—on a par with the Nazis—and you should act as your conscience dictates, perhaps even leaving the country and taking your gold with you.

- Another example of what a government can't physically access is holding assets in other countries. But be aware of any reporting requirements and pay any taxes due! This isn't about hiding assets and evading tax! There's nothing illegal about owning real estate in another country or even holding stocks in a foreign bank account as long as you obey the reporting and taxation laws of your country of residency/citizenship, but your government will ultimately have trouble confiscating it—that's the point. Just be sure that the country you locate the assets in is a solid one, perhaps out of the European Union and American influence, and certainly not a banana republic. Switzerland, Panama, Uruguay, and Singapore are good examples of countries with solid banking systems, and are only obliged to comply with authorities from foreign countries if they can prove that the account holder has broken the law.

And that concludes defending against governments, and brings us into defending against our next "extortioner"...

Defend against Banks

"The rich man's wealth is his strong city: the destruction of the poor is their poverty." – Proverbs 10:15

The above quote is another way of saying that poor people are poor because they're poor; they're poor in terms of *knowledge* as much as wealth. You are no longer ignorant of how the banks work, and that is your greatest defense against them!

And as long as you make payments on any loans you have with them, they will not be able to take your assets... unless you're a guarantor for someone else who gets a loan with them, and that is something to *never* do.

"If thou be surety for thy friend, if thou hast stricken thy hand with a stranger, Thou art snared with the words of thy mouth." – Proverbs 6:1-2

A guarantor is a fool with a pen. Do not guarantee anything for anyone. Do not let anyone "take over" your payments for anything. And even when you're borrowing for yourself, always try to ensure that the loan is not secured against anything, especially your residence. Of course, in the case of real estate, such a lien on the property is unavoidable.

The least obvious bank risk to defend against is failure of the actual bank, or even failure of the banking system itself—we came very close to that recently in 1998 and 2008. Check how much your bank has insurance for against such an event. Keep some cash in the house. Other than that, the precautions taken in the previous section about government confiscation will protect you against bank failure.

Defend against the Economy

"He that gathereth in summer is a wise son: but he that sleepeth in harvest is a son that causeth shame." – Proverbs 10:5

I'm listing all the possible risks to your Freedom Figure here, but in some instances there's not much to say, other than to be aware of the risk. You're now aware of The Great Cycle and The Secret of Seventy, and these two secrets alone will keep you safe from economic recessions. In bear markets and recessions the value of assets goes down, period. Be ready.

And also be aware that recessions are rarely synchronized around the world; not all countries are in recession at once unless it's more like a *depression*, as we saw in 2008. This is another reason to think of yourself as a global citizen, not a national one.

Defend against Lawyers

"Go not forth hastily to strive, lest thou know not what to do in the end thereof, when thy neighbor hath put thee to shame." – Proverbs 25:8

The above quote is saying not to be hasty in suing someone. Unfortunately, modern society does not agree, and many ambulance-chasing lawyers are happy to service such clients. We must defend ourselves against litigation, because when the world suddenly sees your deep pockets, what they will also see is a target on your back. Just like with our taxation discussion, there's no point getting annoyed with lawyers, frivolous lawsuits, and the loopy legal system, we just have to defend ourselves against all this.

First of all, I want you to understand a legal term: "fraudulent transfer." If you transfer assets to protect them *after* a lawsuit is filed against you, that transfer could be considered fraudulent, resulting in a court order that the asset be returned and/or be considered to be yours, and you could even face criminal charges. Therefore, the time to have your defenses in place is *before* a lawsuit is filed.

Lawyers have the means, sometimes through a court order, to find out exactly how much you're worth. They will only usually be able to go back two years though, so any legal transfers of assets you've made before then may not be visible. The rule about not physically being able to confiscate something that's physically unavailable may also help you here, which is why it's preferable not to hold many assets in the country where you reside—your country of residence is most likely where a lawsuit will be filed against you for something.

Carry plenty of liability insurance on everything you own/do that could harm someone else (property, cars, boats, pets, etc.) For not much more money you can get an umbrella liability policy that adds another million or two to your coverage.

It's likely that the most valuable asset you may own in your country of residence is your home, and this can be of considerable value, so you must defend it as you would a castle. The home and umbrella policy I just mentioned is your first line of defense. Another line of defense is to have a corporation own your home and/or to have a large mortgage on it—instead of owning your home without a mortgage consider having a mortgage and using those funds from your home to reinvest somewhere for a greater return than the mortgage interest—The Secret of Seventy would make you much more money, and if you held that asset in a secure way or country, then it would also be less accessible to litigants. Certain jurisdictions also provide some protection for your home; for example, in Florida there is "homestead exemption" where no litigant other than the government or mortgaging bank can take away your home. If you're married or co-habiting, you could also ensure that your home be held in joint names—that way if either one of you is sued the damage to the asset is limited or even negated in the event of attack because there is an innocent party involved (your spouse is likely innocent if you get sued).

But I know what you're thinking: what if your spouse is the one to sue you, as in a divorce? I'm not here to encourage you to hide assets from your spouse and children. Think carefully before you get married, and then work hard at it as a team. If the worst happens and you get divorced, then both parties are to blame and both parties are entitled to what the law provides, *especially innocent children.* Your spouse most likely helped you create the asset, so they should be entitled to their share. If you feel the laws in your jurisdiction are unfair on a certain party (usually the man), then consider moving to a jurisdiction that is fair. For example, in Florida everything is split 50/50—assets and custody—regardless of who wanted the divorce and any wrongdoing. I consider that an equitable divorce law. Make no mistake, the risk of divorce is the most costly (and sadly, most likely) risk to your wealth, happiness, and health. Do not take the decision lightly! And if you must get divorced, please do remember that you're divorcing your partner, *not your children.*

Take a cold look at your situation now, on the way to your Freedom Figure, and when you get it. Then consult with a good insurance agent. And if you really want to be secure, go find a lawyer and ask him to run a simulated lawsuit against you. Poachers make the best gamekeepers!

The best insurance of all though, is one I'll tell you about in the next chapter. You can only be sued for what you *own*, and if you own nothing, what can you be sued for?

But one of the best ways to avoid being sued is not to make any enemies…

Defend against The Fools (and Yourself!)
"The desire accomplished is sweet to the soul: but it is abomination to fools to depart from evil." – Proverbs 13:19

Perhaps the greatest threat your Freedom Figure will face is you, or more specifically, your *ego*, and The Fools you interact with. You will want to spend the money on toys, live the high life, and meet your perceptions of how "rich" people live.

New doors will open for you, but many of them lead to dark places.

"It is an honour for a man to cease from strife: but every fool will be meddling." – Proverbs 20:3

Don't expect most people to be happy for you when you reach your Freedom Figure. They will be nothing of the sort; they will be burning with jealousy, regardless of whether they show it or not. You will lose friends. You will suddenly suffer inexplicable and unprovoked hostility, chips on peoples" shoulders everywhere. *And all those people would love to see you lose it all.* They may even hatch plans against you or at the very least not warn you of something unpleasant coming your way. Jealousy is a powerful emotion, so do not underestimate how it can drive an otherwise pleasant person to evil. But there is a way around all that if you can get the better of your ego.

"I have seen all the works that are done under the sun: and, behold, all is vanity and vexation of spirit." – Ecclesiastes 1:14

Try not to flaunt your wealth in peoples" faces, and don't think about teaching anyone unless they ask for advice. Ideally, on the surface of how your life is perceived by others, it wouldn't change at all. You'd live in the same house, but now it's paid for. You'd have the same lifestyle, only now it's from effortless income and/or capital gain. The outside world—the jealous Fools—would be none the wiser, and that risk is then greatly diminished.

"It is not good to eat much honey: so for men to search their own glory is not glory." – Proverbs 25:27

And in the event you do encounter hostility or even an actual lawsuit, try to "kill them with kindness" and diffuse the situation:

"For if an enemy be hungry, give him bread to eat... for thou shalt heap coals of fire upon his head." – Proverbs 25:22-23

Remember, every enemy you make, whether you deserved it or not, is a potential risk to your wealth in one form or another. I highly recommend you read *How to Win Friends and Influence People* as well as *The Power of Now*.

If you're a man you'll also "mysteriously" encounter more female attention if your wealth is flaunted, and that of course carries the risk of divorce, not to mention the risk of an outright "honey trap" scam:

"I have perfumed my bed with myrrh, aloes, and cinnamon. Come let us take our fill of love until the morning... He goeth after her straight-way, as an ox goeth to the slaughter, or as a fool to the correction of stocks." – Proverbs 7:17/22.

But don't let The Fools get to you to the extent that they ruin the quality of your new life—that's what they want. Diffuse their jealousy and anger, but don't feel any guilt about your accomplishments, for in the final analysis you are in the right, and they are in the wrong, and they will receive what is coming to them, just not at your hand.

"He that is despised, and hath a servant, is better than he that honoureth himself, and lacketh bread." – Proverbs 12:9

When you make it, your best defense against The Fools is to keep your ego in check. When they aggravate you, simply pity them, for "they know not what they do" (Luke 23:34).

The 3+1 Retirement Plan
"There be three things which go well, yea, four are comely in going." – Proverbs 30:29.

Now for that alternative retirement strategy I told you about. If real estate really appeals to you and you'd like a very simple goal for getting to freedom, this could be for you…

It's really very simple. The goal is to find four properties using the real estate secrets I've shared with you so you get a good price, etc. and obviously get mortgages on all of them to spread your starting capital around. One of the properties is for you to live in, so choose that one well. The other three are for rental, so be sure they meet the rental criteria we discussed (smaller units = higher yields). Find them, rent them out at the right time of The Great Cycle.

The next step is to pay off all four mortgages as quickly as possible by any means possible, all guns blazing, and then live happily ever after in your mortgage-free home with the passive income from three mortgage-free rental units. Figure out the numbers so you get the right yields and that match your desired living expenses.

But how do you pay off those four mortgages? You could of course use the stock market secrets I've shared with you. *You could also use the seventh and final secret…*

Chapter 10:
Legacy of
Prosperity

The Seventh Secret

"The just man walketh in his integrity: his children are blessed after him." – Proverbs 20:7

Y ou are evidently a person who *sees things through*, and these days, my friend, that is a rare thing indeed—it will get you far in life. We live in an entitled society becoming increasingly overrun with impatient children who feel the world owes them something, so my congratulations on not being one of them.

The world doesn't owe you a thing. *You owe the world, and you owe yourself.*

You've made it all the way to the final chapter, but there's still so much I have to share with you. But now let's move on to the last secret, as we see how it connects with and fuels all the other secrets:

"But thou shalt remember the Lord thy God: for it is he that giveth thee power to get wealth, that he may establish his covenant which he sware unto thy fathers, as it is this day." – Deuteronomy 8:18

So, what does this mean in our terms? It means two things:

1. When you do make your fortune, don't let pride or arrogance make you forget where you came from. Remain humble, because "pride goeth before a fall." We touched on this last chapter.

2. *What goes around comes around.* If you help others, you will reap the rewards.

Both points are good advice, but it's the second point we're going to translate more into financial terms. How can you help others? You could simply help a senior citizen across the street, or you could give money to charity. Those are the most obvious ways, I strongly recommend both, but this is a course on moneymaking (so that you have the *option* of giving money to charity), so how can helping others make you money?

There is a powerful and proven way, and it also helps defend against the attackers we discussed in the previous chapter, as well as leaves a legacy of prosperity for generations after you.

And remember that "3+1" retirement plan from before? That's the quick and easy retirement plan where you get mortgages on four properties with as little money down as possible. The aim is to live in one and live off the rent from the other three, and to pay off all four mortgages as fast as possible and then retire. Well, this seventh secret is how you could pay off those mortgages.

In fact, The Seventh Secret can grant you a dozen wonderful wishes *if you follow my exact plan:*

1. Help others.
2. Defend against attackers.
3. Pay less tax.
4. Pay less for certain things you want.
5. Help stop your money "flying away."
6. Leave a legacy for generations after you.
7. Pay off the 4 mortgages in the 3+1 retirement

plan.

8. Give you investment capital to build a real estate portfolio with.

9. Get you out of debt quickly with your credit rating intact.

10. Create investment capital for The Secret of Seventy and The Biblical Money Code.

11. Create income streams that could last forever.

12. Build your Freedom Figure.

How would you like all those things? Sounds like Christmas came early, doesn't it? And, if you do things my way, you won't have to give up your day job to pull it off. You can have all this if you use this final secret. Just open your mind, give yourself fresh eyes, and read on.

You Must Cross Over

"For a dream cometh through a multitude of business; and a fool's voice is known by a multitude of words." – Ecclesiastes 5:3

Let's begin with a quick recap of something we began in Chapter Two:

"Imagine two islands connected by a bridge. On one island the people live in slavery, day in, day out. On the other island, the people just sit by their swimming pools without needing to lift a finger if they don't want to.

There are two types of people on the slavery side, and two types of people on the swimming pool side, so let's see which group you're in and how to cross that bridge, shall we? On the "slavery" side of the bridge we have these two types:

1) *Employee*
2) *Self-Employed*

Employee.

The first group is the one most people are in, and they are obviously the most trapped of all four types. An employee has to work for a superior, has limited time off and even needs approval for that, and they are, by definition, a liability on the corporation's profit and loss account. Usually paid an hourly rate as low as the market will stand. Fixed income unless promotions can be engineered through the minefield of office politics.

One of the biggest ways employees are incentivized NOT to be employees is to do with how they're taxed on the (printed) money they earn. An employee must buy many things with money AFTER they've been taxed already. **An employee works for money that the government is continually devaluing, then the government taxes that devalued money, and only then, the employee can spend whatever is left (usually on servicing debt that benefits the banks).**

The benefit, of course, is PERCEIVED security— you go to work, receive a steady paycheck that you "know" will always be there each week. As a legacy of grade school, an employee usually wants to show up and suffer from 9-5, and then be able to switch off for evenings and weekends.

This isn't to say you can't be perfectly happy if you enjoy your work and have no great financial ambition, but I suspect the reason you're here is because you're NOT happy to be an employee.

Eventually, some employees (the smarter, more ambitious ones) wake up. They see themselves being fleeced like sheep by the boss who keeps all the money that their hard efforts are creating, and they decide they'd be better off being their OWN BOSS with their own business. And so it's only natural that this group of people then falls into The Big Trap. Enter the second type of person on the slavery side of the bridge...

Self-Employed

This is where most budding entrepreneurs and professionals get stuck. They now work for themselves, but note the operative word I just said: "work." They still work, only for themselves.

Having a corporation or LLC does NOT mean you're not in this group! Unless you pass a test I'm going to give you now, you may as well be employee or a contractor, I don't care what kind of corporate structure you have. "I have my own corporation/LLC" is a phrase I hear a lot of people boast, but it's a meaningless statement in most cases. They may as well be employees.

So how do you know if you're in this group? Simple. Just answer this question:

If you didn't touch your business for a month and stayed in bed instead, would it still be there when you got back?

Very few people who have corporations/LLCs can say "yes" to this. If you answered "no" to this question, YOU DON'T OWN A BUSINESS, YOU OWN A JOB! All you've achieved is changing employers.

Sure, you may earn a bit more money now. You might even be able to goof off a bit here and there. You're in charge of your own destiny now. So it's certainly better than being an employee in most cases, but you're still a slave. You may be the slave master as well now, but you're still a slave. In fact, many self-employed people work much harder than employees, and in some cases earn LESS. If many self-employed people did the math, they'd be better off going back to having a job, especially when you take benefits into account. Just ask my landscaper.

This is NOT financial freedom. You have to work on your business or you won't have a business. This is why doctors, lawyers, and other professionals will NEVER be financially free. They will NEVER cross the bridge to the swimming pool island. Sure, they may all have swimming pools, but they're unable to sit gazing into it all day (or doing whatever they want).

You pretty much spend what you earn, often because you work so hard and need things like cleaners and childcare. This is The Big Trap for most people who graduate from being an employee for this simple reason: BECAUSE THEY HAVEN'T STOPPED THINKING LIKE EMPLOYEES. And that's where they'll stay in most cases—on the slavery island.

Now, on the swimming pool side of the bridge, we have two groups of people that I'm sure you'd prefer to be with because they don't have all the disadvantages the people do on the slavery side of the bridge...

So now let's pick up where we left this off in Part Two. Here are the two people who live on the swimming pool side of the bridge:

1. Investor
2. True Business Owner

The simple difference on this island is that the natives don't work for money; money works for *them.* Let's look at each one…

Investor

This person doesn't work for money; money works for him. He has built up enough capital to make money in his sleep. Before you enrolled on this course I bet you didn't know how this guy could do that. But now you know The Secret of Seventy, I'm sure you can see how! The Investor is able to sit by the pool because he made enough money to put into stocks and/or real estate. Thanks to the tricks you've learned here, I trust you now see *yourself* as this guy in the near future!

True Business Owner

Contrary to the self-employed person, the True Business Owner has true freedom. He can just sit by the swimming pool all day if he chooses, all thanks to two things: systems and royalties. Let's look at each in turn…

Systems. Does the CEO of McDonald's flip burgers? Does the CEO of Starbucks steam milk? No. Because they systemized their businesses so well that a monkey could do it. They wrote a foolproof manual on how to run their business, and then had other people do it. What's more, once they had a system, they could sell the franchise to their business and make even more money. But the point is this: if they didn't show up for a month, the income would still come pouring in. *They own a business, not a job.*

You don't have to be as big as Starbucks or McDonald's to use the power of a good system.

Now, at this point I hear most people argue and insist that what they do can't be systemized. In some cases this is true, but most times it isn't—they just haven't sat down and written out what it is they actually DO each day in simple language, and/ or invented a way that anyone could do it. That way may not be as perfect as the way you would do it, but McDonald's doesn't care, as long as people buy the burgers, because they understand systems. Again, most people are resistant to this because they're still thinking like employees—it's not in an employee's best interests to figure out a way to be replaced by a monkey!

Next, Royalty. You know what this is—a payment for the use of something you created. Like an App, or a song, or a sales letter and product. Once the initial work is done, you just kick back and collect a royalty while you splash your feet in that pool. People stuck in the employee mindset have trouble with this because there's a feeling of working with no guarantee of payment. Get over it if you want the pass to swimming pool island.

That's the difference between being self-employed and owning a business. A True Business Owner isn't getting paid by the hour like a self-employed accountant, lawyer, or doctor might; a True Business Owner is paid for what he has set up or created, but during that time of creation, he isn't getting paid, so it's a leap of faith that many people struggle with.

Here's an example of how they do things on slavery island. You open up a shop that sells this book to people—all ten chapters in one go. You won't make any money unless people come to you and you open the shop and work in it every single day. I like the product you're selling (!), but you would be *working for money* in this situation. Make sense?

Now let's do things a different way—how they do things on swimming pool island. If you called me up because you knew a friend who'd like to buy this book, and that you'd like 50% of the profit, assuming I agreed to this, all you'd have done is make a couple of calls (one to me and one to your friend), and you'd be receiving checks for the next ten months while you sat back and relaxed. *Now money is working for you, you are not working for money.*

This is the key difference between slavery island and swimming pool island. If you want to cross over you have to understand this difference. You must not get paid by the hour; you must seek *leverage of your resources* to make the most amount of money for the least amount of work.

So, you'll have noticed that I've been talking about owning a *business* that makes money for you (not a business that you make money *for*). And it's this—owning the *right kind* of business—that's going to grant you those 12 wonderful wishes I listed previously…!

1. Help others.
2. Defend against attackers.
3. Pay less tax.
4. Pay less for certain things you want.
5. Help stop your money "flying away."
6. Leave a legacy for generations after you.
7. Pay off the 4 mortgages in the 3+1 retirement plan.
8. Give you investment capital to build a real estate portfolio with.

9. Get you out of debt quickly with your credit rating intact.

10. Create investment capital for use with The Secret of Seventy and The Biblical Money Code.

11. Create income streams that could last forever.

12. Build your Freedom Figure.

Perhaps you already have a preconceived idea about owning a business? Maybe it was a business that didn't work out for you? If so, I understand why you might be skeptical, but, with respect, if it was a business that didn't get you to "swimming pool island," I doubt that the business was a good one, whether it was your fault or not.

You have to go about things a different way if you want different results. The Bible explains this with a beautifully simple verse:

"All the rivers run into the sea; yet the sea is not full."
– Ecclesiastes 1:7

If you keep trying and failing to make money from your own business, you're like a river trying to fill the sea. It will never work, unless you try a different way, and that's what I'm here to give you. So have new faith in owning your own business as I explain how it can grant you those 12 wishes when you enjoy the benefits of *my kind of business…*

Help others.

When you think about it, the system of free enterprise is entirely set up to reward people who help others. How so? Because businesses that solve peoples" problems make a lot of money, and rightly so. Entrepreneurs are therefore *incentivized* to help others. The other kinds of helping others—donating to charity and giving your time to help needy people—is made even more possible by the acquisition of wealth. A successful business helps other people! This is the most important benefit of doing this and, somewhat mysteriously, it is the path that will give you the most rewards in every aspect of your venture. You will sleep well at night, and that's important. And let's certainly not forget that when you own a business you are *creating jobs*, either directly and/or indirectly through the suppliers you're using. If creating jobs isn't helping people, I don't know what is! **Contrary to popular belief, nobody is entitled to a job; jobs are a luxury made possible by a business owner who has a *choice* about whether to open a business or not!**

Defend against attackers.

When you set up your business as a "C" corporation, that is a true corporation and effectively a separate entity to you. We will talk more about this shortly, but suffice to say that a corporation defends you from the attackers we spoke about last time because that is the true purpose of a corporation.

Pay less tax.

A corporation can pay less tax than an individual if set up correctly. It's the corporation that pays tax on money earned, not you. You only pay tax on what you decide that corporation pays you. And governments can't be too harsh on corporations because they know that's bad for the economy (and their political "donations" from larger corporations). And remember, no reason why your corporation can't be a foreign one if justified, and that may enjoy even better taxation than your home country.

Pay less for certain things you want.

More about this shortly, but for anything you use in the line of business, the corporation pays. An employee has to buy things with after-tax money. A corporation buys things with before-tax money, and this means an effective 20-30% discount on those items. Cars, gas, computers, entertaining, business trips, education, anything that can be attributed to business expenses, is now at a big discount provided that the business has a healthy revenue stream to pay for it.

Help stop your money "flying away."

You'll spend less of your personal money when the money is going into a corporation instead of your personal account. Trust me on this one.

Leave a legacy for generations after you.

Another purpose of a corporation is so that it continues to exist long after its founder is dead. It is a separate entity to you, therefore it lives on without you. If you set this up as a business that runs without you (as I will show you to) why should it not continue forever and be a legacy for generations after you? Levi Strauss jeans were first made in 1848, and continue to be sold, making profits for the current shareholders. Do you think Levi Strauss is still alive? No, but he shall never be forgotten.

Pay off the 4 mortgages in the 3+1 retirement plan.

When you have such an advantageous and tax-free revenue stream that a corporation can get you, not only will the money be building up to pay off these four mortgages, but you'll also have a way to accomplish this plan a lot faster! How so? Because the corporation can own the homes for you. Better to do that than pay yourself the money to do so, as this way you pay less tax. Plus, your assets are protected by corporation ownership.

Give you investment capital to build a real estate portfolio with.

By the same token as just explained, your corporation can build capital and then that same corporation can invest in real estate, whether for the 3+1 plan or not.

Get you out of debt quickly with your credit rating intact.

The rapid accumulation of capital will obviously allow you to pay off debts. It may even be possible that your corporation buys the debt from any creditors for pennies on the dollar, and then writes it off.

Create investment capital for use with The Secret of Seventy and The Biblical Money Code.

This one is involving real estate. There's no reason why your corporation can't have its own trading account as a place to park its capital and make money from. Let the corporation own the assets and make the money, and then pay you a salary for managing it. This way you only take out, and get taxed on, what you need to live, not all of the gains.

Create income streams that could last forever.

When you create a stream of royalties or asset income through a corporation, those income streams can continue forever, with or without you.

Build your Freedom Figure.

In this course you wrote down an exact amount of money that would set you free. I've given you a lot of secrets along the way to accomplish this, and your own true business is another. If done correctly, the way I'm going to show you, this could soon make achieving that Freedom Figure of yours look *easy.*

So, if you do things as I propose, you will own a *true* business, and you will do so through a corporation. Now you need to know what that actually means so that you don't negate the benefits or legitimacy of that corporation...

Your New Best Friend

I was giving a seminar a few years ago, and I was explaining the benefits of a corporation when one of the attendees started yelling out, "A corporation is a fiction! A corporation is a fiction! A corporation is a fiction!" The rest of the attendees shuffled away from this guy, obviously frightened that he was having some kind of a mental episode. I stayed silent for a few minutes, waited for him to calm down, and got on with my speech. But I always try to look for meaning and signs in events, and there was a good point in the rants of that attendee.

When most people hear the word "corporation," they imagine a building with people working inside it. They picture something real. But a corporation isn't really real, not in the tangible sense. It's just a few papers sitting in a file in a lawyer's office. So, although corporations aren't quite a "fiction," they aren't far off, and this fine "veil" between you and your corporation can be pierced if you aren't careful.

And yet, corporations can be one of the best ways to save and protect your money IF you understand them. Otherwise, they can give you a false sense of security.

The corporation was born in Roman times and survived through medieval times, in use by the church. This was supposed to represent a community of people with the same interests, but the corporation would live longer than any of those members, thus the corporation would go on forever. But it was the British East India Company in the 1700s that would steal the credit for its invention, which is why some people, perhaps incorrectly, say corporations were a British invention. But it was certainly British maritime ventures that made corporations famous.

The entrepreneurs who sponsored expeditions to the New World developed a way to protect themselves against loss, so that if a ship sunk and the crew drowned the loss and liability would be limited to just that vessel—they used London lawyers to create the modern depiction of what we know today as a corporation. To this day, there's a surviving ancestor in the form of Lloyd's of London still being the world standard for shipping insurance and registry.

A corporation is now an independent entity that had privileges and liabilities distinct from those of its members.

That's the important part above.

If your corporation sells something and a customer tries to sue, they sue the corporation, not you. Thus, the financial damage is, in theory, limited to the assets of that corporation. Great. You probably already knew that. But what happens if the amount of damages claimed exceeds the assets of the corporation? Are the owners (perhaps you) still safe, as the British East India Company had intended?

The answer, like all legal answers, is murky. The answer, as any good lawyer says, is: "It depends... now, are you aware of my hourly rate?" But it's not that hard to decode the common lawyer's answer when you understand the history of corporations and what a corporation truly is, and it's vital that you know these answers if you're to reap the substantial rewards a corporation offers and still sleep at night.

In a way, and somewhat disturbingly, you have to get inside the head of that maniac in the seminar I spoke about earlier because that guy appreciates the fact that *a corporation is not real*, it's not you or him, it's a made up legal thing, **it's an entity all to itself.**

And unless you treat your corporation in this way, you may come unstuck.

Let's take a couple of examples of how *not* to do things. If you "co-mingle" funds between your personal money and your corporation's money, your corporation could be rendered worthless as a shield against your personal assets. By, for example, paying for your daughter's wedding with your corporation's money using some lame justification that suits you mentally ("entertaining clients" no doubt!), you just made a statement to the world that your corporation is NOT a separate entity; your corporation is really YOU. "Your corporation is a fiction! Your corporation is a fiction!" Thus, any attacker would certainly be able to "pierce the veil" that your corporation provides you.

Do NOT co-mingle funds.

You may think you're being cute by putting all number of personal items or "entertaining" down as a corporate expense, but it's not just the tax man who will have a problem with this if you get caught, it's also any would-be claimant. By paying for that baseball game or whatever with your corporation debit card, you just made a useful statement to some lawyer who wants to roll the dice for a frivolous client (and you're required by law to keep all accounts and receipts for six years).

Think of everything in terms of your corporation being a friend, a "business buddy." Do whatever you would do as if it was your friend's bank account, and what would be fair to him in the line of his work.

By that same token then, if you expect your "business-buddy" to be able to operate effectively, you'd give him all the tools he needs to do his job, including dealing with complaints and any litigation. If you don't, and by that I mean you don't provide him with enough operating capital and most of all *insurance*, a suing lawyer could argue that this corporation is indeed a "fiction," and come after you personally, because the corporation was not adequately capitalized (i.e. you sucked all the cash out to avoid loss in any litigation).

But if you bear all this in mind, a corporation will save you tax and allow you to do business safely in an extremely litigious country. Moreover, it will allow you to exploit some of the greatest secrets of the wealthy, and one of the reasons why the rich get richer and the poor get poorer.

When you do something in the name of your corporation, wear a different hat—the hat of your business buddy. And that's a nice hat to wear, because your corporation—your business buddy—thinks a lot clearer than you or I do, and he is without prejudice. And his clarity is what will get you to your goals… *if* you treat him right.

And, from an asset protection point of view, when it comes to creating your "Fortress of Freedom" we discussed in the previous lesson, there's no better way to do the following key thing: **own very little, but control it all.** It's your corporation that owns things, not you. But you're still in the driving seat, because it's your corporation.

That all sounds great, especially all those nice tax-breaks, doesn't it? But there's one thing we're missing to make it all possible: income. So now let's talk about the most important part of your business: how it will create as much revenue as possible for as little of your time as possible.

How to Build Wealth ASAP

Before I pass on to you the greatest business secrets that no business school could ever teach you, I want us to have the spirit of the seventh secret firmly in mind:

What goes around comes around. Our primary business mission is to HELP OTHERS, and to make the world a better place. When we do that, the rewards will take care of themselves.

"Recompense no man evil for evil. Provide things honest in the sight of all men." – Romans 12:17.

Let this and my advice be your guiding light and, I promise you, you will at last be a True Business Owner. Now let's begin, and it all begins with an idea. But let me bust your preconceived notions about an *original* business idea.

Do you think a cup of coffee is an original idea? Wouldn't you say there are plenty of people doing that already—i.e. serving cups of coffee? And yet Starbucks became a national institution. Did they worry about the fact that other people were doing it already?

There are relatively few truly original ideas out there. Most good ideas are just a combination of old ideas repackaged and sold with a different angle.

The next time you start delaying or looking for excuses not to become your own boss, I want you to go to the nearest Starbucks, on your own, for a cup of coffee—out of ear shot of the "naysayers" in your life—and remember this important concept.

Not many people know that Bill Gates didn't become rich by inventing a brilliant idea. He simply bought a prototype program from *someone else* who had the idea and licensed it to IBM for a fortune. That's what I call leverage of resources and how to do business my kind of way. That's a True Business Owner.

Another thing, remember that a business is a means to an end—to make cash for the purposes of investment as well as helping others. McDonald's isn't in the hamburger business as much as the REAL ESTATE business. The plan was to make the burger sales pay for the prime real estate the diners are located on, which is why McDonald's is one of the largest real estate owners in the world.

So, you don't necessarily need a brand-new idea, and very few ideas are truly original anyway. *But you DO need what I'm going to talk about next…*

"Let's say you and I are about to compete against each other with Hot Dog stands. What advantages would you like to have? Whatever it is, just say. Take a minute now to write down what you want to have to beat me. Very important—think about this before continuing...

Ready? OK then. What did you decide on?

Some extra-yummy buns? The world's best selection of toppings and relishes? How about a really cool-looking stand that glimmered in the sunshine? Or maybe the hot dog sausages themselves are the best in world—real frankfurters imported from Germany?

Whatever you chose as an advantage, I will grant you. In return, will you grant me the one advantage I want? Yes? Good. Because I will wipe you out with the thing I want in a single day! What is it I want? Here's what I want...

A crowd of starving people!

Get the point? If you focused on PRODUCT, you LOST the game. If you focused on MARKET, you won.

Would it matter if I didn't have all the relishes, yummy-buns and imported frankfurters? No, because I had a crowd of starving people, so they wouldn't care. In fact, even if my hot dogs were the worst in the world, I'd still have won (important caveat: I absolutely do NOT want to sell bad hot dogs, but again, I'm proving a point).

Your business should focus on where the greatest demand for something is, where it can solve peoples" problems, and help as many people as possible.

I want you to go back now and think long and hard about the little exercise we just did because if you can get your head around it, you will have put yourself in the top 5% of business people in the world. I guarantee it! The vast majority of companies are what's called "product-lead," meaning they think of a product and then think how the market fits in. It's all back to front.

Many, many questions are all centered around finding the right product, when they should have been centered around finding the right *market*. This is an important distinction and is not splitting hairs.

Your aim as an entrepreneur, is to find a MARKET, not a product. Find some hungry fish, THEN find some food for them.

This makes things easy, not hard! Once you find the market, there shouldn't be a question about whether your product will work, as much as "How much will they like it?"

Recall your training on investing and trading in this course. We went with the tide and the current, remember? We didn't swim upstream, we followed the line of least resistance by going with the trend. And remember how buying real estate needed to be synchronized with The Great Cycle?

Business is just the same: we want to follow the line of least resistance, and that means fishing where the fish are.

The companies that embrace this simple concept usually become huge successes. These are the companies that are centered around the market. By the same token, companies that center around a product do poorly or fail.

When a business fails, all number of lame excuses are fired out, when in fact the REAL reason is almost always that THEY DIDN'T SELL THINGS PEOPLE WANTED TO BUY!

And when a business fails you do the exact opposite of helping others.

If you have a business already, or even if you work for someone else, take a look at that business now and ask if it is product-centered or market-centered. Brand this idea into your business mind:

EVERY SINGLE ENTERPRISE YOU EMBARK ON SHOULD BE BASED ON EVIDENCE THAT A PARTICULAR MARKET WANTS SOMETHING!

Also, remember that marketing rewards reality not ego! If there are vast piles of money to be made from male and female libido pills (and there is by the way) *and you sell a pill that actually works and helps people*, marketing will reward you. Marketing doesn't give a hoot about the fact that you won't feel proud to tell people what you sell. Don't let pride stand in the way of what you offer, as long as it's legal and it truly helps others.

Don't even think about a product until you have the market, then make the product fit the market.

Let's return to our Starbucks example as we move on to the next point. What's the difference between Starbucks and the one-man-business on Main St. selling coffee from a truck? Who sells the most coffee and why?

The difference is the man in the truck sells coffee, and Starbucks sells a CONCEPT. That concept being, "You can have your coffee any way you like it in comfortable surroundings with friends and generally be a cool dude." But in both cases the PRODUCT was a cup of coffee. CONCEPT is often entirely different, and a concept will get you across the bridge to "swimming pool island," unlike that poor guy in his coffee truck.

And consider this: Did Starbucks *invent* a cup of coffee? Did Google *invent* the Internet? Did Microsoft *invent* the computer?

No. What the people behind those corporations did was use their *imagination* to come up with a *variation of something ALREADY successful*. And YOU can make a fortune the very same way. Look around you and see examples everywhere of entrepreneurs, large and small, creating wealth by coming up with a variation on something already successful. Why waste time trying to make a market want something brand new?

You just need a concept, and concepts are born of your imagination. And I promise you, all your imagination needs is a specific task you give it and suddenly it goes to work all by itself.

To take an example you can immediately relate to, let's say you're suddenly in the market for a red Honda. That day, as you drive around, you'll suddenly notice red Hondas everywhere! Now, have the number of red Hondas on the road dramatically increased overnight? Of course not, but because you had a specific task in mind (researching red Hondas), your awareness of them was dramatically increased. In other words, it was your perception that changed, not the reality.

Unfortunately, too many people see their imagination as something for children and completely uncontrollable where nothing could be further from the truth. I will prove to you that your imagination is a highly potent force, and more importantly, I'll show you how to harness its power.

The first reaction I usually get from students at this point is "But I don't have an imagination!" So don't worry if this is how you feel at this point. But I put it to you that *we were ALL born with an imagination.* Remember those pictures you drew as a kid? What about those crazy worlds you made from modeling clay?

It's what "the system" did to your imagination on the road to where you are now that's the problem!

Think about it. Your writing materials in kindergarten were blank paper and a box of crayons with colors you never knew existed. By the time you graduated high school your writing materials consisted of a black biro and ruled paper with margins. That's indicative, don't you think? But thankfully, the damage is reversible.

It's been consistently scientifically proven that ALL children are far more creative than adults... and so we can learn a lot from kids. A child has an open-mind, the breeding ground for creative thought.

How open is your mind to new suggestions? Why do you think I constantly encourage foreign travel, and exploring outside your comfort zones?

Name a success story, big or small, and you'll see a person's imagination behind it. The ability to think creatively and correctly perceive situations is the difference between wealth and poverty.

If a person perceives themselves as having a cap on their earning potential, or that they are and always will be poor, that PERCEPTION becomes reality. They will think and act like a poor person and, hence, watch opportunity after opportunity pass them by. Others will perceive them the same way and not invite them on potentially profitable ventures, and so the cycle continues.

Conversely, another person may well be poor in reality, but because they perceive the situation and *themselves* in a different way, an entirely different reality evolves.

So, here's what we've learned so far:

1. Go where the "starving crowds" are.
2. You don't need an original idea, but you do need a good concept for those starving crowds, and that comes from tuning your imagination into that crowd.

Now let me be more specific regarding tuning your imagination into this "starving crowd": you must tune into their WANTS, not their NEEDS. Let me demonstrate with a real example of working with needs and wants, as well as show an example of doing something that does NOT help others...

People NEED to eat spinach. But people WANT to eat hamburgers. Get it? Yes? I'm glad you do, because 90% of most businesses and marketers don't. Here's a story about a man who did get it:

He decided to sell hamburgers, and the restaurant was called, "The Heart Attack Grill." I'm NOT joking, this is a true story and this is a REAL place. You may have heard of it. Here's the menu:

Menu courtesy of The Heart Attack Grill (www.HeartAttackGrill.com)

And I totally admit, I WANT one of those burgers. Do I NEED it though? I NEED it like a hole in the heart.

At The Heart Attack Grill, the manager is dressed in scrubs with a stethoscope slung around his neck, and the waitresses are "naughty-nurses." An ambulance is always parked outside. If anyone can finish the 2-pound "Quadruple Bypass" burger, one of the hot nurses pushes you out in a wheelchair to thunderous applause. They slap pure lard on the burger buns. The fries are fried in pure lard, and they're unlimited, help-yourself at the fries bar (instead of a salad bar). The "butterfat" milkshakes are ALL cream. They aggressively publicize the story if any of their customers pass out on the premises (and they evidently do quite often). And get this: if you weigh over 350 pounds you can eat free FOR LIFE! In an interview, one of these heavyweight customers was asked why they thought they were allowed to eat for free. And do you know what his response was (as he crammed a Bypass Burger into his face)? He replied gravely, "Well... I guess the owner doesn't expect I'll live long enough to make a loss on me eating free forever."

Seriously? So maybe we should be more like that guy and see just how silly we can be with giving people what they WANT, and not bother giving them what they NEED... *except let's help others in the process;* not try to give them a heart attack…

And that, my friend, is probably the most valuable marketing lesson I could ever give you. I have been on both the wrong side and the right side of this truth, and I know which one is more lucrative. Wants and needs. Cater to peoples" wants, not their needs… *ethically.*

When you've got your concept that will help this starving crowd, you'll need to start *marketing* it to them. The good news is that, thanks to the Internet, advertising has never been more **available, efficient, and affordable**. Here's why:

Available:

You can go on Google right now and place an ad, and within minutes, you've cast a net into a deluge of hungry fish. Don't know how to write an ad? Keep reading! You don't need to be one of the big boys with big budgets—on the Internet all trade is done virtually, so it's a level playing field. The customers don't know if they're dealing with a conglomerate or a guy sitting in sweat pants (and as we'll see in a second, the guy in the sweat pants does a MUCH better job…)

Efficient:

It used to be the case that any ad you wanted to place was on a wing and a prayer; you could never be sure if your target audience would see it or not, and how many of them would see it. You'd have to pay for the ad even if nobody bought anything from it. Now? You KNOW that your target audience is seeing the ad AND you only pay for the ad if a customer clicks on it. This is truly amazing when you think of it from the old-school perspective of efficiency! What's more, your ad is based purely on the word a prospective customer is typing into Google. If that person types in "fishing pole" and your ad is for "fishing poles," your ad will be shown at some page in that search. It used to be the case where we just didn't know if people wanted a certain product or not, but now the Internet tells us specifically what people are looking for by what they're searching for. The guesswork is over.

Affordable:

I just explained how you only pay for the ad if somebody clicks on it, which is incredible in itself. But you can also set the amount you'd like to spend each day, and it can be as little as pennies a click.

In short, the little guy has never had such an incredible opportunity. Think back to the "old days" to appreciate this. Get in my time machine and imagine me making this call in 1990 to a newspaper to place an ad:

Newspaper: "Hello, Daily Herd."

Me: "Hello, yes... I'd like to place an ad, 2 columns wide, six inches."

Newspaper: "Okay, that's a thousand dollars according to rate card."

Me: "I never pay rate card."

Newspaper: "Ummm, well I'm sure we can give you a discount if you place a few ads. You see, it takes the customer approximately 7 times of seeing your ad before they recognize your company, and..."

Me: "I think that's nonsense. Have you any solid proof of that?"

Newspaper: "Well... no... it's just an accepted..."

Me: "I thought not. Now, I'm not only not going to pay rate card, I only want readers who are interested in my product to even see my ad."

Newspaper: "What? That's impossible! How can we possibly control who sees the ad!?"

Me: "Well, I want your assurance anyway. And there's more..."

Newspaper: "Oh do please tell me. I can't wait to hear more." (Under his breath to a colleague: "Mandy, we've got a psycho on the phone...")

Me: "Now listen, my good man, I'm only going to pay for this ad if I get any customer enquiries from it, and I'll pay you 50 cents for every enquiry. I think that's fair, don't you? Don't worry, it doesn't matter if those enquiries end up in a sale or not, I'll still pay you the 50 cents per enquiry. Sound good...? Hello? Hello... are you still there? Did we get cut off...?? Hello?!"

That's how lucky we are today. Ah, I hear you say, but it all comes down to writing an ad, doesn't it?

Yes, it does. And that's what I'd like to talk about next, because there's a simple formula you can use. The first thing I need to do though is banish a big myth from your brain regarding what makes a successful ad.

Understand: 99% of the ads you see on TV are AWFUL.

But how can this be? Those ads are created by top agencies on Madison Avenue, costing millions, with major corporations behind them. They win awards!

Don't get confused between an ad that's cute and designed to win awards because it's cute. Ads that are cute and ads that sell products are NOT the same thing. Unlike Internet advertising, TV advertising is completely unaccountable. They really don't know whether an ad works or not because they're still advertising like it's 1990. The phrase, "Advertising Budget" applies to this form of marketing because it's unaccountable. Think about it: advertising is either profitable, or it isn't. The concept of an advertising budget is a nonsense with the Internet.

On any given evening that you're watching TV, look at the ads, and honestly say how many of them make you go out and buy that product the next day. Some ads may entertain you, they may be "very clever," but could you even remember the product name after, let alone go and buy it?

No? Then, by definition, that was a BAD ad, regardless of what some Madison Avenue award ceremony says!

Says the ad agency in response: "Ah, but we raised the product's brand awareness!"

Says me: "do you have proof of that? And guess what? Brand awareness doesn't pay the bills today!"

Last night I saw a TV ad for a new Greek yogurt from a major food conglomerate that presumably threw millions at this campaign that was run through a major ad agency. Picture the meeting between all the high-fiving hotshots: after hours of creative sessions, working late, and spending millions of the clients" dollars, they came up with a slogan... AND they clearly thought the slogan was so hot that they'd better register the trademark, and FAST. You ready to hear it? Okay, here's the slogan below, and I promise you I'm not making this up...

"It is so good ®"

Really? It is so good ®. I stared at the screen in disbelief.

Are they kidding? Not even an apostrophe on the "s" to sound slightly more "cool"? It's so good? No, I guess a focus group somewhere in Nebraska disagreed.

Ads should not be written by committee. Especially a committee of kids that only want to win awards. And the really sad thing is I wouldn't be surprised if that yogurt commercial was nominated for an award. They didn't sell any yogurt, but they won a bunch of awards. Bravo. That is so good. Anyway, enough ranting. Here's the magic formula for writing a good ad:

AIDA.

Really? That's it? And not even a trademark? Is it really "so good"?

Yep, that's it. And the four words these letters stand for will change your life and put Madison Avenue to shame.

"A.I.D.A." stands for (in order of importance): Attention, Interest, Desire, and Action...

Attention

You should tune into whatever is going on in your customer's mind, their wants, and give it to them, only in a provoking way that really stands out. A headline. Snap them out of their apathy. For a quick and dirty example: "Yogurt's an Ancient Greek Anti-Aging Secret?"

Interest

Now you've got their attention, give just a little more detail, back up your headline. For example, "supermodel Swears by Eating It Nightly!"

Desire

Now turn your attention to the customer, how it can benefit them.

"How many years will Greek Yogurt take off YOUR face?"

Action

This part is easy—tell the customer how he can get the product or find out more information. A phone number, a website address, etc. You can also add a "speed premium" here that encourages immediate action—a discount for the next 48 hours, for example. "2 for 1 this week only at www.GreekYogurt.com"

I'm inclined to believe that even my quick-and-dirty ad above would sell more Greek yogurt than the TV commercial I saw, but you be the judge.

When you write a Google ad, it's no coincidence that they give you 4 lines to write on, and that the fourth line is where you put your website address. No prizes for guessing what the other 3 lines represent and in what order!

Don't be intimidated, appreciate the magnificent opportunity, and get on Google or wherever and write an ad. Just try it. It is so good ®. Go to Google.com, look at the bottom left corner, and click on "Advertising":

Advertising   Business   About

(For a deeper discussion on Internet marketing you really need to watch my Instant Internet Income DVD.)

So, back on to the specific subject of helping others in the process of business…

How often have you experienced a great service or product, and then raved about it to people you know? If you're like most people, plenty, I bet. And if the person you've told about this great experience then purchases the same product or service you did, then the business in question gets their due reward.

But do you get yours? Hardly ever, I bet. But you should, because you just became an indirect salesperson for the business you just recommended.

We've all done it. At the time, it seems like we're just tipping off people we know about a good business they should buy from, thus doing both parties a justified favor. Your friend deserves a good recommendation, and the business in question deserves referral business. But you can do both that friend and that business a lot better by negotiating with every good business you come across—you can request a discount for any friends you introduce AND a referral commission for yourself.

You're going around "selling" anyway, aren't you? So why not make it count?

When I mention "selling" to some people (you?), they pull a face as if I'd just insulted their mother, as if "selling" is something to be ashamed of. I remember that feeling, so I thought I'd share with you my early experiences of overcoming this resistance so many of us feel towards selling, because if you want to make money in business, like it or not, you have to sell.

As a child, I once expressed my disinterest with selling to my father (who, for all his faults, was an incredible salesman), and he replied, "People can only have jobs if somebody, somewhere is selling something. Jesus Christ was the best salesman the world has ever seen." I thought that was a fair point, and so I became more interested in this "dirty" business of selling that had previously ranked as low as running a brothel in my young mind.

By the time I'd reached my teens, my Dad had his own car dealership, and guess what my summer job was? Cleaning cars. But it wasn't long after that he had me in the showroom facing those dreaded customers. I was 17 and just wanted to be out with my friends, playing hockey, chasing girls, and anything else other than selling cars. But the cool car that my Dad gave me on my 17th birthday (a 1979 Ford Escort RS2000 for any car buffs reading) came at a price: I was to work on Saturdays in the showroom selling new Fords and used cars. Ugh!

Little did I know at the time, but I was about to acquire an education money can't buy, a training course none of my school teachers knew anything of, and they would have baulked in disgust had I even suggested it. It wasn't just an education in sales though, it was an education about the minds of the general public. And it was terrifying. At 17 years old, I was exposed to all kinds of people and their weird behavior.

The full-time salesmen at the dealership looked at me in awe to begin with: the son of the legendary salesman, their boss. They would race me to customers on the forecourt (and beat me) because they assumed I must be such a killer salesman surely by genetic right, and that they needed to get to the customers before I unleashed my ostensible selling skills on them.

But I sucked at it. I would speak to plenty of customers, show them the cars, I was polite, all that good stuff. But they all walked.

Never wanting to be shown up, my Dad literally pulled me aside one Saturday after watching me lose yet another customer. And as he always reminded me, that customer had just cost fifty bucks through advertising. (Sidebar: how many businesses do you know ask where you heard about them from? How do they know their advertising is working otherwise?) The disappointment was clearly visible in his face. When we started speaking, I realized that he'd actually been secretly loitering around me to overhear my lousy sales pitch.

"I hate this," I said. "Can't I just be a delivery driver, or something?"

Matching the speed of my customary walk of shame back to the showroom from the forecourt, he said, "I heard you speak to that customer. No wonder you hate it!"

I despondently replied, "What?! I didn't do anything wrong. I showed him the car, and he didn't like it!"

Dad said, "Oh really? And what did you **learn** about that customer?"

"Learn about him? What are you talking about?" I said.

Then he said something that stuck with me: "People don't buy products. PEOPLE BUY PEOPLE. And that means learning about them and what they REALLY want. They don't want a car, they want an image, a lifestyle. They want a friend, someone to follow, **something to believe in**. The product is incidental to their desires. I could replace you with a bloody robot!"

End of father/son "chat."

I went home and got on with my Saturday, had an early night in preparation for the big Sunday game as usual. But his words stuck. I would show him next Saturday...

So I stopped selling products and started selling myself. The product almost became secondary. I would ask questions about the prospective customers, ask about their relationships, what they did, establish **how I could help them with their lives.** (The first thing my teen mind noticed was that the wife was in control of the purchase without the guy even knowing it. That put me off marrying anyone ever).

But I soon realized that my Dad was right. His truth dawned on me on the day that I sat an elderly couple's young grandson in one of the cars and made him pretend to drive it instead of yammering on about power steering. The couple shortly wrote a check and refused to speak to anyone else but me forever after. I had established that the elderly couple's pride and joy was their grandson, and that he would be safe driving around with them. I was caring about them as people and helping them find the best car for their wants.

I had forgotten about "selling," which was just as well because I HATED it. I was now just being nice to people, considering them and what was right for them, **solving their problems, helping them.** It was at this point I also realized that my dad, the great salesman, wasn't a salesman at all. He was genuinely just trying to help others.

It was at this point that I also accidentally discovered the power of reverse psychology. Rather than hassle and pressure a customer, I'd say, "Listen, this is a really important decision, so let me sit you down, get you a cup of tea, and give you some time to yourself. I'll be sitting over there when you need me."

Conversion rate: 70%.

And I continued to look after them long after the sale. If a customer of mine had a problem with the service department they would call me and hear me yelling at the service guys in the background. And, as per my training, if a customer complained I would actually listen, apologize, and then ask how I could make it better. (Sidebar: ever come across someone handle a complaint like this lately? There doesn't seem to be a week go by when I get bad service and the person responsible wants to argue with me and make it worse. Where have all the professionals gone?)

My Dad sold the dealership a couple of years later (a great salesman doesn't necessarily make a good business owner), and I landed a job selling BMWs. In 1988 BMWs came without a stereo. When customers (understandably) complained why a BMW came without a stereo, I would walk them to the Blaupunkt stereo kiosk and explain, "Well, BMW understands that you're an individual with your own preferences. You **choose** the stereo. BMW want your car to be yours, to be unique, and tailored. Like a fine suit." I sold a lot of BMWs in the late eighties.

But it was at BMW's training center that I learned something else very important: that each customer has something called a **primary buying motive**. And our objective as salespeople was to discover what that was with each customer we faced. In the case of cars, the primary buying motive could be safety, reliability, fuel economy, performance, etc. etc. Sure, all of these things are important, but there would always be ONE THING, just one, that was foremost in the customer's mind. Their "hot button" was to be discovered and pushed repeatedly, because this was how we could help them the most.

Armed with this new knowledge, solving peoples" problems became even easier and more fun. And in hindsight these times were some of the happiest of my life.

Selling doesn't have to make you shudder. It should only have that effect on you if you're actually selling instead of just trying to help people.

I'm reminded of something the Oscar-winning actor, Ben Kingsley, once said in reply to a question about what his biggest secret to acting was: "I don't act. The camera hates acting." I would translate that into the business world as: "I don't sell. People hate being sold things."

Whether you realize it or not, you're selling every day. Whatever it is you want in life, you will, consciously or unconsciously, be employing sales skills. Even government employees, supposedly safe from the "yucky" world of selling, use selling skills—everyone wants a promotion, right?

When you told that neighbor about how much you enjoyed a product or service, you were being an awesome salesperson without even knowing it. But not getting paid. So you should get paid, and there's an easy way to do so.

It doesn't take long to set up these arrangements, you only have to ask the business owner. If I'm speaking to the person of authority I haven't had a single occasion where they said no, in fact, they were grateful and excited that I asked. You simply say: "If I send more customers your way, do you offer a referral commission? And can I offer them a discount to incentivize them?"

Then the next time you're telling your friends about that great business (and helping them in the process), you tell them to say that you sent them so they'll get looked after. Then make sure the business owner knows whom you're sending ahead of time (in writing by email), so they will pay you. The big ticket businesses are best: new home builders, swimming pool contractors, car dealerships, realtors, etc.

And in no time you'll be representing the best businesses in town, rightfully doing them a favor, doing your friends a favor, and getting a reward. Most valuable of all, you'll be practicing something you need to make money in business: **helping people solve their problems**.

And that also means your customers will come back to you again and again...

When a company is built on sound principles, everyone connected with it becomes enriched; both spiritually and financially...

You must offer a product and service your customers are so thrilled, so impressed with they are eager to buy more from you. Over and over again. **Give more than they expected**—far more. For example, providing unadvertised free bonus gifts can be a powerful strategy. The goal should be to develop the highest possible level of customer loyalty.

The result is the "repeat business factor" which can make you very wealthy. Unprofitable businesses and those that fail have a very low repeat business factor. Short-sighted entrepreneurs often make this mistake. They often try to make a "killing" on the first product sold to a customer by cutting corners on quality and by not delivering good value. It's almost impossible to make money or remain in business for an extended period of time using this approach.

Interestingly, conventional financial statements do not have any category for the repeat business factor. Business schools do not teach its importance. Yet, the repeat business factor is crucial to the financial health of any enterprise. Take Apple; every time they release a new product, there's literally a line of people waiting to buy it before they've even tried it because they know from experience that Apple products help them solve their problems in an enjoyable way.

To build a great company there is one action you can take that helps to build trust better than anything else known. There is nothing simpler, nothing more powerful. It is the secret of great leaders. You must: keep your word!

When you say you will do something, do whatever is necessary to make it happen. No excuses. When people know that whatever you say they absolutely can count on, they will be willing to perform miracles for you. They will move heaven and earth to make your company a huge success.

Customer retention is the key to a successful enterprise. It's a true measure of how a company is doing. If a company has to replace 75% of its customers each year, because they are only retaining 25% of their original customers, they are likely to go under fast. It is so expensive to find this level of new customers.

The successful companies retain 75% or more of their customers. That means they retain customers for a minimum of 5 years. The mega-success level companies retain 90% of their customers. That translates to keeping the average customer for 10 years.

The difference in your profit by retaining 90% rather than 75% of your customers is far higher than you may think. It can be 5 times more profitable to retain a customer for 10 years than 5 years!

Many businesses spend five times as much money finding new customers as they do keeping existing ones. <u>This is a huge mistake</u>. The greater part of your effort and resources should be focused on selling to existing customers. Why? Because customers who already know and trust you are far more likely to buy from you. This is why it is so important to have back-end products. There are really only three ways to improve any business:

1. Attract new customers through sound marketing.
2. Really work on quality and service to keep them.
3. Sell more to existing customers.

Have you ever seen that a new store has opened in town, and you went into it, only to be disappointed? Perhaps you didn't like the merchandise, or the sales assistant wasn't helpful enough. Whatever the reason, you may have decided not to go back into that store.

Then there are those stores where you shop all the time. You like the merchandise, it's reasonably priced and good quality, and the sales assistants are really helpful. It is the same for your business. If your merchandise is disappointing, or your staff unhelpful, they won't order again. Most of your profits will come from repeat orders, so you have to make sure your customer service is top class.

Complaints about lost or damaged goods are inevitable, and you should respond to such a letter within five days, but preferably <u>on the same day</u> it is received.

Try to be fast, friendly and fair when dealing with customers - even if one or two of them are out to fleece you. If you handle a few hundred orders a week, you can quickly build a customer list in the thousands. But if you lose customers every week, your business is going to suffer just as quickly.

If a customer has taken the trouble to write in and complain, then be grateful to them. **You will never know if your customers are unhappy if they don't tell you.** View these complaints as a superb way of ironing out any hiccups in your customer service.

Owning your own TRUE business through a corporation that helps others grants you a lot of wishes that empower all the other secrets, I hope you now see this. So, what about me? What kind of business am I in, and can you draw any special lessons from it for *any* business you might consider getting into?

Fish Where There's Fish

Now I'm going to build on what I consider to be perhaps THE ultimate business secret: go where there's a starving crowd. Several years ago, I gave a series of seminars on something called "direct marketing" (Internet marketing and direct mail). I needed a way to quickly teach students the principles of it, so I developed this analogy that follows. At the time I presented it, even seasoned and successful marketers welcomed its clarity. So let's dive right in...

It begins with a game that I now invite you to play...

You're stranded in the wilderness, and you must catch and eat a fish if you're to survive. For the purposes of this exercise, please consider these 4 things involving catching and eating a fish:

1. Equipment: a fishing pole.
2. Fish processing method: to turn fish into an edible state.
3. Lake: a mass of water with fish in.
4. Bait.

You of course need ALL of these things to catch a fish and survive. The task is to *prioritize* these things in the right order of importance.

Please re-read the above.

Okay, so without cheating and reading ahead, please take a few moments to honestly complete this exercise. Go ahead and place those four requirements in the correct order of importance...

Stuck? Really picture yourself in this situation. Imagine you only had an hour to spend on catching and eating that fish, and then consider how you would allocate these sixty minutes between these four requirements.

No peaking ahead!

....

....

....

Okay, here's the correct order of importance:

1. Lake
2. Bait
3. Fishing Equipment
4. Fish processing method

Surprised? Don't worry, most people are. Let's consider why the priority is this way.

(Sidebar: Please, any fishing enthusiasts reading, resist the urge to correct me, or nitpick. This is all for demonstration purposes only.)

If your fishing pole was an old branch with a piece of string and a rusty, bent nail for a hook, BUT you had superb bait that you dangled in a lake brimming with fish... would you catch a fish?

Yes, you would. That's why fishing equipment is number 3—it's not as important as the lake and the bait.

If you had the best fish processing method in the world, but lousy bait and/or a dead lake, would you catch a fish?

No, of course not. That explains number 4.

So that leaves the bait and the lake...

If you had the juiciest, best bait in the world, but you dangled it into a lake with little or no fish, would you catch a fish?

No, it's highly unlikely, unless the bait was supremely exceptional so that it drew out what fish there were. That's why at the top of the list of importance is the lake. Think about it: you can forget all the other things, all bets are off without a lake full of fish! This is our "starving crowd," but we're taking things further now…

Okay, let's now unmask this analogy. Below is what each of these four things stand for in the marketing sense:

Lake = Market (customers with a specific want—a starving crowd)

Bait = Offer (your CONCEPT)

Equipment = Product

Fish processing method = Product fulfillment, shipping, and support.

Take a moment to digest this…

The key message here is:

You can have the best marketing idea in the world, but unless you get it to the people who want that particular thing, it's dead on arrival. D.O.A. Understand?

Let me restate something, because some people get confused and upset at this stage:

You of course need ALL of these four things to catch a fish and survive. The task is to *prioritize* these things in the right order of importance.

Of course you must have a top quality product! But its *priority* is third.

Now, which two areas do you think most people allocate *most* of their time, especially when starting out?

Yep, number 3 and 4—product and fulfillment!

If you already have a business, which of these four areas take up most of your time? If the time allocation ratio is all wrong, change it immediately!

So, your first goal is to find a marketplace (lake) of people who are proven buyers of whatever. Priority 1.

Next step is to discover what these proven buyers"

hot-buttons are. What are they buying? Why are they buying? What fears and dreams make them buy? You need to get inside their heads so you can help them (bait). If you read a fishing magazine, the ads in the classified section will be for fishing-related products, not cosmetics! This is Priority 2.

Next we need to translate your sales offer into a product. What promise did your sales offer make? What did it claim to do for the customer? The fish have been attracted to the bait, but our equipment needs to keep them on the hook... by not refunding. The product must be of premium quality and value, it must deliver. Again, I am NOT advocating that your fishing equipment be an old branch with a piece of string, the exercise was one of prioritizing.

Finally, we need to deliver the product, we need database systems and support (fish processing equipment). We need the customer to become a REPEAT customer by having a good experience with us.

Is the fog lifting? What I hope this does is allow you to focus on the right things at the right time instead of being overwhelmed with it all, as I know many people starting out are. What you should now clearly understand is that your quest begins with finding a lake, and you'd be amazed how few people do start off that way.

Wait, no. How about one better? **Find fish in a barrel.** Fish in a concentrated area that are circling around impatiently, looking for a very particular kind of bait.

That's what direct marketing gives you: fish in a barrel with very specific bait requirements. Direct marketing makes life easy because there are listings for lakes full of certain fish, and what kind of bait these fish are attracted to. In direct marketing, the customer lists (lakes) are all given to you on a plate.

So let's never forget what occupies the number one spot in this success formula: the customers, or as it's called in direct marketing: **the list**. The man who mentored me in direct marketing told me that the three most important things in this business are:

1. The List
2. The List
3. The List

And he had a point. Perhaps if my mentor had played this little fishing game his answers would have been:

1. Lake
2. Lake
3. Lake
4. Lake

And I probably wouldn't have argued. As a direct marketer armed with this knowledge you could turn up in any Western country, anytime, and make all the money you ever needed… IF you get the priorities in the right order.

And if you aren't a direct marketer, these principles apply to ALL businesses. Plus, if you're not a direct marketer, why not start being one? You've seen all the benefits of owning a corporation, so why not go about giving a corporation what it needs to accomplish all those benefits: revenue? This is also my chosen path as a method of being a TRUE business owner. Maybe you'd like to join me?

Giving Back

Let's take another look at that Seventh Secret, this time from *my* perspective:

> *"But thou shalt remember the Lord thy God: for it is he that giveth thee power to get wealth, that he may establish his covenant which he sware unto thy fathers, as it is this day." –* Deuteronomy 8:18

I need to remember that I wasn't always wealthy; I need to remember that I was once in your position of *striving* to become wealthy. One of the reasons for writing this course was to give something back by sharing what I learned on my journey, and I trust you've enjoyed the ride and now feel empowered to go on and do great things for yourself and others. And, in the spirit of the Seventh Secret, I humbly ask that when you've reached your Freedom Figure you'll pass on the experiences *you've* learned (in your own words, not mine) to people who will listen. What goes around, comes around. Let helping others be your driving force in business, and good things will happen!

You've learned a great deal; everything there is to know about the *only* 3 ways to reach your Freedom Figure (apart from lottery and inheritance):

1. Stock market.
2. Real Estate.
3. Business.

If you want freedom, those are your only 3 tickets to get there. But it's *your own business* that will put the wind in your sails; money pouring into your account will grant you those dozen wishes, which include acquiring capital for investment in real estate and stocks, not to mention building your Freedom Figure outright.

One last piece of business advice before you go: **the most profitable start-up businesses are *home* businesses.** The main reason for that is because the overhead is so low, so that's how I recommend you start.

But now you're still left with that question about what business to be in and what idea you could run with. Don't worry, that's perfectly normal! Most new entrepreneurs get stuck at this point, but if there's one major point that you take away from all this information, I hope it's the understanding that God wants to provide you with riches...

Made in the USA
Lexington, KY
21 December 2018